Tom Pinder,

A Story of the Holmfirth Flood

D. F. E. Sykes

Alpha Editions

This edition published in 2024

ISBN : 9789357956499

Design and Setting By
Alpha Editions
www.alphaedis.com
Email - info@alphaedis.com

Contents

INTRODUCTION

Tom Pinder, Foundling is a romance and moral tale, set in the early part of the 19th Century, to the backdrop of the Greenfield and Holme Valleys when both were a part of West Yorkshire. It deals with the life of a foundling, Victorian values, the burgeoning of the cooperative movement and the Holmfirth flood. The book was first published c.1902 and subsequently published under the title Dorothy's Choice (A Rushing of the Waters).

Sykes is one of few novelists who chose to portray the lives of common people in this period and for this reason alone it is a valuable resource as a social history. His use of the local dialect, ability to sketch interesting characters and their relationships adds greatly to its readability.

CHAPTER I.

THE *Hanging Gate* is a public-house of venerable aspect. It stands at the corner of one of four cross ways, where the road from the summit of Harrop Edge cuts the turnpike from Leeds to Manchester. It pays rates in the township of Diggle, and to Diggle it properly belongs; but the small cluster of tumble-down cottages that constitutes a very small hamlet rejoices in the name of Wakey, a name whose origin has hitherto baffled the researches of local antiquarians. The inn itself is a low, two-storied, rambling building. Its rooms are so low that a moderately tall man must dodge the oaken rafters. There is much stabling, now largely abandoned to the rats, for the pristine glory of the *Hanging Gate* departed with the stage coach. A long horse-trough by the side of the inn front still stands to remind the wayfarer of the days when the highway was quick with traffic, but the sign itself bears eloquent testimony of decay and fallen fortunes though it still flaunts its ancient legend on a miniature crate that rocks and creaks over the narrow doorway:

"This Gate hangs well and hinders none;

Refresh and pay and travel on."

But on a certain winter's night of 183—, when this story opens, the guest more bent upon refreshing than travelling on might have pleaded good excuse. Outside, the snow lay upon field and road knee-deep, the thatches, gables, and very faces of the scattered houses of Wakey were splashed and bespattered with snow, which for days had fallen in big flakes, silent and sad as the grey leaves of latest autumn, making thick the air as with the lighting of grasshoppers. The moon in the low-hanging sky was veiled by heavy masses of dark cloud that stole across the heavens like mutes oppressed by the sombre garb of woe. Signs of life about the Wakey there seemed none, save the mellowed light that shone across the bisecting roads from the curtained lattices of the *Hanging Gate.* It was eight o'clock and the hand-loom weavers or mill-hands habiting the small stone-build houses that straggled from the valley up the bleak sides of Harrop Edge had gone to bed, not so much because they were weary as to save fire and light. The village smithy flanking the stables of the *Hanging Gate* was closed and the smith himself, big burly Jim o' Little Hannah's had forged his last shoe and blown the last blast from his bellows, poured his last pint down his throat in the neighbouring taproom and trudged home to his little wife and large family. The few frequenters of the tap-room had tarried till tarry they might no longer, for times were bad, money was scarce and the credit given by the best of innkeepers has its limits.

Mrs. Betty Schofield, the buxom hostess of the *Hanging Gate* was no wise dismayed by the slackness of her custom. Rumour had it that Betty was a very warm woman. She had been some years a widow, and her husband had left her, as the gossips said, well worth picking up. Look at her as she sits in the long kitchen before a roaring fire of mingled coal, peat and logs. Below the medium height, with wavy brown hair, a soft brown eye, a dimpled chin, now inclined to the double, a full and swelling bust, a mouth not too small and smiling lips that parted only to display a perfect set of teeth—it does one good to look upon her rosy cheek.—Happy the man, you say, who shall own those ample charms and for whom shall beam the ready smile or soften the warm brown eyes.

There are another two seated in the brick-tiled kitchen. Mary o' Stuart's commonly called Moll o' Stute's, and Mr. William Black. Moll shall have precedence in honour of her sex and calling, a noble calling, of a verity, for Mary was the midwife of the valley. She is scantily clad for the time of the year, yet you judge that it is not from cold that she huddles by the fireside, but rather for convenience of lighting the black clay pipe she so intently sucks, one long skinny brown arm resting on her knee, her eyes fixed upon the glowing fire that casts its flickering light upon the sharp hard-featured face. Her black hair is long and though streaked with grey is still abundant, and rebellious locks, escaped from the coil, stray over the scraggy shoulders, round which a shabby, faded, flannel shawl hangs loosely. No one knows where Moll lives, if it be not at the *Hanging Gate*, which, if not her home, is for Moll a sort of *Poste Restante*, and if not there to be always seen there she can always be heard of. Moll has less need of fixed abode than ordinary mortals. She has reached the age of fifty or more, and still bears her virgin name and owns to neither chick nor child, though there were that breathed mysterious hints of wild passages of thirty years gone bye, when Moll's cheek was soft and rosy and her form, though tall, lacked nought of grace and suppleness. "A saucy queen," the village grannies said, "and one that always thought herself too good for common folk; but pride had had its fall,"—a reflection that seemed to bring comfort to the toothless, hollow-cheeked beldames as they wheezed asthmatically of the scandals of a youth long fled, when Mary's foot light upon the village green and her laugh was readiest at feast or wakes.

On the opposite side of the hearth sat Mr. Black, the village Schoolmaster, a little lean man well past his meridian, his hair sparse and thin, and sparse and thin all his form and frame. He is clean shaven, but his lips are firm and his eye bright and keen. Though he has the lean and hungry look of the born conspirator, never did such a look so belie a man; for a gentler being never breathed than William Black, nor one more secure in the affection and esteem of high and low for many miles around. He was not a that country man and how or by what fate, driven by what adversity or sore mischance, he had drifted to that wild neighbourhood none presumed to know. He kept a day school for boys and girls, whose parents paid fourpence a child per week when they could afford it, and less when they couldn't—generally less. Then on alternate week-nights he kept a night-school where strapping and ambitious youths from loom or farm or bench, whose education had been neglected in their tender youth sought painfully to learn to read and write and sum. These were known to pay as much as twopence a lesson. Mr. Black—even in those irreverent days and parts, where few even of the better sort escape a nick-name, he was always called *Mr.* Black,—was a bachelor, and his modest household and Mr. Black himself were ruled by a spinster sister, shrill of voice, caustic of speech, with profound contempt for her brother's softness, but unceasing and untiring in the care of the household gods, and happiest in those "spring cleanings" that were not confined to spring. But to-night Mr. Black has fled before his sister's voice and twirling mop, and a look of seraphic content rests upon his face as he meditatively puffs his long churchwarden and sniffs the fragrant odour of the mulled ale that simmers in the copper vessel, shaped like a candle-snuffer, or, as Mr. Black reflected, like a highly burnished dunce's cap, and which the plump hand of Mrs. Schofield had thrust nigh to its rim in the very heart of the ruddy fire. The schoolmaster's thin legs, clad in stout stockings of native wool, knit by Miss Black's deft fingers, were crossed before the blaze and the grateful warmth falls upon them, the while the clogging snow slowly melts from his stout boots.

"Redfearn o' Fairbanks is late to-night," he said at length, after a silence broken only by the click of Mrs. Schofield's steel knitting needles.

"Aye, it's market day in Huddersfilt, yo' know, Mr. Black, an' th' roads 'll be bad to-neet. But Fairbanks 'll win through if th' mare dunnot fall an' break his neck."

"Th' mare's nooan foaled 'at 'll break Tom o' Fairbank's neck," said Moll o' Stuart's, grimly. "It's spun hemp that bides for him, if there's a God i' heaven."

"Whisht yo' now, Moll, an' quit speakin' o' your betters, leastwise if you canna speak respectful."

"Betters! Respectful! Quo' she," retorted Molly with a defiant snort, pulling hard at her filthy cuddy.

"Aye betters!" snapped the landlady, or as nearly snapped as lips like hers could snap. "It's me as says it, an' me as 'll stand to it. Wheer i' all th' parish will yo find a freer hand or a bigger heart nor Tom o' Fairbanks? Tell me that, yo' besom."

"Aye free enew," said Molly curtly.

Mrs. Schofield bridled indignantly.

"Oh! It's weel for yo' to sit by mi own fireside an' eat o' mi bread an' nivver so happy as when yo're castin' up bye-gones 'at should be dead an' buried long sin."

"Aye, aye, let the dead past bury its dead," put in the schoolmaster soothingly.

"An' what if Redfearn o' Fairbanks ware a bit leet gi'en i' his young days," went on the irate hostess. "He's nooan th' first an' he'll nooan be th' last. He's nobbut human like most folk 'at ivver I heard tell on. He's honest enough now, if he's had to wear honest. An' it's weel known....."

But what was so well known that the voluble tongue of Mrs. Schofield was about to repeat it at large shall not be here set down, nor was destined that night to enlighten the company; for the outer door was opened, and a gust of keen wind laden with feathery flakes of snow whirled up the narrow passage, well nigh extinguishing the slender light of the oil lamp on the wall, and causing the great burnished metal dishes and the very warming-pan itself to sway gently on their hooks.

"It's Fairbanks, hissen," said Mrs. Schofield "Talk o' the de'il," muttered the irrepressible Moll but no one heeded.

Then was heard much stamping of feet in the outer passage and kicking of boot toes on the lintel of the door and not a little coughing and clearing of the throat.

"Ugh! Shut the door to, man," cried a hearty voice; "do yo' want me to be blown into th' back-yard?"

The heavy bolt-studded door was pressed back and there strode into the room a tall well-built man. Top-booted, spurred, with riding-whip in hand, and wearing the long heavy-lapetted riding-coat of the period—a hale, hearty man fresh-complexioned, with close cropped crisping hair, the face clean shaven after the fashion of the times, a masterful man, you saw at a glance, and one who knew it. Though he was over the borderland of his fifth decade, time had neither wrinkled his ruddy face nor streaked his crisp brown hair. Behind him as he strolled into the kitchen, shambled a thick-set, saturnine, grim-visaged churl, who knew more of his master's business and far more of his master's secrets than the mistress of Fairbanks herself. It was Aleck, the shepherd and general factotum of Fairbanks farm, Aleck the silent, Aleck the cynic, Aleck the misogynist, against whose steeled heart successive milk-maids and servant wenches had cast in vain the darts and arrows of amorous eyes and who was spitefully averred to care only for home-brewed ale, and the sheep-dog, Pinder that now, already, was shaking the snow oft his shaggy coat preparatory to curling himself up before the fire.

"Sakes alive! It's a rough 'un, good folk," said the master of Fairbanks, "Good night to yo' Betty, an' to yo', Mr. Black. I was feart aw should miss yo'. Give me a stiff 'un o' rum hot wi' sugar an' a splash o' lemon; an' yo' Aleck, will't ha' a pint o' mulled?" Which redolent compound Mrs. Schofield was now pouring into a capacious pitcher.

"Tha knows better, mester," was Aleck's blunt reply. "A quart o' ale, missis, an' nooan too much yead on it—no fal-lals for me, mi stummack's too wake."

This was an unusually long speech for Aleck, and he sank exhausted on a settle that ran beneath a long narrow window, whilst the dog prone upon the hearth, his jaws resting on his fore paws, feigned sleep, but blinked at times from beneath twitching eyebrows at the rugged visage of the tanned, weather-beaten herdsman.

"An' yo' stabled th' mare aw nivver heerd th' stable door oppen?" queried Mrs Schofield.

"Nay, I left Bess at th' *Floating Lights*. She cast a shoe coming over th' Top. So we'n walked daan an welly up to mi chin aw've bin more nor once—it's th' heaviest fall aw mind on."

"But you're late Fairbanks," said Mr Black. "I looked for you this hour and more. Have you had a good market?"

"Aye nowt to grumble at, an' we Aleck? Sold forty head o' beast an' bought thirty as fine cattle as ever yo' clapped e'en on, eh, Aleck? An' we're nooan strapped yet," he laughed, as he drew a leather pouch from an inner pocket and cast it jingling on to the table. "Here Betty, put that i'th cupboard."

"Have yo' counted it?" asked Mrs. Schofield, handling the greasy bag gingerly.

"Count be danged," said Mr. Redfearn, "saving your presence, schoolmaster. Gi' me another jorum. Sup up, Aleck."

Aleck supped up and silently handed his pewter to Mrs Schofield.

"But it wasn't the market that kept me so late," went on Mr Redfearn. "There were a meeting o' th' free holders o' th' district to consider the new Reform Bill. We met i' th' big room at th' *George*, but it all came to nowt; though Harry Brougham talked and talked fit to talk a hen an' chickens to death. Gosh! Our Mary's a good 'un, but she couldn't hold a can'le to Brougham."

"Aye, did you hear Mr. Brougham?" asked Mr Black, with interest. "What manner of man is he?"

"Why nowt much to look at—aw could blow him away like thistle down; more like a monkey up a stick nor owt 'at I can think on. But talk! You should hear him! But he didn't talk my vote out o' me for all that. King and Church for me, say I. Th' owd ways were good enough for my father an' my father's father an' aw reckon they'll do for me."

"But he's a marvellous man," said Mr. Black. "Who but he could leave the Assizes at York, travel, there and back, over two hundred miles after the rising of the Court, address half-a-dozen meetings and be back next day taking his briefs—I think they call them—as fresh as new paint."

"Aye, but that wern't Brougham," said Redfearn. "It wer' Owdham browies."

"Eh?" queried the schoolmaster.

"Aye, Owdham browies. I had it from a sure source. Th' other day i' th' Court Harry wer' fair done an' it wer' getting late. 'Won't your ludship adjourn, now?' He says, as mild as milk."

"'No, sir,' says th' judge,'I shall finish this case if I sit till midnight.' Yo' see he knew Harry only wanted to be off spoutin' an' th' owd judge wer' a Tory."

"'Very well, my lord,' says Harry an' turns to his clerk, an' in a jiffy there war a basin o' haver-bread wi' hot beef drippin' poured on it an pepper an salt an' a pint o' old port wine stirred in, an' Harry spooinnin' it into him like one o'clock, slap under th' owd Judge's nose. Th'owd felly wer' a bit hungry hissen, an' th' smell set his mouth a watterin' an' he jumped up an' adjourned th' Court, an' if he didn't say 'curse yo',' they say he looked it. But what ails Pinder?"

The sheep-dog had pricked its ears, then listened intently, then gone into the passage whining and growling.

"Pinder thinks it's time to be goin' whom'," said Aleck, as he followed the cur into the passage. The dog laid its nose to the bottom of the thick door; whined and began frantically to scratch at the door beneath which the snow had drifted in thin sprays. When Aleck neared the dog it leaped on him and then with looks more eloquent than speech compelled him to the door.

"Ther's summat up," said Aleck, as he opened the door. "Bring th' lantern, missus."

The dog bounded out, set its head to the ground and howled dismally. Aleck stooped, his big hands swept away a big mound of snow and he lifted something in his arms. "Mak' way theer," he cried, as nearly excited as ever Aleck had been known to be; "mak' way; it's a woman an' oo's dead, aw'm thinkin'."

He bore his burthen, almost covered with its cold winding sheet of snow, into the warm kitchen, and laid it before the fire. Mrs. Schofield had snatched a cushion from the settle and placed it under the head of the lifeless figure. The men had risen to their feet and gazed helplessly at the rigid form. They saw the fair young face, marble white and set, fair tresses, sodden through. Upon the feet were shoes of flimsy make, the heel gone from one of them. A slight cape covered a thin dress of good make and material, but far too tenuous for winter wear, and all was travel-stained and soaked through.

Moll o' Stute's thrust the men aside. "Go whom," she said, "yo're nooan wanted here." She put her hand into the woman's bosom. "Gi' me some brandy," she said. It was there already, held in Mrs. Schofield's trembling hand. A little passed the lips and gurgled down the throat. A little more and the potent spirit did its saving work. The white thin hand twitched, the eyes partly opened, then closed again as a faint sigh breathed from the pallid lips.

"Put th' warming pan i' th' best bed, an' leet a fire upstairs," commanded Moll. "I'st be wanted afore mornin' or aw'st be capped."

"Shall Aleck fetch Dr. Garstang?" ventured Mr. Redfearn.

"Garstang fiddlesticks," snapped Moll. "This is wark for me, aw tell yo'. There'll be one more i' this house bi morn, and happen one less, God save us. But get you gone an' moither me no more."

CHAPTER II.

MR. Black did not sleep well that night. He had fevered visions of Alpine crevasses, of St. Bernard dogs and of fair blanched faces set in long dank tresses of clinging hair. He had had, too, before seeking his narrow pallet, a rather bad and disquieting quarter of an hour with his sister, who had demanded in acrid tones to be told what made him so late home. He was losing his character, the irate Priscilla had declared, spending every spare moment at the *Hanging Gate*, whose landlady everyone knew to be a designing women and openly and unblushingly "widowing." A nice howdyedo it must be for him, a scholar, to have his name bandied about in every tap-room between Diggle and Greenfield. But she would see Mr Whitelock the vicar of St Chad's, and perhaps her abandoned brother would take more notice of his spiritual adviser than he did of those that were his own flesh and blood so to speak. But if he meant to go on that gate, drinking and roistering and maybe even worse, she, for one, wouldn't stand it, and nevermore would she set scrubbing brush to desk and floor or duster to chair, no not if dirt lay so thick, you could write your name in it with your finger—and so forth. Mr. Black had smiled when Mr Whitelock was mentioned, for well he knew the worthy vicar's cob stopped without hint from rein as it reached the *Hanging Gate*, and no one knew better than the reverend gentleman the virtues of those comforting liquids Mrs. Schofield reserved for favoured guests. Priscilla, however, had been somewhat mollified and allowed the cauldron of her righteous wrath to simmer down, when her brother told her he had been detained by Mr. Redfearn of Fairbanks, and that she might expect a basket of butter and eggs, with maybe a collop, as a mark of friendship and esteem from Mrs. Redfearn herself.

Mr. Black struggled hard with his early breakfast of porridge and milk, but it was no use. He pushed away bowl and platter and murmuring something about being back in time to open school he seized his beaver, donned frieze coat and made off to the *Hanging Gate.*

His heart sank within him when he found the door closed though not bolted, and every window shrouded by curtain or blind.

Mrs. Schofield was rocking herself in the chair and looked, as was indeed the case as if she had known no bed that night. There were marks of tears upon her, cheeks, and her glossy hair, was all awry and unkempt.

"Eh, but Mr. Black," she half sobbed, "but it's good for sair e'en to see yo' or any other Christian soul after such a time as aw've passed through this very neet that's passed and gone. Glory be to God. And oh! Mi poor head, if it doesna crack it's a lucky woman Betty Schofield will be. If it hadn't been for a cup o' tay goodness only knows but what aw'd ha' sunk entirely, and Moll o Stute's wi' no more feelin' nor a stone. But sit yo' down, sir, an' drink a dish o' tea."

Now black tea in those days was 8s. a pound and a tea-drinking was almost as solemn a function as a Church sacrament. Tea was not to be lightly drunk, and indeed was reserved chiefly for funerals and christenings. The women folk of the middle classes drank it at times to mark their social status, as people now-a-days emblazon emblems of spurious heraldry on the panels of their broughams. The men held it in derision as a milksop's beverage and swore by the virtues of hops and malt. But Mr. Black was fain to forget his manhood nor resisted over much when a certain cordial, darkly alluded to as "brown cream" and commonly supposed to mellow in the plantations of Jamaica, was added to the fragrant cup.

"And the poor woman?" he asked timidly at last.

"Ah! Poor woman well may yo' call her, though mebbe now she's richer nor any on us, for if ever misguided wench looked like a saint i' heaven she does—an' passed away as quiet as a lamb, at two o'clock this mornin' just as th' clock theer wer strikin' th' hour. Eh! But she's a bonnie corpse as ever aw seed but she looks so like an angel fro' heaven aw'm awmost feart to look at her. Yo'll like to see her, but Fairbanks 'll be comin' down aw doubt na an' yo'll go up together."

"Did she speak, is there anything to show who or what she is?"

"Not a word, not a sign, not a mark on linen or paper; but oo's no common trollop that aw'st warrant, tho' she *had* no ring on her finger."

"Maybe her straits compelled her to part with it," suggested Mr. Black.

"Weel, weel, mebbe, mebbe, tho' it's th' last thing a decent woman parts wi', that an' her marriage-lines. But, as I said, th' poor thing med no sign. 'Oo just oppened her sweet e'en as Moll theer laid th' babby to her breast, an' her poor hand tried to touch its face, an' just th' quiver o' a smile fluttered on her lips, an' then all wer' ovver, but so quiet like, so quiet, 'twere more a flutterin' away nor deein'. Eh! But awm thankful 'oo deed i' my bed an' not o'th moor buried i' a drift"—and the tears once more trickled down Mrs. Schofield's rounded cheek.

Mr. Black took the plump left hand that rested on the widow's lap and gently pressed it in token of the sympathy his lips could not express. Could mortal man do less?

"It's times like these a poor widow feels her lonesome state," murmured Mrs. Schofield.

Mr. Black withdrew his hand, and the grim visage of Priscilla flashed across his vision.

The twain had been so absorbed that Moll o' Stute's had glided into the kitchen, and now was seated on her accustomed stool by the fireside. She had a soft bundle of flannel in her arms and as she sat she swayed gently to and fro murmuring, not unmusically, some crooning lullaby of the country side.

"The babe?" whispered Mr. Black, and Mrs. Schofield nodded silently, and then, sinking her voice, "Moll's got another maggot i' her head. She thinks th' poor lass 'ats dead an' gone wer' seeking Tom o' Fairbanks. Yo' know how daft she is when 'oo sets that way."

"Aye, give a dog a bad name and hang him. An old saying and true. We all know Fairbanks was a sad fellow in his young days, but bar a quip and maybe a stolen kiss from ready and tempting lips, he's steady enough now".

"Aye, aye, worn honest, as they say," acquiesced the hostess. "But here he comes. Aw med sure he'd be anxious to know the end o' last neet's doin's—an' wheer Fairbanks is Aleck's nooan far off, nor Pinder far off Aleck."

Nor was Mrs. Schofield wrong in her surmise, Mr Redfearn came almost on tip-toe through the passage into the kitchen. The presence of death needs neither the whispered word nor the silent signal. Its hush is upon the house of mourning as the Sabbath stillness rests upon the fields. Even the phlegmatic Aleck had composed his rugged features to a more impressive rigidity than was their use, and the very dog stole to the hearth with downcast head and humid eyes.

"It came to th' worst then?" asked Mr. Redfearn, after a solemn silence. He needed no reply. "Well, well, we all mun go someday; but she wer' o'er young an' o'er bonnie to be so cruel o'erta'en."

"Aye it's weel to hear you talk, Fairbanks," broke in the irrepressible Molly, as she strained the child closer to her shrunken breast. "But there's someb'dy 'll ha' to answer for this neet's wark an' who it is mebbe yersen can tell."

Redfearn checked a hasty retort. There were, perhaps, reasons why he must bear the lash of Molly's tongue. "Is she i' th' chamber?" he asked.

"Yo'd like to see her," said Mrs Schofield.

Softly, the farmer and the schoolmaster followed their guide up the narrow creaking steps that led from the passage to the best bedroom, the room of state of the *Hanging Gate.* Upon a large four-poster lay the lifeless form fairer and more beautiful than in life. Mrs. Schofield drew the curtain of the window and the morning light streamed upon the couch and cast a halo on the pure child-like face. The long silken hair, deftly tended, had been drawn across each shoulder and in rippling streams fell about the bosom. It was hard to think that Death was there—'t was more as though a maiden slept.

The men stood by the couch side gazing reverently on the fragile form. Redfearn drew a short and gasping breath and passed his hand furtively across his eyes.

"A good woman, schoolmaster, a good woman. I'd stake my life on that."

The dominie moved his head in silent assent, then with broken voice breathed low, "Let us pray," and Mrs. Schofield flung her apron over her head as she sank upon her knees, and Redfearn and Mr. Black knelt by the bedside. 'Twas but a simple prayer that God's mercy might have been vouchsafed to the sister who had passed away, far from her friends and home, a nameless wanderer, with none to help but the Father who had called his wandering child to the land where the wicked cease from troubling and the weary are at rest,—His own sweet home; a prayer, too, that God would raise up friends for the orphaned bairn that would never know a mother's love nor perchance a father's care. And as he prayed Redfearn's hand pressed heavy on his arm and in hoarse tones the farmer muttered.

"God forgive me all my sins—I'll find the wee lad's father, if he's in the three Ridings, an' if aw dunnot th' lad shall nivver want for bite nor sup." Then as though ashamed, he groped his way down the dingy staircase and flung himself into the big oaken arm-chair that none ventured to dispute with him.

But it was not in the nature of the man to be long oppressed by brooding thought or to abandon himself to the bitter-sweet reflections of sombre-visaged melancholy. His active, restless temperament was impatient of reflection and his practical mind turned to the present need.

"Aleck, yo'll go to Sam Sykes's an' order th' coffin, an' tell him to see about th' grave i' Saddleworth churchyard. Gi' my respects to th' vicar an' ask him to fix all about th' buryin', an Sykes 'll see about th' undertaker. Yo'll see th' poor lass put away, Betty, an' yo' too, Moll, an' yo'll want a black gown, aw dessay. Well, thank God ther's a shot i' th' locker yet. Give us th' bag out o'th cupboard, Betty. It's weel aw left it last neet, aw med ha' known. An' now what wi one thing an' another awm fair done an' yo mun bring me summat to put a bit o' heart i' me."

"It's weel talkin' o' puttin' folk away," broke in Moll, in no way softened by the prospect of a new gown. "Th' dead's soon away wi'; but what abart th' child here?" and Molly turned aside the flannel covering the infant face.

"Dooms! Aw'd fair forgetten th' bairn," said Fairbank, "Let's ha' a look at it bi th' winder mi eyes are none so good as they used to be."

Molly reluctantly placed the little one in the farmer's outstretched arms and he bore it to the light.

"A fine child as ivver yo' seen," said Mrs. Schofield. "It's gotten my Benny's things on, leastwise them at 'aw made for him wi' my own fingers, but it warn't to be, for th' poor lad nivver breathed but once. Eh! It's a queer warld; them as could do wi childer an' thank the Lord for 'em cannot ha' 'em, an' them as sudna ha' 'em,—they come a troopin'. It passes me altogether."

Mr. Black was casting anxious glances at the long sleeve clock, its long brass hand now marching upwards to that ninth hour of the morn that every schoolboy dreads.

"I must be going," he said.

"Nay, rest you," urged the widow. "Gi th' childer a holiday—. Yer' none yersen tha morn, an' to be sure which on us is? I'll ha' some ham in th' pan i' a jiffy, an' it's Fairbanks fed, an yo know what that means."

"Nay, nay, tempt me not, tempt me not. Those lads o' mine e'en now are up to their eyes in mischief. There'll be a crooked pin in the cushion of my chair, a chalk drawing of Priscilla, none too flattering, on the map of Europe, and those of them that are not playing cots and tyes for buttons will be playing 'Follow mi leader' over the forms and desks. It's much if the windows arn't broken and there wont be a button left on some of their clothes—inveterate gamblers as though they shook a box at Brighton Spa." Mr. Black's tone was harsh, but there was a gleam in his eye that took away the sting of his speech.

“Yo’re a good Churchman, aw know,” said Redfearn, “for yo’ do as th’ owd Book tells us—yo’ spare the rod an’ spoil the child. But we mun settle summat about th’ bairn here, an’ aw’ll be down to-neet as soon as I can get.”

Mr. Black bent over the sleeping babe nestling in its nurse’s arms. “Come early,” whispered Molly, “aw’ve summat to say to yo’ partic’ler.”

It was but a distracted mind the teacher gave that day to the budding genius of his school. He was lost in conjecture as to what Moll might have to say to him, and not less in surprise that she should have aught at all, for though that hard-featured damsel of the rasping tongue treated him with a deference shown to no other he could think of no subject demanding the secrecy Molly’s manner had seemed to ask.

He did not fail to be early at the *Hanging Gate*, indeed Mrs. Schofield, her wonted serenity restored by an afternoon’s nap on the settle, had but just sided the tea-things, after that meal which is locally called a “baggin’”—(another term whose origin is shrouded in mystery) and was still in the sacred retreat upstairs, where she was accustomed to array herself as beseemeth the landlady of a thriving hostelry, with money in the bank, and that could change her condition by holding up her little finger.

Molly no longer held the child in her arms. It had been transferred into the highly polished mahogany cradle, which Molly worked gently with her foot, and which also had doubtless been purchased for the use of that disappointing Benny.

“Eh! Aw’m glad yo’n come,” she said eagerly, as Mr. Black removed his wraps. “Speak low, th’ missis is upstairs, an’ these rafters is like sounding boards.”

She thrust her hand deep into one of those long linen pockets beneath the upper gown and that only a woman can find.

“Here tak’ it,” she said, “tak’ it. It’s welly burned a hoil i’ mi pocket. Dunnot let me han’le it again or aw’ll nooan answer for missen. It’s gowd, man, gowd, aw tell yo’ an’ there’s figgerin on it i’ some mak o’ stones at glitter an’ dazzle till yo’d think the varry devil wer’ winkin’ at yo’, an whisperin’ i’ yo’r lug to keep it quiet an’ say nowt to nobody.”

She placed a trinket in the schoolmaster’s hand and heaved a sigh of relief. It was a locket of gold, heart-shaped. On the one side was worked, in small diamonds, a true-lovers’ knot, on the reverse, in pearls, a monogram.

The like neither dominie nor nurse had ever gazed upon before, save, perhaps, through the tantalizing barrier of a jeweller's window in Huddersfield or Manchester, and, it is safe to say, never before had either held in hand article of so much value.

"Yo' know aw helped to put her to bed," whispered Molly, with a motion of head towards the best bedroom, "an' aw undressed her, an' when th' missis wer' airin' a neet-gown for th' poor thing aw' spied that teed round her neck wi' a bit o' velvet. So aw' snipped it off, for aw seed weel enough oo'd nivver want it again. Aw'd meant to keep it till aw could mak it i' my way to go daan to Huddersfilt; but aw stood at th' bottom o' th' stairs when yo' wer prayin' yesterday, an' oh, Mr. Black, it wor' a tussle, but aw couldna keep it, aw couldna keep it after that."

Mr. Black was much moved. He took Molly's hand in his and bowed over it. "You are a good woman Molly, and One who seeth in secret will reward you openly."

"Dunnot tell th' misses," urged Molly, flushing even through the tan of her hard face at a tribute seldom paid to her. "Oo'll mebbe think aw sud ha' gien it to her; an' though aw've no patience wi' her airs an' her greetin' (crying) an' settin her cap at's aboon her, thof poor they may be, but still oo's reet at t'core, an awd be sorry to fa' out wi' her."

Mr. Black nodded, and carefully placed the locket in the pocket of his vest.

"I must think over this. I don't like secrets; but you shall go harmless. This trinket, valuable as it doubtless is of itself, may be more precious still as a clue to that poor child's parentage and I must take counsel with Mr Redfearn."

Molly shook her head in emphatic dissent.

"You wrong Fairbanks, indeed you do, Molly."

"Ah, yo' ken, yo' ken," said Molly, brokenly, "who but Fairbanks ruined my young life?"

"And hath he not repented and would have made amends? As you stand in need of forgiveness, Molly, learn to forgive. 'Tis a lesson we all must learn."

The entrance of Redfearn himself precluded the further discussion of a delicate and painful subject. Molly assumed with some difficulty the control of her features, but there was lacking, for a time at least, that resentful defiance and general contrariness his presence seemed generally to arouse. Drawing back into the shade of her favourite corner she devoted herself to the assiduous care of the cradle, whilst Mrs. Schofield, now resplendent in her evening finery of black silk, with massive gold brooch and long gold watch chain that reached in double folds from neck to waist, with her own fair hand decocted the soothing compound demanded by the master of Fairbanks, nor disdained to pump the humming ale that was the nectar of the attendant herdsman.

"Well, Aleck, tha wer' tellin' me," said Redfearn, "tha's seen Mr. Whitelock an' th' sexton an' th' undertaker, an' all's arranged?"

Aleck made no reply till he had lowered the pewter two-handled quart measure, and wiped his lips with the back of his hand—a good pint had disappeared, and you might have heard it gurgling down his throat like water down a bent and choked drain. He nodded his reply: then gruffly:

"To-morrow, three o'clock. Th' hearse an' coaches here at two."

"An' now what's to be done about th' little 'un?" queried the farmer. "I've thowt an' thowt, an' better thowt. An' aw'm nooan a bit nearer. Aw thowt mebbe yo' could tak' care on it, till its own folk wer' found. What ses ta, Betty?"

But Mrs. Schofield shook her head. "It wouldn't do Fairbanks, it 'ud nivver do. Aw met manage if Moll wor allus here to look after it an 'oo could give a hand i' th' taproom o' Saturday neets and Sundays. But wi' her, nivver to be depended on five minutes together, knocked up i' th' middle o' th' neet when least yo' look for it, an' nivver knowin' when oo'll be back or wheer oo'll be next more like a gipsy or willy-wisp nor a regular lodger, an' me a sound sleeper—yo' can see for yorsen it 'ud nivver act."

"Why dunno yo' offer to tak' him to Fairbanks?" Molly could not forbear asking, with some malice. "One more or less 'll mak' no differ to yo', an' th' lad 'ud sooin be o' use on th' farm."

"Not for a thousand golden guineas," exclaimed Redfearn. "Our Mary's th' best o' women; but if 'oo has a fault it's jalousin' about every bye-blow that's born i'th' village. There's her an' your Priscilla, schoolmaster, bin collogin' o'er this job already, bi what aw can speer, an Mary looked sour enough to turn a field o' red cabbage into pickles, when aw started fro' Fairbanks to-neet. Didn't 'oo, Aleck?" concluded Redfearn, with his usual appeal to his faithful henchman.

"Oo did that," said Aleck, starting out of a deep reverie.

"Yo' might lay it to me," at last Aleck said, "awst nooan mind, an' aw say Pinder 'd get used to it in a bit."

"What could yo' do wi' a child i' th' hut, you numskull?" laughed the farmer.

"Well, settle it yo'r own gate—it's all a price to me. Best chuck it i' th' cut an' ha' done wi' it."

If a look could have blasted man, as lightning blasts the oak, never more would Aleck have herded flock on the lofty heights and stretching moors that edge Diggle valley and its rippling brook.

"Out on yo', Aleck no-name," cried Molly, springing hotly to her feet. "Eh! But if aw could nobbut see mi way, yo' bonnie bairn, none sud ha' yo' but mysen. These hands received yo', an' these hands sud tew for yo', if aw worked 'em to skin an' bone. But it canna be, my bonnie pet,"—she apostrophised the unconscious babe—"An' Moll o' Stute's nooan fit to ha' th' rearin' o' such as thee, quality-born if ivver ther' wor one."

"That reminds me," interposed the schoolmaster, as he drew forth the locket and told its tale.

"Well, aw nivver did," gasped Mrs. Schofield, eyeing the keepsake and with some difficulty prizing it open with the point of her scissors. "Black hair an' leet, crossed an' knotted. Th' leet coloured 'll be th' poor lass's, silk isn't in it for fine, an' th' black 'll be th' father's, aw'll be bun'."

Even Aleck could not refrain from admiration. "It'll come in handy some day," he predicted, "aw sudn't wonder if it fot enough to breech th' lad, when th' time comes."

"Breech th' lad, in sooth; hear him. Why, yo' stupid, it 'ud buy twenty o't best sheep ivver tha seed i' pen. Our Mary's nowt to marrow it, wi her mother's an gret-aunt Keziah's thrown in."

"Twenty ship!" repeated Aleck. "Weel, weel, fooils an' ther brass is soon parted."

"But we get further off i'stead o' nearer th' point," pursued the farmer. "Yo'n said nowt, Mr. Black; what's to be done wi' th' child?"

"Well, first and foremost we must advertise i' th' *Leeds Mercury* an' th' *Manchester Courier*, for you see we've nothing to guide us which way she came. It may well be sorrowing parents, perhaps a conscience-stricken lover, or indeed, perchance, a distracted husband, at this very moment is seeking far and near for the poor wanderer. What tale of wrong those sealed lips could tell we may not even surmise. But the locket and these initials may put us on the right track. Anyway it won't cost much, and it's our clear and bounden duty to both the living and the dead."

"It's reet weel thowt on, Schoolmaster. See what it is to be educated. Thof aw will say aw hannot much hope. Aw onest lost a cow for three week—yo' moind on it, Aleck?"

"Three week an' three days," muttered the shepherd.

"An' aw 'vertised an 'vertised but nowt cam' on it. But Pinder fan her didn't ta, lad?"

Pinder winked his dexter eye and lazily stirred his tail.

"An' if th' advertisin' comes to nowt, what then?" said Molly.

Aye, what then! There was indeed the rub.

"Mr. Black's nooan finished yet," said Mrs Schofield.

The schoolmaster thoughtfully stirred his rum toddy with the metal crusher.

"I should dearly like to take the child as my own and rear him up to follow me when I've closed the school door for the last time and the long vacation begins for the old dominie. I could bring the lad on in arithmetic, grammar, the use of the globes, mensuration, algebra up to quadratic equations, Latin as far as Caesar *De Bello* and the Greek Testament as far as Matthew," and Mr. Black's eyes glistened at the alluring prospect.

"To be sure yo' could, no man better," assented Mr. Redfearn, none the less stoutly that he did not know what Mr. Black meant. "Aw'd a dog once called Caesar, but Bello's beyond me."

"It's to 'prentice him to th' blacksmith, can't ta see?" said Aleck.

"Aw see, an' a very gooid notion too."

"But I cannot take the child on, though fain I'd be to do it. You know Priscilla's never wed. She says it's for my sake, and doubtless she knows best. But she isn't as young as she was, and those plaguy boys have tried her temper. I wouldn't say it to anyone, but Priscilla is a little, just a little, mind you, tetchy, so to speak, and certain sure I am she'd neither be willing nor able to do for a helpless bairn."

"Aw see how it'll end," cried Molly. "Sakes alive! Farmer, missus, an' schoolmaster all backin aat, like those folk i' th' Bible 'at wer' bid to th' weddin', an' nooan on 'em could come. There's nobbut one end for yo' an' that's th' work'us, th' big hoil o'th' hill yonder, as weel say it as think it," and the incensed virago bounced out of the kitchen and joined the company in the taproom in a game of "checkers" and sparing neither partner nor opponent the rasp of her biting tongue.

"Yo' could make it, easy for th' bairn?" went on Mr. Black.

"An' th' matron's a motherly body wi' childer o' her own," put in the hostess.

"An' we needn't lose sight o' th' lad," added Mr. Redfearn.

"And I could spare an hour or two a day, when he's big enough. I'll make a course of study this very day. It's the very thing. Good Molly, *rem acu tetigisti*, as we say in the classics."

"Exactly," assented the farmer. "By the way, Aleck, did yo' say owt to Mr. Whitelock about th' chrisenin'? Aw'd welly (well-nigh) forgetten it."

"After th' buryin', t' same day," said Aleck the terse.

"Yo'll be god-mother, Betty, na' who'll stand godfather?"

"I've always understood in case of a foundling it takes the finder's name," said Mr. Black.

"That's Aleck," said the landlady.

"Nay it wer' Pinder theer," protested Aleck.

"The very thing," exclaimed Mr. Redfearn, smiting the table so the glasses danced. "Tom Pinder, fit him like a glove. We'll weet his yed i' glasses round an' then whom (home) and bed, say I."

Mr. Redfearn glanced at the schoolmaster, the schoolmaster at Mr. Redfearn.

"You're the chairman of the Guardians," said the teacher mildly.

"An' th' biggest ratepayer, worse luck," said his crony.

CHAPTER III.

THE Workhouse for the Saddleworth Union is a low stone building of no great dimensions, standing on about as bleak and cold a site as could well I have been selected. It stands on the hill-side on your left hand as you walk from Diggle to Saddleworth, part of that dorsal Pennine Range we call "the back bone of Old England." Its exterior is grim and forbidding, nor is the external promise redeemed by any extravagance of luxury inside. It is in unenviable contrast to the palatial structures modern architects design for the option of the sick and destitute. But it is healthily situated, and that counts for much. All in front as you look down the valley, are the green fields; at its rear stretch the moors on which sheep graze and lambs bleat and gamble conies sport and burrow and where the warning "Go-back, go-back" of the grouse salutes the ear as summer softens into autumn, and the purple heather hides the luscious bilberry.

At the time of which I write no mill chimney belched their smoke into the air and the breezes that swept the Workhouse on every side though blowing at times with unwelcome force, were pure and sweet. The Workhouse kine yielded milk so abundantly that adulteration was never thought of; the kitchen-garden, tended by the pauper hands, was rich in its herbs and vegetables, and a small flower garden gave forth the fragrance of the hardier roses, of musk and mignonette, whilst sweet williams, forget-me-nots and stocks gave colour and variety, dear to the eye of the female paupers. It is true the wards were low, the benches hard, the light and ventilation far removed from modern notions; but in this respect they differed in no wise, or if they differed, differed for the better, from the houses of the well-to-do farmers and tradesmen of the district.

Anyway there the young foundling of my story was in babyhood and boyhood tended, petted, and made much of. Consigned to the charge of an elderly pauper he had a not unkindly foster-mother. Rare, thank God, the women whose hearts do not soften to the helpless child. Tom sucked his bottle like a hero, waxing chubby and rosy, "poiting" with his legs on which the flesh lay in creases, and crowing lustily as he grew. Mr. Redfearn, it has been said, was the Chairman of the Guardians and did not conceal the interest he felt in the lad; Mr. Black, a privileged visitor everywhere for miles around, had to be restrained by the nurse from gorging his protege with lollipops. The story of his birth had spread in all those parts and lost nothing in the telling. For anything the master and matron knew the Workhouse might be entertaining, if not an angel, unawares, at least a baronet. The lad, when able to run about, was transferred to the particular care of "Workhouse Jack," a pauper of some thirty years of age, supposed to be "not altogether there," or as it is sometimes put, to have at least a half slate off. Jack was the messenger or Mercury of the Workhouse. He fetched the masters newspaper from the village post-office, he was entrusted with commissions to the grocer and draper by the matron, and smuggled snuff and twist and forbidden luxuries to the inmates. He knew every farm-house and every shop for miles around, and never wanted for a meal or a copper when he went his rounds. But, best of all, he knew the habits and the haunts of every bird that nested in the tree or hedge, on the greensward or, like the stone-chat, in the crevices of the long, grey dry-walling of the pastures. He knew, too, to an inch, the curvature of the field drains, their exits and their entrances. He kept surreptitiously in the old, two-stalled stable of the House a sharp-toothed ferret, which he oft-times carried in his pocket and that allowed him to handle and fondle it with quite appalling familiarity. It took Tom a long time to overcome his shrinking awe of that lithe and stealthy ferret, but he did it, and once nearly sent Mrs. Schofield into convulsions by insinuating it from his own into the capacious pocket of this steadfast friend. For I regret to say that Jack was a daily visitor at the *Hanging Gate*, and was doubly welcome when the little Tommy toddled, *haud aquis passibus*, by his side. But Jack had a seasoned head and though he called, on one pretext or another, at many an hostelry, was never overcome and had the rare good sense to inculcate sobriety on his admiring charge by many a precept if not by example. To Tom, Jack was the very incarnation of wisdom, and his very first battle was fought at the back of the Workhouse stable with another foundling who had called his guide, philosopher, and friend by no less derogatory a title than "Silly Billy." From that encounter Tom emerged with streaming eyes and nose, but in the proud consciousness of victory. Nor was Jack's lore confined to the creatures of the air and land. Down the mountain sides trills many a gushing stream to join the Diggle Brook, pellucid waters murmuring over the worn pebbles and larger fragments of volcanic rock that still, to this day, resist the action of the fretting air and pelting storm. Who so deft a hand as Jack at tickling the shy trout that darted among the sedges and rushes of the banks or lurked beneath leaf and boulder motionless as the stones themselves. And if the matron, when the dainty fish graced her table was not scrupulous to ask whence came this toothsome addition to the dietary approved by my lords in London town, whose business was it to interfere?

Ah! It is grand upon the billowing hills to wander idly in the sweet spring-time; to mark the lark rising above its nest high in the azure sky, trilling joyous melody, to hear the lambs calling to their dams, to see the kine cropping pensive, in the meadows the sweet new blades of the greening grass; sweet is it to bask at mid-day nodding on the heather and lulled to sleep by the hum that, like distant muffled music, just falls upon the ear, and sweet too, is it as the western sun drops to its rosy curtained couch, to call the cows with their swelling udders from pasture to their byre; sweet to stand by rustic maid of rosy cheek and buxom form as, piggin betwixt her knees and head pressed on the flanks of patient and grateful beast, she strains the warm and frothy fluid to the can. Glorious, too, to hearken to the whetstone drawn by practised hand across the scythe, to bear its swish as the swathe lengthens out before the steady strokes of the mower; glorious to strew the damp, green grass upon the ground to catch the morning sun, and grander still to mount upon the load of fragrant hay and be borne triumphant with the gathered harvest of the fields. Who that has passed his early youth on the hill sides of Marsden and Diggle can ever forget the changing raptures of those early days or weary in recalling them when the brain is distraught by the turmoil of the town, and the heart turns sickening from the searing sorrows of thwarted schemes and fallen hopes.

It may seem to the reader that Tom Pinder's workhouse life was not the life depicted by the immortal genius who told the piteous tale of a pinched and bruised Oliver asking for more. But be it remembered that all masters were not and still less are not Bumbles. The Saddleworth Workhouse in the thirties of last century had few inmates. The people on the sparsely populated hill-sides were mostly hand-loom weavers; not a few of them had a patch of land, a cow, a pig, and poultry. They were as clannish as the Scotch and when age, infirmity, or affliction overtook the declining years it was counted shame even of distant kin to suffer one of their name and blood to go to the big House. The poor then were mindful of the poor, and though the pinch of want was felt in the long winter days it went hard with folk if a neighbour's cupboard was left bare or his grate without the mountain peat. Add to this that the master and matron were good, easy-going folk; that the Guardians knew well every inmate of the House; had perchance played truant with them in their youth and been birched by the same cane, or employed them in their prime, and, to cap all, forget not that Saddleworth was an obscure Union, scarce worth the expenditure of red-tape or the visit of an inspector.

Mr. Black did not forget his promise to see to Tom's education. Almost before the child could lisp he was at him with the alphabet, and with his own hands designed alluring capital letters and emblematic animals so that to his dying day Tom never saw the letter D without thinking of a weaver's donkey going "a-bunting," or in other words, taking in his master's warp. At six Tom could read big print, and at seven was set to read chapters of the Bible to the old grannies of the women's side of the House; at eight he could do sums in Practice and was not afraid of Tare and Tret. But beyond this he stubbornly refused to budge. In vain Mr. Black wooed him to decline *Rosa*, a rose, or to conjugate *Amo*. Tom feigned indeed an interest he did not feel, but promptly forgot on one day all the Latin he had learned the day before. Mr. Black was fain to confess with a sigh that Tom was not bent by nature to a clerkly calling.

"Well, he's none the worse for that," said Mr. Redfearn, consolingly. "Look at me, schoolmaster. I can read a newspaper, make out a bill though it's seldom called for i' my trade, thank the Lord, write a letter, and what more do I want? How could I tell the points of horse or beast if mi head wer' allus running on th' olden times an' chokefull o' a lot o' gibberish, saving your presence, an' no offence, Mr. Black, as well yo' know. We can't all be schoolmasters, nor yet parsons an' as for lawyers and doctors aw've very little opinion o' awther on 'em, an' th' less yo' have to do wi' 'em th' better. Not but what a cow doctor's a handy man to ha' wi'in call; but th' lawyers! Aw've had three trials at th' Assizes abaat one watter-course on another. An' lost one case an' won two, an' th' two aw won cost me no more nor th' one aw lost. No! Th' lad's fit for better things nor a black gown. He's getten th' spirit o' a man choose wheer it comes fro'. Aw put him on Bess's back t'other day, wi'out a saddle an' his little legs could hardly straddle fro' flank to flank, an' he catched her bi th' mane an' med her go round th' field like a good 'un. He rolled off into th' hedge at th' Bottom Intack, an' 'steead o' sqwawkin' and pipin' he swore at Bess like a trooper an' wanted puttin' up again. Oh! He's a rare 'un, that he is. Larnin's thrown away on him. It 'ud nobbut over-weight an' handicap him, so to speak."

"I'm sorry to hear of the lad swearing," interposed Mr. Black.

"That's Work'us Jack's teachin'," commented Mrs. Schofield. "It's surprisin' how easy th' young 'uns 'll pick up owt they shouldn't know, when ther's no brayin' what they should know into their little heads."

"Well, well," went on Mr. Redfearn, to get out of a sore subject, for he had recognised some of his favourite expletives in Tom's scholeric words; "th' point is, th' lad's handier wi' his hands nor his head piece. Yo' can tak' a horse to th' watter but yo' cannot mak' him drink. An' talkin' o' watter, th' young scoundrel gave me a turn t' other day an' no mistake. Yo' know th' dam aboon Hall's papper-mill? Weel it's th' deepest dam bi a seet for miles round here. Aw'd gone up wi mi gun to see if aw could pick up a rabbit or two for th' pot an' theer wor Tom reight i' th' middle o th' dam, throwin' up his arms an' goin' dahn like a stun, and then he cam up blowin' like a porpus. Aw' sent th' retriever in after 'im an' th' young devil, 'at aw should say so, cocked his leg over th' dog's back an' med him, carry 'im to th' bank, an' 'im laughin' all th' time fit to crack his young ribs. He'd nobbud pretended to drown to fley me."

"Jack's doing again," said Mr. Schofield.

"Well, but, what's to be done with him?" persisted Mr Black. "Can't you take him on to th' farm, Fairbanks?"

"'Tisn't good enough," said Fairbanks. "He's fit for better things. At best he could never be much more nor a sort of bailiff an' *they're* noan wanted about here. If we could send him out to Canada now, or Australey, theer's no tellin' what he med come to be. At least so they sen. But i' th' owd country farmin's nowt wi'out brass, an then it's nowt much but a carryin' on. Nah, I've thowt o' a plan. We could 'prentice th' lad out to a manufacturer. Th' lad's sharp an' 'ud sooin sam up owt there is to larn. Th' Guardians 'ud pay th' premium for him' an' nobbut a fi' pun note or so an' aw think aw know th' varry man to tak' him an' sud do well by 'im if ther's owt i' religion?"

"Who is it?" asked Mr. Black.

"It's Jabez Tinker, o' th' Wilberlee Mill, i' Holmfirth. He's the main man at Aenon Chapel,—a pillar they call 'im an' preaches hissen o' Sundays, so he suld be fit to be trusted wi' a lad."

"I'd rather he'd ha' bin Church," commented Mrs. Schofield. "Aw've often noticed 'at those 'at put it on so mich o' Sundays tak' it aat o' th' Mondays. Devil dodgers, aw call 'em."

"There are good men among the Dissenters." Mr Black's spirit of fairness compelled him to testify, "though I wish they could find their way to heaven without making so much pother on earth." The days of the Salvation Army were not as yet, and sound and salvation were not convertible terms.

"There's one gooid thing abaat it," was the landlady's opinion. "Holmfirth's nobbut over th' hill, so to speak, an' th' lad could come to see his old friends at Whissunday and th' Feast, when th' mills are lakin'."

"Aye, aye, a lot better nor them furrin' parts," agreed the farmer. "Owd England for me, say I."

"And I have not lost hopes of clearing up the mystery of the boy's birth," concluded Mr. Black. "He must stay near us."

To this time nothing had been said to Tom about his parents. He knew he had no father and no mother—that was all. He knew other lads had fathers and mothers, and how he came to be without did not concern him very much. Once, indeed, one of the village lads had jeered at him as a love-child. He did not understand what this might mean, but he had sense to perceive something offensive was meant.

"What is a love-child?" he asked Mrs. Schofield one day, suddenly.

"All childer's love childer," fenced Mrs. Schofield, but Tom was not satisfied.

"What's a love child, Jack?" he asked his bosom friend.

Jack ruminated. Definition was not his forte.

"It means a lad's mother's nooan as good as she should be."

Tom flushed hotly, and said nothing: but that night a village lad with lips much swollen slept with a raw beefsteak over his eye.

The germ of thought had been sown in the youthful mind. *Why* was he different from other lads? Time had been when in some confused sort of fashion he had looked on Mrs. Schofield as his mother and Mr. Black as his father.

"Mr. Black," he asked one day, "where is my mother?"

It was a question that the Schoolmaster had looked for at every recent visit that he courted and yet dreaded.

It was on a Sunday noon as the congregation left the porch of St. Chad's some lingering by the gateway to exchange neighbourly greeting, others sauntering with an air of unconcern to the door of the Church Inn across the way, whilst yet others still made with leaden foot to a recent grave to pay the tribute of the mourner's tears.

Tom had been with other pauper lads in the gallery, a spot of vantage screened from the verger's eye, and where it mattered to nobody what heed you took of the service or sermon so long as you did not make too much noise. He had made haste to get outside the churchyard so that he might not miss his ever gentle friend, the schoolmaster, and now stood by the village stocks outside the graveyard wall and watched the stream of worshippers pass slowly by. Presently his hand was in the schoolmaster's, who turned his face to the road which led past the workhouse boundaries down to his own home at Diggle.

"Mr. Black, where is my mother?"

The schoolmaster paused, hesitated. They had left the rough and narrow road and crossed a stile into the fields. They were on the higher ground and could plainly see the churchyard. The loiterers had gone their homeward way or drifted into the Inn to seek a solace that is supposed to be appropriate alike in the glad hours of rejoicing and the heavy time of affliction.

"Your mother lies yonder," said Mr. Black, solemnly and sadly.

"Show me," said the boy, simply.

They retraced their steps and sought the ancient burial ground with it's sunken crosses and mouldering mossy stones, and those little mounds without a name that cover the humble dead. In a distant corner Mr. Black stood with uncovered head by a small marble cross and stone slab.

sacred to the memory
OF
A. J.
AN UNKNOWN WANDERER WHO DIED IN CHILDBED
AT THE HANGING GATE, DIGGLE.
JAN. 11TH, 183—.

Tom gazed upon the simple monument till he could gaze no more, for blinding, scalding tears welled into his eyes and trickled down his cheeks.

"Let us go home," he said, "let me stop with you to-day."

In the evening of that peaceful Sunday the school-master told the foundling all he knew: he placed in his hand the precious locket taken from the mother's neck and promised that it should be transferred to Tom's, keeping when he should be old enough to keep it safely.

"You will treasure it as the immediate jewel of your soul," he said; "for thereby you may clear your mother's name." Then, falling on his knees he read the evening prayer, and with his blessing dismissed the lad.

CHAPTER IV

THE ancient village of Holmfirth on the river Holme was, in former days, of considerably more pretension than it is to-day, when the neighbouring town of Huddersfield dwarfs the surrounding communities. Holmfirth stands near the head of the valley of the Holme, and at one time was looked up to as a petty capital by the straggling hamlets that intervened between the river's head and the spot where, some nine miles below, its tortuous course joins the river Colne at King's mill in Huddersfield, whence the united currents sweep in broader stream to blend with the Calder at Cooper Bridge, and so onwards to the capacious bosom of the Humber.

Best known and best accustomed of all the shops in Holmfirth was that of Ephraim Thorpe, sometimes; known as Eph o' Natt's o' th' Thong, but more as "Split," from a tradition current in the village that he would split a pea rather than be guilty of giving over-weight or measure. The shop was low and dark, it's floor of blackened stone seldom scrubbed. The two counters were not cleanly, their surface much worn by the friction of heavy vessels and the testing of doubtful coins. But what article of household provision you failed to get at "Split's" you might despair of purchasing anywhere nearer than Huddersfield itself. A candle rack ran round three sides of the shop, just above the counters, and the sickly odour of tallow pervaded all the spot, dominating even the smell of treacle and "shilling-oil" as the oil used for lamps was called. Flitches of bacon hung from the rafters; bags of flour and of oatmeal with open necks were propped up in corners. Bars of soap, piles of soft-stone and white stone, tins of tea and coffee, pats of butter, skins of lard, papers of blacking and black-lead, pots and pans, and brushes hard and soft, eggs and herrings, peas and beans and Indian corn for poultry, gridirons and porringers, thimbles and shoelaces, clogs and pocket-handkerchiefs—all these and sundry others were the articles of commerce retailed at fifty per cent, profit to a grateful public by Mr. Ephraim Thorpe. That public consisted for the most part of those employed in the neighbouring mills, and few were the families of the humbler sort entirely out of Ephraim's debt. He was always willing to trust a man that he knew to be fairly sober and in fair work, and to his regular customers at the crisis of a funeral or a wedding, lend a guinea or so at the easy interest of sixpence in the pound per week; so long as the interest was paid regularly he never pressed for the principal. But woe betide any housewife who took her ready money to a rival tradesman, or ventured to go shopping at the flaunting stores of

Huddersfield. The Court of Requests and the "Bum" were words of terrible portent, and Ephraim knew every trick of the law. He knew, too, the wages of every working family in the district how much they ought to spend when they bought in for the week, and how far it was safe to trust when work was slack or sickness rife and ready-money not forthcoming. Truly no lord of the manor in the good old days of dungeon-keep, thumb-screw and rack, was held more in awe than the red-headed, freckled, yellow-fanged, parchment-skinned, ferret-eyed "Split," general dealer and deacon of the Baptist Flock that gathered at Aenon Chapel, Holmfirth, "the altar by the rushing waters."

For Ephraim was as zealous in his chapel-going as in his shop-keeping. Sunday morning and afternoon saw him in his pew, dressed in sable doeskin, but with a subtle flavour of soap and chandlery exhaling from his pores. He rented a high, uncompromising pew, in which he could coop himself up and barricade himself from the non-elect. It was a capital sentinel-box, whence he could espy the gaps in the ranks of the faithful. He could note when Ned o' Ben's, or Bill o' Sue's absented himself from service, and speculate at his leisure whether a bull-baiting or a cock-fight had lured to sinful delight, and recall to a nicety the amount that stood to the delinquent's debit in the long narrow, greasy, skin-bound ledger of hieroglyphics that only Ephraim understood, and at whose sight the stoutest good dame's heart would sink and the shrillest-tongued virago's voice be hushed.

Mr. Thorpe was a widower, and though it is possible—such is the amiable of a women for the bereaved and afflicted—that more than one might have been willing and lend attentive ear had he wooed again, a widower, Ephraim announced, he meant to live and die. His daughter, and only child, Martha, was old enough to keep the house above the shop, in which the father and daughter dwelt. The spiteful gossips of the village said she was not only old enough, but ugly enough. But said gossips suffered their critical judgment of the daughter to be warped by their unfavourable opinion of the father. It cannot be denied that Martha's hair was not only of somewhat harsh and coarse texture, but of hue from her sire. It is true also that her face was angular and pinched, and freckled to boot, and that her form displayed none of the graceful curves so suggestive of clinging warmth and seductive softness; nor was her voice the soft and dulcet fluting that disarms not less than melting eye or witching smile. Poor Martha had been crushed and stifled and starved all her life. She had never loved nor been loved but the timid, wistful, yearning look that stole unbidden from her grey eyes told of a heart that hungered for the love that makes a woman's life. Though she lived, and had lived for years under the same roof with her father, she could not remember to have heard from his lips one caressing word, to have received from his hand one gentle touch, or; seen from his eye one glance of affection. He was not unkind to her, save in the negative way which is the withholding of kindness; nay, if in any way. Ephraim could be said to be extravagant it was in the lavish adornment of his daughter's person. The vicar's wife had not a richer silk or costlier shawl; no manufacturer's daughter finer feathers or more elegant bracelet. But Martha would have preferred a much homelier garb and a necklace of beads or jet; she asked only to slink unnoticed through her chill life, and had an half-formulated idea that her father dressed her as he did his shop windows, in the way of trade and to abash his neighbours.

Martha had practically no friends. The daughters of the manufacturers could, of course, not be expected to have more than a go-to-meeting, bowing acquaintance with a shop-keeper's daughter, though that shop-keeper was popularly supposed to be able to buy up any two mill-owners put together. To be sure the Rev. David Jones, the pastor at Aenon Chapel, and Mrs. David Jones and Miss Lydia Jones called at times and dutifully partook of tea and muffins in the sitting-room above the shop from which no ingenuity had been efficient to bar the insidious blend of many odours from the store beneath, and true also Martha was a constant attender at Dorcas meetings, class meetings, prayer meetings, and Chapel and Sunday School tea-parties, called by the scoffing and ungodly herd, "muffin-worrys." But Martha was constrained, awkward, *gauche*, and though her heart, was ready to go half-way to meet an overture, she could not make an advance. Little children were not allured to her, girls of her own age ridiculed whilst they envied her dress jewellery, staider matrons thought it shame that grasping miser's scarecrow daughter should "peark" herself out in dainty raiment whilst their own well favoured ones went in cheap cottons or plain home-spun.

Of all the worshippers at Aenon Chapel, none was more considered than Jabez Tinker. There were many reasons for this. One undoubtedly was that Jabez Tinker was one of the leading manufacturers in the valley. No one, not old Daft Tommy, who was reputed to be over a hundred years old, could remember a time when the Tinkers were not a great name in Holmfirth and when Wilberlee Mill was not run by them. The very name of Tinker is, curiously enough, significant the family connection with the staple industry of the valleys of the Colne and the Holme. It is said to be derived from the Latin, *tinctor*, a dyer, and to have come down from those far off times when the Roman conquerors introduced the arts of civilisation to the aboriginal Celts of these northern wilds. Certainly Jabez Tinker's father and grandfather and great-grandfather before him made cloth and doubtless dyed it. And they had made good cloth, buckskin and doeskin of the best. They were not a pretentious nor an ambitious race. They worked hard made shrewd bargains, paid their way expected to be paid, and put by money slowly but steadily. They had mostly married money too, not, perhaps marrying for money, but taking care to marry where money was. They were just to their work people and were slow either to put a man on or to take a man off. Once get a job at Wilberlee Mill and you were there for good, if you behaved yourself—or, as the heads said, if Tinker didn't know when he had a good man, the man knew when he had a good master. It was not that the Tinkers paid more than ruling prices for their labour. They made no pretence at being industrial philanthropists—that would not have been business; but they contrived to keep the mill running, shine or shower. Times must be parlous bad indeed if the great water-wheel did not turn at proper times in the race at Wilberlee; and constant employment is more to a man than high wages, with slack times in between, if men had only the sense to see it.

It is not necessary to go far back into the ancestry of the Tinkers, though, in a quiet way, they were not a little proud of it. Old William Tinker had left two sons, both of whom had been brought up to the business, and to both, as partners, the business had been left. Jabez, the elder, I shall have much to say. Richard, the younger, might not have been a Tinker at all. He did not "favour" the Tinkers, who were traditionally tall lean, wiry, big-boned men, somewhat sallow of complexion, with dark straight hair, scant of speech, inflexible of will, their word their law, neither grasping nor prodigal, and as strict at chapel as the counting-house. But Dick Tinker, Dick o' Will's o'th Wilberlee, had been a "non-such." He had blue eyes that always sparkled with mirth; curling chestnut hair, that affronted Puritanic sense; and he was a sad spendthrift. He had a hearty word for everyone. He liked to go of a night to the *Rose and Crown*, and led the revels there. He never missed a meet of the harriers, and he kept his own game-cock. He had a very appreciative eye for a pretty face, even though it was half-hid under a weaver's shawl, and for a neat ankle, though cased in clogs. During his widowed father's life he had gone dutifully to chapel, when he couldn't make any plausible excuse for shirking attendance, for it was no small matter to stand up against the old man's will. But when the father died, Dick stoutly declared, with not a few oaths, that he was sick to death of the Hard-bedders—such was his irreverent term for the Particular, very particular, Baptists—and contented himself by going to the Parish Church, on those rare occasions when he felt need of spiritual solace. Then he capped all his follies by marrying the pretty, penniless, governess at the Vicarage, a girl said to be from down Lincolnshire way, who spoke with refined accent, had gentle, graceful ways, and was so clearly a lady that every woman in the district, save the Vicar's wife and the working folk, resented it. But the moors were too bleak for her and she had the grace to die after two years—which had been like Paradise to Dick—leaving him an infant daughter, Dorothy.

Jabez had not liked his brother's marriage. He had nothing to say against his sister-in-law, except that it would have been better if she had been a "that country's" woman. Why couldn't Dick have done as the Tinker's had done from time immemorial, and married in the valley. "There were lasses anew, and to spare," he said, "well favoured, and only waiting to be asked." Then Dick's bride had brought him nothing but the clothes she stood up in, and that was another grievance. But Dick had laughed, in his careless way, and said it was time to mend the Tinker breed, by bringing some grace and beauty into the family, and "my Louie has that, you can't deny." And Jabez could not deny it.

"Why don't you marry yourself, Jabez? You, all alone i' th' old homestead, with nobody but old Betty to look after you! Dreadful lonesome you must be. Th' house is none too cheerful at th' best o' times. But a woman's pretty face, an' a soft voice, an' th' patter o' little feet 'll lighten it up if now't else will. And tak' advice, Jabez, look further afield, not among th' Wrigleys, an' Wimpennys, an' th' Brookes. Their lasses are weel enough, an' there's money with all on 'em. But they run too much to bone, an' they've been chapelled, an' missionarized, an' dragooned till religion 's soured on 'em, an' when they love they love by rule o' three."

But Jabez had winced, and changed the subject.

After his wife's death Dick had gradually fallen back into his old courses. He loved his little wench, as he called his daughter, passionately; but a full-blooded, hearty man, still in the very pink and flower of his manhood, one used all his life to the bustle of the market, the free and easy ways of an inn and the sports of the field is not very much at home in a nursery. So Dick, who had felt, when the cruel blow fell, that life had nothing left for him was once more to be seen o' nights at the *Rose and Crown*, roaring out a hunting song, or arranging the details of a coursing match, a pigeon shooting, or a cock fight—and the maidens of the valley of the Holme took heart once more, and began to feel a lively concern for the poor orphaned babe in the lonely house. They forgave Dick—handsome, rollicking Dick—his passing aberration, his one overt act of treason to their charms, and reflected, with satisfaction, that his married life had been so brief, it might be considered as not counting at all—an episode, not a history.

But the rising hopes of these speculative spinsters were rudely dashed. One bright winter's morning, when a sudden thaw had softened the iron fields and promised the scent would lie, Dick rode forth cheerily on his hunter to the meet at Thongsbridge. There was a substantial breakfast at Mr. Hinchliffe's a brother manufacturer and a county magistrate. Dick did ample justice to the cold beef and ham but declined coffee for old October. Then he must needs drain a stiff glass of brandy and water "to warm the old ale," he said; and in very merry mood was Dick when the hounds broke covert. Now save the stone walls of Galway there are no worse fences than those of the Valley of the Holme. You must clear them at the peril of your neck. There is no crashing through a dry-walling,—a "topping" *may* give once in a way; but it is odds that it wont. Dick—Dare-devil Dick they called him in the hunting-field,—rode straight. The ground in the higher reaches had not yielded to the thaw or the morning sun. His horse baulked at an awkward fence, slipped, and failed to recover itself, and before Dick could disengage boot from stirrup, fell upon its side, with Dick crushed beneath. The broken ribs were pressed into the lungs, and though he lingered a few days at Mr. Hinchliffe's house, he was borne from it a corpse.

"You will be good to Dorothy?" he said to Jabez and Jabez had pressed the clammy hand in silent promise.

"You'll take her to live with you. She's a bright little lass, like a ray of sunshine in the house. You wont let her forget her mother or her worthless dad, will you, Jabez? You'll be taking a wife someday yourself, lad, an' have childer o' your own. But you won't be hard on th' little lass, will yo', Jabez?"

And Jabez said she should be as his own.

"She won't be bout brass, yo know, Jabez," gasped the dying man, the sweat standing in heads upon his pale brow. "There's my share i'th' business, and odds and ends. Yo' know all about 'em. I'd never no secrets fro' yo, Jabez, though yo' wer' always a bit close, weren't tha, lad? I've left everything to Dorothy an' made yo' her guardian an' th' executor. I know yo'll do right bi th' little 'un. I'm none feared for that. Th' Tinkers aren't that sort; but don't be hard wi' her. She's nooan as tough as some, her mother's bairn, God bless her."

And so poor Dick was gathered to his fathers and lay in the old churchyard at Holmfirth by the fair, fragile wife's side in the grim vault of the Tinkers. Not a mill worked in the district as they carried him to his grave. Men and Women "jacked work" with one accord and lined the route from the dead man's house to the very side of the grave. For Dick with all his faults, perhaps, because of them, was dear to the simple folk of the valley, and many, a tale was told in the village inns, of cheery word and ready jest, and helping hand in time of need; and many a buxom housewife, as she stirred porridge for good man and bairns, smiled sadly and gave a gentle sigh as she saw herself again a sprightly wench chased at Whitsuntide round the ring at "kiss in the ring" Or "choose the lad that you love best," and found herself a willing captive, but panting and struggling still, whilst Dick saluted the rosy cheek. For at the Sunday School treats at "Whis-sunday," all classes were on a level, and even the parson himself must run as fast as legs could carry him if tap of maiden greatly daring fell upon his shoulder, or her kerchief dropped at his feet.

Whether it was the necessity of having some other companionship than old Betty for the young niece so solemnly committed to his charge, or whether he was weary of his bachelor solitude and felt the need of a woman's presence in the old homestead in which he had been born and which he had inherited on his father's death, certain it is that Jabez Tinker began seriously to think about a wife. He was now nearing his fiftieth year, and the romance of youth—love's young dream—he sadly told himself was not for him. Perhaps he had never been young; but be that as it may he was now a staid, prosaic man, who looked all his years and more, his whole soul in his business, in parish affairs and in other spheres in which the gentler emotions have no concern. Business was with him as the breath of his nostrils. Had he liked, he could have retired on a fair competence; had he been asked he could have given no solid reason why he should continue to toil and moil and put by money. Dorothy was his nearest relative, though of remoter ones—cousins and half-cousins, agnates and cognates as the Roman lawyers said, he had them by the score. But it certainly was neither for Dorothy nor other relative, near or distant, he spent more and more time in mill and counting-house, planning fresh outlets for the produce of his looms, building additions to the old mill, and watching eagerly every improvement in the machinery of his trade. He did it simply because he must, as a successful lawyer takes briefs upon briefs, or a popular doctor case upon case. And he resolved that in his choice of a bride he would look for money that would buy out Dick's share in the business, and leave him sole master of Wilberlee mill.

And in this mood his thoughts turned to Martha Thorpe; he scarce knew why, except, perhaps, that he was used to the sight of her Sunday after Sunday, and at the weekly services and social functions of the chapel and Sunday school. All the world knew that Martha would have money, but none the less did all the world—of Holmfirth—gape and exclaim with its "Did yo' evver? "and its "Aw nivver did," when the reserved master of Wilberlee was seen, not once or twice, but, in time, Sunday after Sunday, pacing slowly by Martha and Old Split's side from the chapel gates to the modest home above the shop in Victoria Street. But when it become known that Jabez Tinker actually took his roast beef, and Yorkshire pudding, and apple pie (with cheese) at Splits, the spinsterdom of the village was divided between wrath and scorn.

"Such a letting down to th' Tinkers," declared one.

"I'll never believe it till I see it," affirmed another.

"It's money he's after," a third alleged.

"He's enough o' his own."

"There's no telling. Happen he's speculated. Besides, much will have more, an' Tinkers wer' allus rare 'uns for th' main chance," was the general conclusion.

"All but poor Dick," said his old cronies of the *Rose and Crown.*

"By gosh! But Ginger o' Split's 'ud be a pill as 'ud bide some gilding for my taste," vowed the jolly landlord. "Jabez mun ha' a good stomach."

And what thought Martha?

It was inconceivable to her at first that the visits of Mr. Tinker, of Wilberlee, could be anything but visits of business to her father; doubtless some matter connected with the Chapel or the Sunday School. But Ephraim dropped hints.

"How would ta like to be wed, lass?

"Father!"

"Aye, it's father now. It 'll be happen gran'father afore long," and the old man chuckled a greasy chuckle.

It could not be true, murmured Martha to her heart. That anyone should come a wooing to her, unless, perchance it were some needy parson after her money, seemed preposterous. And yet everyone said Mr. Tinker was more than well-to-do. And, after all, was she so very plain? Is there in this wide, wide world a woman's glass that does not tell a flattering tale to one, at least? And, as she looked, a warm glow tinged the pale cheeks, and a light shone in her eyes they had never known before. To be loved! To be loved for her own sake! To get away from that horrid shop; to be Jabez Tinkers lady; to queen it over those who had sneered at her behind her back! There was rapture in the thought. And oh! She would love him so; she would be his very slave; no house should be like theirs. Never did the heart of Andromeda leap to meet the coming Perseus, as Martha's heart went out to this prince, come, if come indeed he were, to break the chains that bound her to the cruel rock of barren life. Her heart overflowed with gratitude, and humbly she thanked her God that His handmaiden had found favour in this great Lord's sight. She did not ask for the fervent worship of an ardent wooer's love. She only asked to be allowed to love, and to be loved a little—oh! just a little, in return—as the parched ground thirsts for the grateful shower, so thirsted the heart of the patient Martha for a good man's love.

CHAPTER V.

HAPPY'S the wooing that's not long a-doing, and Jabez Tinker, his mind resolved, was not the man to let the grass grow under his feet. Martha was not the one to insist on all the formularies of a protracted siege; she surrendered the citadel of her heart at the first blast of trumpet. She only insisted that the wedding should be a quiet one. As this jumped entirely with her lover's notions she had her own way, though Ephraim protested.

"We don't kill a pig every day, and blow th' expense. If aw pay th' piper surely I ought to chuse th' tune."

But he was not suffered to choose the tune, though none questioned that he paid the piper, and paid him handsomely. Exactly how many thousands of pounds made over his humble counter went to swell Mr. Tinker's balance at the Bank no one but he and his son-in-law and the bankers knew, and is no concern of ours.

Jabez took his bride to London for the honeymoon. The wool-sales were on at the time, so that the manufacturer was able to combine business with pleasure, and to avoid that exclusive devotion to his wife which even more ardent husbands are said to have found somewhat irksome. But he took care that Martha should see some of the sights of London—the Houses of Parliament, the Abbey, St. Paul's, and the Tower. Theatres were, of course, not to be thought of, but on one never-to-be-forgotten Saturday, the two went up the river to Hampton Court. Then for the first time Martha realized that the world is very beautiful and often amid the bleak hills and stone walls and hideous mills of her mountain home, her thoughts would dwell upon the green fields and rich hedges and rustling, swaying, leafy branches and deep flowing waters of the fair valley of the Thames. The portraits at Hampton Court shocked her, and she hurried through the rooms with crimson face.

But her heart was very light and glad as she entered her own home at Wilberlee. The ancient homestead of the Tinkers was hard by the mill. It was a long two-storied building of rude ashlar, now dark with age. There was a sitting room or company room, low and gloomy even on a bright day, for the windows were overhung by the ivy that covered the house front. The furniture was massive, dark mahogany. There were but few pictures or ornaments in the room, the pictures mostly oil-paintings of dead and gone Tinkers in stiff stocks, precise coats, with thick watch-chains and seals hanging from the fob; the women with smooth plaited hair, long stomachers, and severe looks. By the looking-glass over the mantel-piece were deep-edged mourning cards, in ornate frames, recording the deaths of defunct ancestors, with pious texts and verses expressive of a touching confidence in the departed's eternal welfare.

The bedrooms of the upper story were furnished in the same enduring fashion, were even gloomier than the dismal sitting room, the vast four-posted mahogany bedsteads with their voluminous drapery casting heavy shadows, and as the narrow windows were never opened, the chamber air, in summer time, was heavy laden with the blended smell of feathers, flocks, and lavender. It is marvellous what a dread our forefathers, who lived so much in the open, had of fresh air and thorough ventilation in the sleeping rooms of their homes.

But, after all, the kitchen or living room was the main thing. A roaring fire in winter time, walls yellow-washed, floor ochred and sanded, dark rafters overhead, flitches, hams, ropes of onions, dried bushes of sage and parsley, burnished tins that caught and reflected rays of fire and gleam of sun, a long table, its top white as soap and scrubbing brush can make the close-grained sycamore, long shelves laden with Delf and ancient crockery—ah! It was a paradise for a good housewife.

And a good housewife Martha proved to be. There was not a cleaner house in all that country side. She had kept on Betty for Dorothy's sake, and there was besides, Peggy, scullery maid and general help. Betty and Peggy would very much have preferred that their mistress had been neither so keen of eye nor sharp of tongue—for the Mistress who, as callers said, could not say boh to a goose, could talk thirteen to the dozen, so Betty averred, anent a grease spot or an iron-mould.

Martha's lot, it may be said, if not an ideal, was now a serene one. Had she but had child of her own, she thought no happier woman could have been found in the wide West Riding. But in this Fate was unkind, and the withholding of the crowning blessing of a woman's life, to hold her own babe to her breast, was all the harsher measure, that Martha knew her husband in his secret heart brooded over their long disappointment and nursed it as a grievance. Poor Martha! How many prayers, how many vows, were thine for this boon so freely granted to your husband's poorest workman!

It was in vain that Martha tried to stay her heart's longings by filling a mother's place to the little niece left by that graceless Richard. All that duty dictated Martha did; did ungrudgingly conscientiously. But there is one thing in this world that is absolutely beyond the human will: it is the human heart. Love knows no reason, and is uninfluenced by the sternest logic. It is like the wind that bloweth where it listeth. School herself as Martha would she came, in time, to have a smouldering jealousy of little Dorothy, and the child's quick perception taught it to shun the eye, and soon the company, of her aunt, and turn for comfort to buxom, homely Betty.

It is a Sunday afternoon in the Summer of the year '45—a glorious summer's afternoon. The garden at Wilberlee, stretching below the parlour window right down to the river-side—no great stretch, indeed—is ablaze with colour. The sky overhead is of rich deep blue, flecked with trailing wisps of feathery cloudlets. The lark sings high in mid ether. From the meadows round about comes the scent of the hay, and the garden gives forth its fragrance of musk and rose. In a low basket-chair, placed beneath the shades of an umbrageous chestnut tree, Mrs. Tinker sits, stiff, erect, unyielding. She is dressed in rich dark silk, and the lace of collar and cuffs have come from the skilled fingers of the nuns of Belgian convents. A religious periodical, the "Baptist Magazine," lies unheeded on her lap, for Martha is watching, with wistful eyes, the graceful movements of a young girl, who flits from flower to flower, and bends occasionally to snip a bloom or leaf.

"Why are you getting flowers of a Sunday: Dorothy? You know your uncle would not like it. I'm sure we don't want any more in the house—the parlour smells almost sickly with them—besides, it's Sunday."

"I don't want them for the parlour, aunt Martha. They are for poor Lucy Garside."

"Who's Lucy Garside?"

"Why, aunt, how can you forget? She worked in uncle's mill till she had to leave. It is something the matter with her legs and spine. Don't you mind that pretty, rosy Lucy Garside, that used to be in your class at the Sunday School? But she isn't rosy now—oh! so pale and thin, and has to lie all day on the settle."

"You mean the sofa, child."

"No, aunt, the kitchen settle I mean, they have no sofa; but they try to make it comfortable for her with shawls and things; and her mother is making a list hearth-rug for her to lie on, and then, may-be, she'll be easier—and she loves flowers. You will let me take them, aunt Martha, won't you?"

"Well, they're gathered now, and it's no use wasting them. But, in future, you must ask my leave before you cut more. And I don't quite know how your uncle would like you going trashing about among those low mill-girls."

"But, aunt"—and here Dorothy lowered her voice and glanced timorously at the opened window of the parlour—"but, aunt Martha, they say—in the village, I mean, not Lucy's mother—that Lucy's hurt her spine and crooked her legs working too long in the mill—hours and hours, and hours, they say, all the day and nearly all the night, and sleeping under the machines because she was too tired to go home to bed; and that, and not enough to eat, the doctor says, has made poor Lucy a cripple for life."

"Then Dr. Wimpenny ought to be whipped for saying such things, and I won't have you listening to these tittle-tattling stories. You ought to be ashamed of yourself, to let folks tell you lies about your uncle's mill. Folk ought to be glad they can send their children to work, to earn their own living. How would they live if they couldn't? But there's no gratitude left in the world—that's a fact. But there's your uncle finished his nap, and you'd best be off; and don't let me hear any more of your silly tales about things you don't understand."

It was a very prim and demure maiden that walked sedately from the side-gate of the house at Wilberlee, a large bunch or posy of flowers grasped in one little hand, a basket in the other. Dorothy had coaxed sundry delicacies from the not reluctant Betty—a loaf of bread, some slices of meat, a pot of jam, a glass of calves'-foot jelly, and a small packet of tea.

"Bless her bonny face," remarked Betty to Peggy, the underling, "it isn't i' my heart to refuse her owt. But it's to be hoped th' missus 'll never find it out."

"Saints preserve us," devoutly ejaculated Peggy, who was shrewdly suspected to have Milesian blood in her veins.

"Isn't she a pictur'?" said Betty, as her eyes followed her little mistress until the gate shut her from admiring gaze.

"'Deed, then, she is—an' as good as she's purty," assented Peggy.

"It's Mr. Richard's own child, she is," went on Betty, reminiscently—"th' same dancin' e'en, an' gladsome look, an' merry smile; and yet, sometimes, when she's thoughtful-like, an' dreamy, you'd think she wer' her own mother, as I could fancy her as a lass,"—and Betty heaved a very deep sigh, from a very capacious bosom.

And, indeed, Dorothy was a picture to gladden the eyes of man. The small coal-scuttle bonnet of Leghorn straw, with its drab strings, could not hide the pure oval of the face, nor its shade conceal its rich, warm complexion. The auburn ringlets, not corkscrewed to mechanic stiffness, but loosely curling, fell in clusters about her shoulders; and the child moved with an instinctive grace. Once out of the view of the garden and the house windows her pace quickened, she began to skip along joyously, her bonnet thrown back from the head, and her little feet, peeping and twinkling from beneath her shortened skirts, beat measure to the snatches of songs, that were not hymnal in their wording or their melody. As she passed the cottage doors, the good folk—standing by their thresholds to breath the air, or bask in the grateful sun, or while away the sleepy hours of unwonted rest in friendly gossip with "my nabs"—would turn to look upon the sweet and glad young face, and not one but had a hearty word and a friendly greeting for Miss Dorothy.

"Eh! But oo's a bonny wench. A seet ov her 's fair gooid for sore e'en. Oo'll be a bright spot i' some lucky chap's whom some fine day, please the pigs." And Dorothy had a nod, and a smile, too, for everyone; for she knew them all by name, and most of them worked for her uncle, either in the mill, or at their own loom in the long upper chamber of their little cottages.

"Oo's bahn to see poor Lucy Garsed, Ben's lass, aw'll be bun; an' oo's noan empty-handed noather. See th' posy oo's getten; an' mi mouth fair watters when aw think o' what there'll be i'th basket—noan o' th' missus' sendin', aw'll go bail."

"Aye, there'll be summat beside tracks, if Miss Dorothy's had a finger i' th' pie,"—and so the old wives' tongues ran on.

The cottage of Ben Garside was barely furnished, but all was spick and span. Ben was a hand-loom weaver, and, of a week-day, by earliest day, til sunset in the spring and summer-tide, you could have heard the clack of his loom overhead as the nimble shuttle with its trail of weft sped across the warp. But to-day Ben has gone to stretch his legs on the moors, and it is Lucy's mother who bids Dorothy welcome and relieves her of her parcels.

A long oaken settle runs under the deep window of the "house" or living room. The window ledge is full of pots of geranium, fuchsia, musk and rose that turn their petals to bathe in the glorious sunshine that streams with tempered warmth through the thick glazing of the long low window. Poor Lucy lies upon the couch, her cheeks so hollow, her skin so transparent, her brown soft eyes so unnaturally large and her look of patient suffering, and of the resignation of abandoned hope so heart-rending when it is stamped on the face of youth. But the large eyes brighten as Dorothy comes to the couch, and her thin hand, so white and bloodless, rests in loving, lingering caress upon Dorothy's glossy tresses as she stoops over the invalid and leaves a kiss upon the pallid lips.

"Better to-day, I hope, Lucy."

And Lucy, with a suspicious catch in her voice, says:

"Oh! Yes, better to-day, Miss Dorothy, almost well."

Alas! There will be no well for Lucy till that best of all days shall dawn for her, where sickness and suffering enter not, and tears forget to flow.

"See what Aunt Martha has sent you," said Dorothy presently,—may heaven forgive the fib,—"no, not the flowers. I gathered them all myself because I know just what you like best, and now all the afternoon, when I'm gone, you know, you must just do nothing but arrange them in that big glass on the drawers there. And this jam is for you, too, and the calves'-foot jelly to make you strong, you know, and the tea is for you, Mrs. Garside, when you've been washing and feel just like sinking through the ground, as I've heard you say you do."

"And thank the missus kindly, Miss Dorothy, my respects; but whativver's this?" and Mrs. Garside extracted the bread and meat.

"Oh! I'd forgotten them. These are for Ben."

"Eh! But aw'm feart they'll nivver keep till next Sunday i' this welterin' weather. To be sure aw might rub 'em wi' salt, but Ben do want such a power o' ale a'ter salt meat. But we'll see, we'll see. Eh! Miss Dorothy, but it's yo' that thinks o' ivverybody an' thof yo' say it's yor aunt, it's well aw know—but least said, sooinest mended. But sit yo dahn an' aw'll dust that cheer i' hauf a tick-tack—it's fair cappin wheer all th' muck comes fro' this warm weather, fit to fry yo' like a' rasher o' bacon; sit yo' dahn, do, an' throw yo'r hat off an' yo'll read ith Book a bit; not 'at aw held so much religion but Lucy theer likes it an' it's cheap, that's one gooid thing or th' poor folk 'ud get little enew on it."

Mrs. Garside, who, it will be observed, did not allow her power of speech to rust for want of use, paused to draw breath for another effort.

"What shall I read, Lucy?"

"Oh! Just that story about Jesus at the pool of Bethesda. How I wish I could have been there."

Mrs. Garside composed herself to listen, putting on that look of impenetrable stolidity and unreceptiveness that a good many people seem to think most appropriate for a Scripture-reading.

"In these lay a great multitude of impotent folk, of blind, halt, withered, waiting for the moving of the waters.... 'Sir, I have no man, when the water is troubled, to put me into the pool; but while I am coming, another steppeth down before me.'"

"Nah! If that isn't Holmfirth all ovver, my name's not Hannah Garsed" broke in that lady. "Holmfirth all ovver. Aw can see just how it wer'. Th' poor man wer' ligged theer all bi hissen, an' nobbudy to help 'im. Then fust one an' then another comes up an' thruts 'im o' one side. An' if them watters wer' owt like th' Booik says, yo may mak' sure 'at there'd be th' rich folk theer wi' their sarvants, an' lackeys, an' nusses an' lady's maids, to put 'em i'th' watter an' they'd ha' th' pick o' ivverything. An' yar Ben sez 'at if th' heealin' o' th' man wi a infirmary wer' a miracle, it's a bigger miracle 'at someb'dy hadn't bowt that pool up an' med a fortin' out o' it. Not 'at aw hold wi' all yar Ben says, for there's gooid folk amang th' quality, as we'd no need to look further nor Wilberlee," she concluded, with a penitent glance at the table.

"But I've some news for you, Mrs. Garside," interrupted Dorothy, "and I hope it will be good news."

"It'll be summat fresh if it is," murmured the irrepressible dame, "weel, out wi' it."

"You know uncle has been very busy lately, putting in new machinery?"

Mrs. Garside nodded. *That* did not concern her, except perhaps that it might mean either more or less country-work to the hand-loom weavers. But that would be to try for.

"And he is going to take another apprentice," continued Dorothy. "I heard him tell Aunt Martha so and ask her where she should lodge him. Aunt Martha said she hadn't an idea, anywhere would do for an apprentice. So I managed to catch uncle all by himself, and I said perhaps you would be glad to do for a boy."

"And that's what yo' ca' gooid news, is it, Dorothy? As if aw hadn't enough to do wi' th' house-work and th' cookin', though that's easy enough, God knows, an' me bobbin-windin' to keep Ben agate at th' loom, an' th' little lass theer at might ha' been a help an' a comfort laid o' her back fro' morn to neet an' neet to morn an' all to do for, not but what it's a pleasure to do for yo', my pet, an' it's more aw wish your owd mother could do, an' aw wodn't swap her agen ony lass i' all th' valley; but a noisy lad a rampagin' all abaat th' haase an' whistlin' an' happen stoppin' out o' neets till all hours, an nivver' wipin' his feet except upo' th' fender rails, an' makkin' enough noise to wakken th' deead, an' eitin' enough for two! Not but what th' bit o' brass 'ud be welcome, an' thank yo' kindly. We'll see when th' time comes; its no use meetin' trouble hauf way nor lawpin' afore yo get to th' stee, an' doubtless yo'r aunt 'll be speikin' to me or yar Ben, an' that 'll be time enough, which awm obliged to yo' all th' same, miss, for givin' a thowt o' us an speikin' a gooid word for us, though yo'r aunt knows weel as if aw *did* ha' a boy aw'd do for 'im as well as here an' theer a one, though aw say it, mebbe, as suldn't."

Who can unravel the tangled skein of life and say, as the foolish say, "This is fate," or as the wise, "This the foreordaining of God, the will and fashioning of the great Designer, from the foundation of the world?" But call it Fate or what you will, certain enough it is that the very day after Dorothy's visit to Dame Garside's cottage, Jabez Tinker mounted his stout cob and rode up the road that leads past the Bilberry Reservoir, past the Isle of Skye and far-famed Bill's o' Jack's, past the grey pile of St. Chad's, and so to the Workhouse On the hill. His horse was taken at the gate by Workhouse Jack and Tom Pinder, and led to the stabling in the rear to have a draught of meal-and-water and a feed of oats. Jack and Tom lingered in the stable admiring the gloss of the horse's coat, running fingers through its mane, smacking its warm flanks with many a "Whooa hup" and "Stan' ovver, lass," examining its hocks and its teeth, and generally doing those knowing things affected by the veriest tyro who would be thought wise in the deep and subtle matter of horseflesh.

But presently came the Workhouse Porter:

"Tom Pinder, th' Master wants you in th' office. No, not you, Jack; you can go into th' potato patch and don't let me catch you here again or you'll know about it."

The porter was a much more dignified man and more important in his own esteem than the master himself, so it is just as well he had not eyes at the back of his head to see that sign made by a certain application of thumb and outspanned fingers which in all times and countries has been deemed significant of contempt unutterable.

Tom followed the Porter wondering to the office. The Master was closeted with a tall, broad-shouldered, sparer, man, with clean shaven face, keen grey eyes, and hair tinged with grey at tee tell-tale temples. He sat by the table, a tankard of ale at his side, and his hand swinging his riding whip idly to and fro.

"This is the lad, then, Mr. Redfearn wrote to me about? He seems a likely lad enough, but somewhat overgrown. How old are you boy?"

"Rising fifteen, sir."

Mr. Tinker eyed the youth from head to foot and turned him round and round, feeling the muscles of his arm and the thews of his thigh and calf as though he was appraising a horse at the Cattle Fair.

"Sound in wind and limb, I should judge," he concluded, "but his age is against him. A lad should go into a mill young, Master, before his bones are set and his fingers stiff, if he's to be any good. I'm not in your Union or I would have seen to this. The Guardians have no business to keep a big lumbering lout of a lad lazying about the House and eating his head off. It's demoralising to the lad and is enough to pauperize a whole neighbourhood. What's his name?"

"Pinder sir, Tom Pinder," answered the Master, and, whilst Tom stared with all his eyes on the stranger, wondering vastly who he might be and what this interview might portend and wondering too if Workhouse Jack would remember to feed his rabbit and find a fresh sod of grass for his lark, the Master made apology for Tom's height and girth.

"You see, Mr. Tinker, Pinder's been kept longer than usual. There's a sort of mystery about him, and both the Chairman and Mr. Black have taken uncommon interest in him. Indeed the Schoolmaster's so wrapt up in him he couldn't have been more if th' lad had been his own son, which I'd almost think he was myself if it wasn't so ridiculous. But there's never no telling, is there, Mr. Tinker? these quiet uns is often as deep an' dark as a pit, bu' we're all human, eh?" And Master winked a wink meant to be a summary of profound knowledge of the universal fallibility of the human race.

But Mr. Tinker was not a man to be winked at or joked with, nor apparently was he disposed to discuss the tempting topic of man's—and woman's—depravity—with a Workhouse Master, the sole audience a Workhouse foundling.

"Pinder,"—he said musingly, strumming meditatively on the table, and somewhat brusquely declining the Master's hospitable offer to have in another jug of October ale, or something shorter if a cordial for the stomach would be more acceptable.—"Pinder—Tom Pinder? it isn't a this country name. There was a Pinder at Marsden, a clothier in a small way—took to drink, banked, and showed his creditors a clean pair of heels; but you wouldn't have a Marsden brat in this Union."

"But he wasn't called after his father," said the Master, somewhat curtly, for if Jabez Tinker could be curt, curt too could the Master be, and any way, he was sovereign there except on Guardian days. "Damme, I can crow on my own dunghill," he thought, "or I'm th' poorest cock ever crowed this side of Stanedge."

"Oh! I forgot, Mr. Redfearn said something about his being a bastard, a chance child—a rambling tale. I didn't mind it, I was thinking about something else. 'Twill be his mother's name?"

"No, nor his mother's," said the Master. "I don't rightly know who he was called after. It had something to do with Mr. Redfearn's shepherd. But it's a long time since, and I forget. But what's the odds? There th' lad is. You can either take him or leave him, it's all a price to me, and I reckon to th' Guardians too."

"When can he come?"

"Next week. There'll be th' papers to make out. Th' overseers will sign th' indentire. Five pounds they've to pay, I think t'was settled."

"Yes, five Pounds; but if I'd known his age and size I'd have stood out for more. But it's too late for haggling you'd send him over this day week. I'll arrange about him. Tell him to bring the cob round, Tom, and so good day to you, Master. Time's money these days, and I've wasted a whole forenoon over this job. Pinder, Pinder, it's a strange name and yet there seems a look i' the lad's eye I've seen before somewhere. My respects to Mr. Redfearn when you see him, and tell him he should be too old a farmer by this to keep his cattle till they're almost too far gone for the market."

The Master smiled the official smile at a Guardian's jest; but it was no very friendly glance that followed the erect form of the Holmfirth manufacturer as he turned his good mare's head over the hills. "Tom's in for a bad time of it, I'm thinking," said the master.

It was Mr. Black who conveyed the lad with a father's love from the Workhouse to Holmfirth. And the lad went with a heart light enough, though on his cheek the tears were wet he had shed at parting from the faithful Jack. He had solemnly made over to the lamenting Workhouse drudge his boyish treasures,—the lark, that obstinately refused to sing, the lop-eared rabbit, and the hedgehog he had rescued from the clogs and sticks of a posse of village urchins—captive not of bow and spear, but of fist and toe. Moll o' Stuarts, too, had been to bid him farewell, and, as a parting gift, had bestowed on him a child's caul.

"Keep that all th' days o' your life; nivver part wi' it, wet or fine. Yo'll allus know th' weather by it, as guid as a glass an' better nor bi a mony on 'em. An' as long as that caul's thine, drowneded bi watter yo' canna be. There's mony a fine spark at sails the seas 'ud be main glad o' that same. Hanged yo' may be, tho' God forbid, but drownded nivver." And in after years, of which the reader shall read in good time, Moll o' Stuarts was able to invoke her prophetic soul, and to attribute to her own prescience the wonderful deliverance this story shall narrate. Moll, too, brought a pair of stout stockings knit by the widow Schofield's own plump hands, and a crown-piece, that the night before had jingled in Tom o' Fairbank's well-filled leathern purse.

Over the hills trudged the Schoolmaster and his ward; the dominie thoughtful, and not a little sorrowful.

"Pray God we've done for the best," was his pious hope, as they reached the low wall of the Church of St. Chad's, and one at least thought of the fair unknown, whose son was setting forth into the untried paths of life, with all the glad, unquestioning undoubting confidence of eager youth. Hard by the Church Inn they turned to the face of the steep ascent of almost unbroken moorland, threaded by a rude and rutty path, strewn with rubble and boulders, torn and wrenched from the crags above by the driving storms and angry raging winds of the rolling years. On the lower face of the hill they passed, here and there, the rude shelter of a moorland cottier, whose cow and pig and poultry gained precarious living in the lean enclosures won from the sweeping stretch of heather and coarse grass or the lowly cottage whence the familiar clack of the hand-loom told of swaying beam and scudding shuttle. Anon they reached the summit; Mr. Black, notwithstanding the help from Tom's sturdy arm, fain to rest upon one of the vast rocks belched forth from the bowels of the earth in some angry vomiting of the prisoned airs, and now, rounded and smooth-worn and dark with the gloom of ages, resting massive on the commanding summit called Pots and Pans.

"Yes, that indeed, is Bill's o' Jack s," panted Mr. Black, in answer to Tom's eager questioning.

"That is where the murder was done, murder most foul. Poor hapless Bill and Tom, I knew them well, a hale and hearty farmer, and his son a strapping gamekeeper. Done to death, whether for gain or revenge, none knew for certain, though it was shrewdly guessed, but nothing was ever proved and for ought is known, the murderers may dwell in our very midst. See yon little window left of the door, 'twas the old man's bedroom. There, in a pool of blood, his lifeless body was found; his son,—his head cleaved by a heavy bill-lay lifeless in the kitchen. It was a little wench, who went betimes for milk, gave the alarm."

"Was it long gone sir?" asked Tom, gazing spellbound at the farmhouse in the valley's dip.

"In '32—the year of the great Reform Bill. You were a bouncing baby then, Tom. But see how thick the bilberries lie snugly in the heather, and how a film settles on the ripened fruit as though the mist of the hills had kissed them with a lingering kiss. Better fill your kerchief, for well I guess they'll be right welcome at Mrs. Garside's, where you must make your home.

"And now, lad, turn your eyes once more upon the old church and towards the fields you know so well. Remember in that valley you were born and bred, and in that valley are those that love you well and who have knit you to their hearts. Yonderwards, in the other valley, is your future home; what trials, what labours there await you, who shall say? but as David said to his *son*, say I to you:

"'Be thou strong and shew thyself a man, and keep the charge of the Lord Thy God, to walk in His ways, to keep His statutes, and His commandments, and His judgments and His testimonies that thou mayest prosper in all that thou doest, and whithersoever thou turnest thyself.' And now, come, lad, 'tis a brave step from here to Holmfirth and the way will be long for me when I come back without thee."

CHAPTER VI.

Tom Pinder was "apprenticed"—so the phrase ran—to Jabez Tinker with all the form and circumstance and not a little of the verbal exuberance of the law. The manufacturer bound himself to the overseers of Saddleworth who stood to the foundling in *loco parentis*, to teach his apprentice the art and calling of a clothier—so manufacturers were then styled, when men were less fond of high-sounding terms and preferred plain English to foreign-fangled names. He also undertook, under his hand and seal, to feed the said Tom and provide him one new suit of clothing each year until he should attain the age of twenty-one years. The overseers, on their part, engaged that the "said Tom should faithfully serve the said Jabez Tinker and his wife and family, his and their lawful orders should do, his secrets should keep, and his goods protect," likewise that the said Tom, so long as his indenture should endure, taverns should not frequent, bowls nor dice should play, fornication should not commit, and marriage should not contract. As the delicate subject of wages was not so much as hinted at in this formidable document, it seemed pretty certain that the ingenuous apprentice would not be exposed to much temptation either from tavern or dice-box; and Mr. Black, after reading, no less than three times, the articles of this solemn covenant could not withhold his admiration of the zealous care the law manifested for the morals of the young. He should think better, he averred, of lawyers ever after, and was inclined to believe they must be a much maligned body of men. If there had only been some mention of the catechism, he said, the deed might have been framed by a Bishop. Mr. Redfearn to whom he thus unbosomed himself said nothing, but there were volumes in the wink he conveyed to the stolid Aleck.

"I could ha' thoiled th' absence o' ony mention o' th' catechism if there'd been some mention o' wage," was his only spoken comment.

"But think of the immense advantage of learning the whole art and commerce of a clothier under such a teacher as Mr. Tinker," urged Mr. Black.

Mr. Redfearn apparently did think, and what he thought was again conveyed to Aleck by a surreptitious wink.

Tom was not long in proving for himself the advantages of being an apprentice. They consisted, so far as he could make out, of being harder worked and more harshly treated than a paid hand, and as for instruction or initiation into the mysteries of the clothier's craft, he was left to learn so much as his own eyes could teach him and his gumption acquire. It was fortunate for him that Ben Garside, with whom he lodged, lived at no great distance from the mill, for he had to be at his work by daybreak in the summer months, and long before the first uplifting of night's black curtain in the cold winter morns. Many who worked in the same mill, young boys and girls not yet in their teens, had to trudge in all weathers from distant homes on the raw hill sides, often by lanes and footpaths deep in mud or slush, often by the light of the many stars, sometimes by the pale glimmer of the lanthorn, sometimes in Egyptian darkness, feeling their way by the touch of walls or hedges or trees, drenched by rain or sleet, pelted by hail, sinking into deep ruts or forging through the drifted snow, lightly clad, the warmest garment of the girls the shawl about their head and ears, their faces pinched and blue with cold, their fingers aching with the shrewd wintry pinch, starting from home without breakfast and hurrying with empty stomachs to their dreary work, ill-clad, ill-shod, worse-fed, and still worse paid. The hours of labour were long. Wilberlee Mill was, though not exclusively, mainly a water-mill, the motive power being led from the mill-dam by a head-goit to the great waterwheel, and from the wheel-race restored by the tail-goit, little diminished, to the river's course, to serve the turn of mill owners lower down the stream. Often in dry seasons the supply of water was scant enough and hence it came that when the dam was flush of water the manufacturer reversed the process of making hay while the sun shone by making pieces while the rain fell. There was little or no restriction in the age at which a child might be sent to work, or the hours for which it might be kept there. It was of so common occurrence as to be almost regarded as a matter of course, not calling for comment, that a child nine or ten years of age should stand to its work sixteen or seventeen hours at a stretch, cramming its meal of water-porridge down its throat in the fluff-laden air of the weaving shed or spinning room, afraid to break off work even to eat a hurried and unsavoury meal. Sometimes the children were locked in the mill all night, and many would fall asleep as they stood, or drop exhausted by their machines only to be roused by a kick from the slubber's clogs, a blow from a roller, or a resounding smack from the slubber's strap.

Tom had been set to billy-piecing, but it was found that his fingers were too big and his joints too set for such work, so, to his great delight, he ceased to rub the skin off his knuckles till they bled again, and was transferred to the "scouring-hoil" and in time had charge of a willey, or as it was sometimes called a "devil," or "fearnowt," an iron monster into whose maw he threw the scoured wool just fresh from the "drying-hoil," to be torn and "teased" by the hundred fangs of the insatiable mouth, digest as it were, in its mechanic stomach, and thence cast out in a light and airy fluff ready to be scribbled, slubbed and in time spun into warp and weft.

But though, for a time, Tom escaped the most arduous and confining and debilitating part of an operative's daily lot, his lines were hard enough. He looked back upon his workhouse life with a sickening yearning, and when he remembered the regular and abundant meals of the House, his gorge rose at the ever-recurring surfeit of water-porridge to breakfast, water-porridge to dinner, water-porridge to supper, and water-porridge between meals.

But for all that Tom grew apace, and his was not the willowy, weedy growth of the towns. If the advocates of vegetarianism want to press their proofs, let them recur to the country-bred, porridge-fed youngsters of a by-gone generation, when they were not cooped up in mills and worked beyond the endurance of Nature. As Tom was often sent out with the lant-barrel to collect from the cottages for miles around the scouring liquid for which ammonia is the modern substitute, he had ample opportunity to stretch his legs and broaden his chest and brace his sinews; so that when, as time went on; he attained to the dignity of a loom, he was as well-set-up a youth as one would meet in a day's march, straight, old Hannah Garside vowed, as any "picking rod," with strong limbs and corded muscles, and, best of all, with a sound head and a warm heart,—a happy contrast to the many of his comrades whose shoulders were rounded, and backs bent and legs curved by weary hours of standing and stooping at tasks and under burdens beyond the immature powers of ill-nurtured bodies. It was a common saying in those days that nine out of every ten of the mill-hands of Holmfirth could not stop a pig with their legs.

But the happiest chance that befell the young apprentice was that which made him a lodger with Ben and Hannah Garside. It was long enough before he had much more than a nodding acquaintance either with them or their invalid daughter; for, of weekdays, he took his meals at the mill, and at night he was so dead-beat that he was fain to wash himself and steal to bed; and on Sundays, for many a week of his early apprenticeship it was his glad custom to bolt his morning meal and make off as fast as his legs could carry him over the moors to Saddleworth, generally arriving at St. Chad's Church in time to be late for the morning service, but ample time to accompany Mr. Black or Mr. Redfearn home to a better dinner than Hannah Garside had ever seen, or even dreamed of.

But as the summer mellowed into autumn and the autumn drooped to Winter, there came Sundays when wind and rain made the tramp over the storm-beaten moors a matter not to be undertaken merely for a jaunt's sake, and Tom had, perforce to put up with the somewhat meagre fare furnished by Hannah Garside.

Sunday was the one day in the week when there was meat hot and fresh to dinner-roast beef and Yorkshire pudding with pickled cabbage, and sometimes rice pudding. One can imagine what a welcome day that weekly day of rest and feasting was, the day when the village "knocker-up" forbore to rattle at the door or tap the chamber window with long stick, calling out belike: "Ger up, Tom, an' howd th' dog while aw wakken thee." Daily use would break the morning sleep of the wearied toiler, but, oh! how sweet to remember with your first yawn that it was Sunday, and that if you liked you could spend the livelong day in bed, or at least, forego your morning meal and stretch between the blankets till the steaming fragrance from the revolving spit saluted your nostrils and sent you with yearning stomach down the rickety steps to cozen a sop from Hannah, stooping with reddened face over the spit, basting the revolving joint as it shed its dripping over the Yorkshire pudding, whilst Lucy, propped up with many pillows, peeled potatoes, or, on rare and great occasions, pared the apples for pie or pudding, chatting pleasantly, and soothing the ruffled temper of her mother.

And it was of Sunday afternoons that began those long talks with Ben Garside that had no less influence on Tom's destiny than the earlier monitions of Mr. Black, or the shrewd worldly axioms of Tom o' Fairbanks.

It had been a matter of less surprise than delight for Ben to find that Tom could not only read, but read without having to spell out or slur over long words. The joy of Hannah was great thereat, for so was Ben deprived of any pretext for sneaking out of a Sunday morning to the nearest public to hear the paper read. Now, she managed to produce each week a penny, by virtue of which Ben became one in a partnership of six, whose united contributions purchased a weekly paper. It mattered not at all that when it reached Ben's house it was much thumbed and soiled and beer-stained, for in virtue of receiving it when truly it was a week old and much the worse for wear, Ben was allowed to retain it in perpetual proprietorship, and, had made a cover of "rolling boards" in which the copies were tenderly hoarded up and treasured.

Now Ben was a great politician, and if pressed upon so close and home a matter would profess and express himself an Owenite. Add to this that he very rarely troubled either chapel or church except on Christmas Day, and that he made a point of slinking out of the house if he chanced to be in when the vicar of the parish or the shepherd of a dissenting fold called at the cottage.

"Aw cannot abide parsons," he confided to Tom one day. "Though aw wodn't let yar Lucy yer me say so for worlds."

Now Tom, as we know, had been taught to respect the Church, and he was absolutely against when Ben Garside, a little wiry, keen faced, middle-aged man, eager of speech and not a little fond of the sound of his own voice, went on:

"Weel, Tom, aw'm nowise minded to hurt yo'r feelin's, an' if th' parsons wer owt like that Mister Black 'at yo set such store by, an' well yo've a reet to by all accaants, if they tuk after him, aw'd happen ha' cause to alter mi mind. But "ifs" an' "buts" ma' all th' differ i' this world, an' they simply isn't."

"Well, they couldn't be better," said Tom, pleased with this tribute to his benefactor.

"Noah, but they set up to be. Nah aw'll nooan go as fur as some folk 'at aw know, 'at say as parson's bun' to be oather a rogue or a fooil."

"That's strong, Ben, isn't it?"

"Aye, lad, it's nooan exactly what yo'd call meeat for babes; but aw reckon it meeans summat like this—'at if a parson believes all he preeaches he's a fooil, an' if he dunnot he's t'other thing."

"But surely," began Tom.

"Aye, aye, aw know what yo'd say—'at they *do* believe. Weel then aw'll tell yo' I'm too mich respeck for their intellec's to think at them, wi' all their college larnin', can believe one hawf o' what ther paid to teach. Nooah, nooah, religion as them mak' o' preachers mis-ca' their teachin' is nobbut fit for women an' childer, an' to keep th' ignorant i' awe. Nah! *aw'm* a *reely* religious man missen, an' that's why aw dunnot hold wi parsons."

This seemed a somewhat novel reason for discrediting ministers, and Tom could but look his surprise, which was exactly what Ben wanted.

"Nah! aw'll gi' yo' a hinstance," he said, sitting on a low wall—they were out for a walk—and bidding Tom follow his example. "Aw'll gi' yo' a hinstance. Yo'n bin to th' Baptis' Chapel, wheer Jabez Tinker goes?"

Tom nodded.

"Nah, then, if yo'll swallow all th' parson says at Aenon yo' mun believe that afore aw wer' born aw wer' predestined awther to heaven or hell—yo' follow me?"

"Weel, tak' it 'at aw wer' predestined for hell, just for argyment's sake."

Tom thought it more than probable that this dreadfully free-spoken man was at least in danger of the fire, so he conceded the postulate.

"Nah! Do yo' think it fair o' God Almighty to send a poor weak sprawlin' infant into th' world, knowin' full weel 'at after mebbe sixty or seventy yer o' moilin' an' toilin' an' scrattin', he'd end up wi' weepin' an' wailin' an' gnashin' o' teeth for all eternity. Aw put it to yo' Tom, wod yo' ha' done it yersen?"

"But if you were to go to Church, Ben, or even to Chapel," began Tom.

"That doesn't touch th' point. Th' point is at One they sen is Love, suld suffer a bairn to be born i'to this world, weel knowin' its awful end."

"And don't *you* believe in God?" asked Tom, sinking his voice almost to a whisper and edging a little further off his companion.

"Aw do that, lad, but nooan i' siccan a God as that'n. But aw'n nooan done wi' th' parsons yet—one thing at a time. Yo' know aw can read th' Bible, though nooan so glib-like as yo' can, but aw think on what aw read. Nah chew this tex' ovver th' next time yo' go to th' church. Yo'll find it i'th' General Epistle o' James:—

"'For if there come unto your assembly a man with a gold ring, in goodly apparel, and there come in also a poor man in vile raiment, an' yo' hav' respec' to him 'at weareth the gay clothin', an' say unto him, sit yo' here in a guid place; an' say to th' poor, stan' yo' theer, or sit under my fooitstooil.' Well, lad, tha's bin a Workhus lad thissen, an' yo' know weel enough wheer they towd yo' to sit."

Tom did know, and reflected that on the whole he had very much preferred the dark corners of the gallery to the chief places in the synagogue; but he had the sense to know his reasons were not of grace.

"Aye, an' it's th' same all through," went on the little hand-loom weaver, growing excited and warming to his topic. "It's th' same all through. They're all tarred wi' th' same brush, or welly (well-nigh) all on 'em. They uphowd th' rich, an' they patronize th' poor, aw' most to a man. Why, see yo', we'n been feightin' for th' Factory Act i' this district ivver sin Sir Oastler tuk his coit off an' put his neck to th' collar i' 1830, afore yo' were born. How many o'th' parsons i' this district, dun yo' think, has sided wi' th hand agen th' maisters? Ther' wer th' Reverend

Madden, o' Woodhouse, *he* com' aat like a man, but he had to dare to be a Daniel an' dare to stand alone, as th' hymn says. Yo'st take all th' progress 'at's bin made i'th' world sin th' days o' Adam, an' tak' it broadly speikin' yo'll find 'at th' parsons ha' bin agen it. There's Stephen's th' Wesleyan minister an' Chartist he cam' to Huddersfield wheer had he to talk do'st think? I'th' Parish Church? Not he, faith. I'th' Wesleyan Chapel? Not he. I'th Hall 0' Science, man, i' Bath Buildings, a infidel shop, th' bigots ca'ad it."

"But surely, Ben, you believe in something. You say you believe in God. You believe in Christ too, don't you?"

"Aye i' th' *natural* Christ, but nooan i'th' travesty o' Jesus o' Nazareth 'at th' owd monks twisted an' fashioned out o' th' natural man till his own mother wouldn't ha' known him. *Aw* believe in him, but th' parsons don't."

"Nay, nay, Ben," expostulated Tom, bewildered, shocked, but interested.

"They dooan't. They sen they do, an' they happen think they do, for it's wonderful, just fair cappin', how folk can cheeat their own sen. Nah! Aw'll just ax yo' if yo' wer to steal th' vicar's cooat, or poise his shins for 'im, wheer do'st think tha'd sleep to-neet? I' th' towzer,* wouldn't ta."

Tom thought this highly likely.

"But that's nooan what Jesus towd folk. An' what abaat heeapin' up stores o' riches i' this world wheer moth an' rust doth corrupt an' thieves break through an' steal? Weel, if there's a chap i' all this valley at's keener after brass nor some o'th' parsons *aw* know an' some o'th' deacons *yo'* kno, aw dooant want to have ony truck wi' 'em for one."

Tom thought of Ephraim Thorpe, and was mute.

"But that's nooan th' warst aw han agen th' parsons. They're nobbud men, though they set thersen up for saints, an' there's good an' bad amang 'em same as there is amang other folk, aye, an' allus will be as long as th' world goes round, but ther's just one doctrine 'at sticks i' my gizzard waur nor all th' others."

Tom thought it must be a particularly lumpy doctrine, if this were so, for Ben seemed to have a narrow and constricted throat.

"Yo' heard th' parson tell folk to be content wi' that station i' life to which it has pleased Providence to call 'em."

"Well, it's no use being anything else that I can see," said Tom, getting tired of being talked down and jumped on, in a manner of speaking.

"A'm ashamed on yo', Tom. Aw thowt better things on yo', after all my talkin' to yo'. Nah, my motto is, Be content just as long as yo' can't better yo'sen; but it's yo'r bounden duty to yo'r sen an' yo'r fam'ly, when yo' get one, an' yo'r fellow-men, to be as discontented as ever yo'n reason to be, an' to try all yo' know to better yo'sen an' them. Discontent, lad, 's th' basis o' all progress, an' yo'll nooan be a reformer till yo'r chock full on it. Look at Moses, nah!"

But Mrs. Garside might be seen at the cottage door beckoning them to tea, for there was ever a cup of tea on Sunday afternoon with wheat bread and fresh butter, and lettuce or watercress and radishes and spring onions, when the season served, and these fresh pulled from Ben's little garden patch, or gathered from the brim of the purling brook.

Tea over, Ben seated himself by the hearth on which was spread the large warm list rug, like Joseph's coat of many colours, lists which Lucy had herself cut and her own mother stitched into the stout canvas backing. Ben justly regarded this rug as a work of art, and when he ventured to plant his feet upon it of a Sunday night, did so, as it were, apologetically.

"But we hannot finished our talk yet, Tom," he began, puffing vigorously at his clay pipe to assure that well-gripped glow that permits of soliloquy or monologue. "Aw wer' sayin' when Hannah ca'ed us in."

"Now, father," interrupted Lucy, "remember what day it is, don't let us have any o' those horrid politics, they only put yo' in a fash an' a tantrum."

"Tom 'll ha' to bide it," said Hannah, who was pleased to see her husband settle down by his own fireside and cross his legs upon his own hearth, as what wife is not. "Tom 'll ha' to bide it. Yo'r father's like a eight-day clock. If Tom's wun' 'im up, Tom mun let 'im run daan."

"Well, aw wer' sayin'—at what wer' aw sayin'?—guise-'ang-me if aw hannot forgotten wheer aw left off—Oh! Abaat Moses. Nah, tak' th' Book theer. Reick it daan, Hannah, reick it daan, Tom 'll happen mash a ornament or crumple a fal-de-lal" and Ben winked at Tom in token that this must be taken as a subtle innuendo at Hannah's over-tidiness.

But Hannah was impervious to innuendo, and carefully lifted down the ponderous family Bible, bound in stout leather covers with brass corners, and containing on the front leaf in faint ink and sprawling characters the brief records of marriages, births and deaths. The book had been given to Hannah by her grandmother on her death-bed, and never did priest of Levi touch the Ark of the Covenant with more reverent hand than hers as it held the sacred volume.

"Nah, lad, read that abaat th' ovverseer an th' Hebrew."

Tom looked at Lucy for further explication.

"Father allus picks th' fightin' bits i' th' Scriptures," she said.—"I like th' stories o' Jesus best, myssen—but as long as it's i' th' Bible it must be good, so best humour him. It's wheer Moses felled th' taskmaster."

And Tom read:

"'And it came to pass in those days, when Moses was grown, that he went out unto his brethren and looked on their burdens: and he spied an Egyptian smiting an Hebrew, one of his brethren.

'And he looked this way and that way and when he saw that there was no man, he slew the Egyptian and hid him in the sand.'"

"Aye, aye, blood's thicker nor watter, all th' warld ovver," commented Hannah, who sat rocking herself softly before the dying embers of the fire, her nervous fingers playing with the corners of her apron, lacking the knitting needles that are to a woman what a pipe is to a man.

"Eh! That Moses wer' a man after mi own heart," burst in Ben. "Just think on it; theer he wer', browt up o' th' fat o' th' land, wi' th' best o' ivverything to eit an' drink, an' brass for owt; an' nowt to do but scrape his leg to th' powers 'at be an' he wer' a made man for life. There isn't one man in a thaasand, pampered an' fed an' thrussen up as he wer', but thrussen up as he thrussen up as he 'ud a left th' poor bondslaves to shift for theirsens, yo' needn't go aat o' Holmfirth to see that e'ry day o' yo'r life. Gi' a workin' man a bit o' power an' a bit more wage an' set 'im ovver t' others an' he'll what-do-you-ca' it?—'out-Herod Herod,'" and Ben paused in evident gratification at this rounding of his period, but added on reflection, "or mebbe, aw sud say, out-Pharaoh Pharaoh. But Moses nah" ...

"Yes but, father," said the gentle voice of Lucy, as she laid her thin white hand caressingly on her father's knee—"Yar Lucy can leead th' father wi' a threed o' silk," thought the mother.—"Yes but, father, Moses had a direct order from God; 'I will send *thee* unto Pharaoh, that thou mayest bring forth my people out of Egypt.'"

"True enough, lass, true enough: but yo'll obsarve 'at th' angel o' the Lord didn't appear to Moses till he'd shown th' stuff he wer' made on.

Aw tak' it God likes to know summat abaat folk afore He sets 'em on to gaffer a job. Us workin' folk didn't go to Oastler i' that gret haase o' his at Fixby, aboon Huddersfilt yonder, till he'd written to th' pappers an' spokken aat like a man abaat th' ill-usage o'th' little childer. It's a long day sin' but we'st win yet, as sure as God's i' heaven, for He has surely heard the cry of the little uns, an' He has seen the oppression wherewith the Egyptians oppress them."

"But, Ben," said Tom, "we aren't living in Egypt, an' Queen Victoria isn't Pharaoh, and we aren't bond slaves."

"Oh! th' warst kind o' slave's him," retorted Ben, "as doesn't know he is a slave. Look at Lucy theer, her 'at sud ha' bin, aye an' wod ha' bin', as strong as a young colt, on' what is 'oo nah, a lily brokken on its stalk—mi poor lass, mi poor lass"—and the father's voice broke and the mother's face was turned aside.

"Dunno greet, father I'm very happy, for aw nivver knew till aw wer bed-ridden how sweet life can be wheer love is."

"Wheer's yo'r een, Tom? "went on Ben very fiercely, to hide his softer feelings, "wheer's thi e'en? aw say. Isn't Sam Buckley th' spinner at Wilberlee yet?"

Tom nodded.

"Weel, aw know Sam. 'As to ivver seen him peilin' an' cuffin' th' young 'uns abaat th' yed, wi' them big fists o' his'n, little, wee, puny, ramshackle things o' scorn an' eight yer owd, all skin an' bone, so to speak, an' precious little bone at that. Hasn't ta seen 'im strappin' 'em an' layin' abaat 'im reet an' left wi' a roller as thick ay yo'r shackle, an' crack'd 'em abaat t' poll till th' blood's come, when he's getten 'is skin full o' four-ale? Things ha' altered strangely if tha hasn't, or else tha'rt stone-blind and past prayin' for."

Now Tom had seen this and felt it too; but he had supposed it was all part of the day's work. He saw others put up with it, and he had put up with it—it might, for aught he knew, be involved in that all-controlling indenture of apprenticeship.

"Aye, it's true enough," he said, "I've wondered about it, Ben. Isn't ther' a law against it? Mr. Black says there's one and the same law for the rich and the poor."

"Then Mr. Black's nooan as knowin' as aw tak' 'im to be. Law! Law fiddlesticks! Tak' an' overseer afore th' magistrates—most on 'em manufacturers theirsen—for beeatin' a child, nivver name a 'prentice—why, yo' might as weel fall out wi' owd Harry an' go to hell for justice.—

But it's time yo wor i' bed, lad, if tha meeans to gooa to-neet, an' nivver tha forget abaat Moses. Gooid neet to yo'."

Now it so befell that on the afternoon of the very next day it was Tom's ill-fortune to become embroiled with that same Sam Buckley. The foreman spinner was a big, burly fellow, broad-shouldered and vast of paunch. He had the fishy eye and mottled face of the heavy drinker and a short and uncertain temper; not, perhaps an ill-meaning man, but quick and heavy with his shoulder-of-mutton hands. It chanced that Mr. Tinker had been obliged to go to Huddersfield that day and was not expected at the mill till late in the afternoon. As the day lengthened, the sky had become overcast, the air sultry with the unseasonable warmth and closeness that tells of a brooding storm or the artillery of the heavens. The upper room of the mill, where the billy-pieceners were mostly engaged, was a long, low chamber. Its walls had once been whitewashed but were now a dull, dirty colour from mingled grease and fluff and dust. The floors were cased with grease. There was little ventilation, except the air that entered when the door opened or through an odd broken Window; pane or so. The inner air was hot to sultriness, laden with the breath of a score or so of workers and with the rancid smell of machine oil. The spinner had gone to his dinner, and it was seldom he missed "calling" on his way back to the mill. It was a toss-up whether he would return in a good or a bad temper. If in a good one he would probably spend a half-hour or so in the weaving-shed among the grown-up girls who worked there, making jests and taking the coarse liberties they dared not resent if they would keep their looms. If in a bad temper he would make for the "billy-hoil," where it would be safe to vent it. Now this afternoon he was in a particularly bad temper.—Monday is often given up to bad temper. The overeating of Sunday conduces to it, the fact that Monday is, in the parts of which I write, as sacred to the wash-tub as Sunday is to the chapel, does not soothe it. The moment Sam shoved open the door, with thunder on his brow and lightning in his eye, the quick-witted hands, sharp beyond their tender years, sniffed the threatening storm, and bent with intent looks and nimble fingers over their work. But little "Billy-come-a-lakin" had succumbed to the drowsy influences of the time and place. Sat upon the floor, his little legs outstretched, his back against the greasy wall, his dinner can by his side, Billy slept. He had just time to start from his slumber and his dreams when Sam pounced upon him and dragged him to the central gangway of the long chamber, the lad shrinking within himself, cowering and whimpering, and but half awake.

"So aw've caught o', have aw, yo' young gallows bird? This is th' way yo' rob yo'r mester, as soon as a man's back's turned."

"Please sir aw couldn't help it; summat cam' ovver me, an' mi legs seemed to ha' nooa feel in 'em, an' oh! aw wer so tired. Don' beeat me, Sam, it'll mak mi mother greet so, if 'oo sees th' marks on me when aw doff missen to-neet."

"Aw'll mark yo' nivver fear, aye an' gi' yo' summat 'at 'll keep yo wakken, too, yo' idle good-for-nowt," and Sam swung in with a piece of belting thicker and broader than a navvy's belt.

Now it was at just this moment that Tom took the door. He had come from the dyehouse to match a cop.

"Hold," he cried, and strode quickly up the room, "you won't beat that child, Sam, wi' that strap. Drop it, I say."

"An' who'll stop me?" roared Sam.

"I will."

"Then tak' that for thi' impudence yo' d——d, meddlin' workhouse bastard," and Sam brought the stinging leather right across Tom's flashing cheek.

Then, quick as lightning, sped a downright blow, straight from the shoulder true between the eyes, and Sam fell like a stricken ox, ignominious, into a skep of cops. There was the quick catching of breath from a score of throats as two score eyes watched the bully's fall, and Tom, as he looked about him, felt prouder and gladder than all his life before.

"Eh! but aw'st catch it for this," whispered Billy-come-a-lakin. "Aw'll run for it whilst aw've th' chance," and he fled the place, and his billy knew him no more that week.

"Yo'n nooan heerd th' last o' this," said Buckley, as he slowly picked himself up, dazed and scowling. "Aw'll mak' yo' pay for this day's wark, if aw swing for it, mind yo'r piecenin', yo' young limbs o' Satan, an' quit yo'r gapin'," and the irate spinner stalked out of the "scribbling boil."

Tom did the errand on which he had been sent by the dyer and made his way down the outer steps to return to his own work. He had to cross the mill-yard. Mr. Tinker had just ridden in at the gate and now was bending his head from the saddle to hearken to the tale Sam was pouring into his ear. Tom saw his master's brow contract.

"Send him to me," Tom heard, "I'll deal with him. It's rank mutiny."

Tom stepped forward and stood by the horse's side.

"I'm here, sir," he said quickly, tho' he could hear the beating of his own heart.

The riding-whip was raised with quick and angry menace. Tom never flinched, he only dug his nails into his palms to stay his tingling nerves. But the blow fell not.

"*Where* do you say you come from?"

"Diggle, sir," and Tom's quiet grey eye looked his master in the face. "You hired me yourself at the Workhouse."

Jabez Tinker peered, in the falling autumn light, into the lad's pale set face and scanned it searchingly.

"How came that weal across your cheek?"

"Sam can tell you best," was the quiet reply.

"You said nothing of this Buckley," said the master. "Mind when you come to me again, you don't come with half a tale. Go your ways, Pinder, but let me have no more of this broiling or you'll soon regret it."

And Jabez Tinker dismounted, threw the reins to Buckley, who stood surlily by, waiting the upshot of his complaint, and walked without another word to the office. But he had sighed as he watched Tom's upright, sinewy figure cross the mill yard, and a lingering, longing look followed the unwitting 'prentice.

CHAPTER VII.

TIME passed, as it will pass even in Holmfirth. Tom is still an apprentice, but in no fear of stick or strap from Sam Buckley, or any other Sam. The first Factory Act has become law, Ben Garside had a grievance the less, though when the night drew long it was still delight fighting his battles o'er again, to tell the oft-told tale of that famous march to York, when from Huddersfield, and all the parts contiguous, men, women, and little children made their weary way to York, to cry aloud that the iron-heel of capital might not crush out the infant life of the nation's self. Ben's limbs are stiffer by many a year since that historic tramp, but he straightens them and erect with flashing eye, as he dwells upon the heroic patience, the grim resolve of those who trod the long, long miles, and tells how weary men stayed with their arms the feeble, halting steps of bent and grey-headed sires, and worn and foot-sore women carried in their arms drooping children, not their own; how the rain fell in torrents, and the wind beat the cold showers in upon their drenched garments and many stole behind the hawthorn hedges, and the gray low stone walls, and slept the sleep of an exhaustion that was well nigh unto death; of how, as they came by some kindly waggoner, carting sacks of corn, or bales of wool, or barrels of good ale, the women and the children were taken up and given a sore-needed lift; how, as they passed through village and hamlet, hard-featured men and homely women came running into the road, and pressed upon them meat and drink, and wished them God-speed, and a safe return; of how when they reached the Castle yard in York itself, the clogs of many were clotted with the blood of their bruised and lacerated feet, and last, of how when their hearts were sick with hope deferred, the glad hour of triumph came, and the groans of the workers pierced the ears of Parliament, and the joy-bells rang to herald in the great Charter of the Toiler's freedom.

But Tom had that to protect him which was better fashioned than any statute ever made, incomprehensible by amplitude of words. Now, in his nineteenth year, he is nearing the six feet of manhood, and his frame is well knit and strong. Simple fare has agreed with him, anyway, simple, fare and simple, cleanly ways. He is the delight of Hannah Garside's eyes, and of eyes, too, younger and brighter than hers, though the winsome mill-hands of the valley declare that Tom Pinder is as dateless as a stone. "It's time wasted on him," they say, "he thinks o' nowt but his books an' his wark, an' maybe o' that poor ill-shaped Lucy Garsed."

It is Saturday afternoon, and Hannah's cottage is all "red up," and Hannah herself is washed and dressed and ready to don herself, and sally forth a-shopping, when the clacking of Ben's loom shall cease in the upper chamber. Lucy still tenants the settle under the window, but it is a stronger, bonnier Lucy than the wan frail Lucy of former days. Deformed she will always be, but some measure of bodily strength has been vouchsafed to her, and the bobbin-wheel by her side, presently to be put by, and a basket of bulky cops, and another of plenished bobbins tell that Lucy is no longer an unwilling divine in that busy hive, but can, with nimble fingers and pliant wrist, do the winding once her mother's care.

"Now stand you there, Beauty, and stir a foot if you dare," a voice is heard outside, a pleasant girlish voice; and without knock or ceremony the latch is lifted and a merry face, all smiles and sunshine, roses and dimples, peers in at the half-opened door.

"May I come in, and *do* you mind my fastening Beauty to the door-hasp, he is so restive, and always in a hurry to rush off home," and without waiting for permission the speaker trips into the room and kisses Lucy on both cheeks, and gives Mrs. Garside a hearty hug.

"Why, if it isn't Miss Dorothy!" exclaimed the good old dame. "My word, how yo' dun grow, miss, to be sure. Deary me, an' it only seems t' other day aw held yo' i' mi arms an' nussed yo' o' mi lap, an' yo' a wee-bit babbie kickin' an' croonin' an' little dreeamin' o' what yo'd lost upstairs, an' yo'r father awmost off his head wi' grief—deary, deary, how time dun fly, to be sure. But sit yo' daan, nah do."

How beautiful, how utterly bewitching and distracting a picture was Dorothy Tinker my art would utterly fail to tell. Image to yourself a lissom maiden of sweet seventeen, just of that happy medium height that reaches to a tall man's heart, and of that rounded proportioning of form, with outline of graceful curve that company with health and exercise; dream of an oval face in which the blush rose dwells, a rounded dimpled chin, violet eyes dancing with mirth, carnation lips and ivory teeth, and the small head crowned with wealth of auburn hair, rippling in waves like a dimpling streamlet;—dream of all this, and still 'tis but a dream, and only eye and ear could tell you how sweet and dainty a maid was Dorothy. Men drew their breath sharp when first they looked on her, and young men ravished and betook themselves to poetry and woeful sighs, and wandering far and lone by moonlit ways.

"We don't see much of you now-a-days, Miss Dorothy," said Lucy, smiling fondly at her visitor.

"An what mak' o' a gown do yo' ca' that?" said the mother.

"Oh! this, Mistress Hannah Garside, wife of Benjamin of that ilk, is my riding-habit and to be respected accordingly. It is, I believe, the only one in Holmfirth. Neat, isn't it?"

"Yo' look like a lad i' petticoits. Is it quite decent for a wench?" asked Mrs. Garside, somewhat anxiously.

"Decent! why, it's the very pink of the latest fashion: the only wear, in fact, though I *think* I would rather be without the skirt on a windy day. *Then* there'd be an uplifting of hands and a searching of hearts, if you like."

Mrs. Garside only looked half-satisfied.

"Yo'r th' same, an' yet not th' same," she said.

"Not the same! Hannah, why I should hope not indeed, or my good uncle's money would be sadly wasted, and you know that wilful waste makes woeful want. I know or should know, for Aunt Tinker dins it in my ear every time I buy a new ribbon or a pair of gloves. The same, indeed! Why do you know, Hannah, I'm being *finished*," and Dorothy dropped her voice as though she spoke a word of doom.

"Finished?" queried Lucy, "finished?"

"Aye finished, in very sooth. Fashioned, moulded, formed taught carriage and deportment, and several other extras at Miss Holmes's highly fashionable, strictly select academy for young ladies in Huddersfield, and thither and thence I ride on Beauty every day of the blessed week bar Sundays and missin's—but that's an improper word and not to be spoken in genteel society."

"A 'cademy! lor, think o' that now," said Hannah much impressed "an' what do they larn yo' now, furrin languages I'll be bun."

"Oh dear, yes! I can already relieve my feelings to my aunt in French that she cannot understand, and which I dare say, would puzzle Mons. Feugley, our French master, and I know some German words that sound so like swearing that Aunt Tinker gasps and grows pale when I use them, and I can tinkle on the piano and sing indifferently well for a screechy voice."

"That's nooan Gospel, my word," put in Hannah, stoutly, and Lucy held up a reproving finger.

"And oh! tell it not in Gath, publish it not in the streets of Ascalon."

"More furrin' parts" groaned Hannah.

"I can, sh! speak low my voice, bend your heads and lend your ears.—I can dance!"

"Dance!" gasped Hannah.

"Yes, *vraiment*, which is French or German, I forget which, for of a verity and in good sooth—but they don't know at home. It's an extra extra, dancing is and Aunt Martha wouldn't hear of it, and Uncle declared it was a vanity. But I learn all the same."

"How do you manage it?" asked Lucy, with an admiring, caressing but wistful look at the beaming face.

"Why the other girls teach me, silly, in the bedroom. We dance in our nightdresses, when *Fraulein* has put out the gas. But it isn't as nice, they say, as dancing with Professor Blanc, *de Paris, vous savez*."

"Oh, Dorothy, how can you say such things!" and Lucy looked really shocked.

"But you, Lucy, you are altered too. Ah! How my tongue runs on. But there, it is such a relief to let it run just once in a way, for at school, it's 'Miss Tinker, give silence, if you please,' and 'Miss Tinker, less noise.' and 'Miss Tinker, cease laughing,' till I'm Miss Tinkered to death, and you know what it is at home. I vow if it weren't for old Betty and Irish Peggy, I'd soon be competent to conduct a school for the deaf and dumb. Yes, Lucy, you are altered too; you're stouter and rosier, altogether happier looking, what's come over the child, Hannah!"

"Ah! that's all Tom's doing," said Hannah, "and God's, mother dear," softly added Lucy.

"Tom?" queried Dorothy, "who in the name of goodness is Tom?"

"Why, Tom,—oh, Tom is just Tom," said Lucy, "you can't have forgotten him, Miss Dorothy, you must remember to have seen him."

"Not a remembrance!" exclaimed Dorothy emphatically; "but it's an ugly name enough. Tom what? or maybe it's the cat."

"Ah! now aw see you're only playing, miss," said Hannah. "Noah, sen yo'? why, wheerivver han' yo'r e'en bin not to see yar Tom, Tom Pinder, yo' know—he's warked for yo'r uncle these how mony years is't, Lucy, lemme see, aye these five year an' more, an' if yo' hannot seen him I'se warrant yo're th' only wench i' Holmfirth 'at ha not.

"But what's this Admirable Crichton to do with Lucy's better looks?"

"Why, ivverything, if truth be spokken, as ever it shall be i' this haase whiles Hannah Garsed has a tongue to speik. Yo' mind what a pale peaky helpless critter 'oo wor five yer back, none fit to do a hand-stir for hersen. That wer' after 'oo'd worked 'at yor' uncle's for a spell—but that's nother here nor theer. An' then, who but yo'r own sen up an' spak' to yo'r uncle 'at aw could, mebbe do wi' a lodger, an' didn't he come—yo'r uncle, aw meean—an' 'gree wi' me to tak' Tom an' do for 'im, an' he—yo'r uncle aw meean—wer' to pay me hauf-a-craan a week for him, at first, an' rise to four shillin' afore Tom wer' out o' his writin's, which awm sure it's little enough when th' weshin's considered, an' 'im that hearty yo'd think sometimes he'd eit a man off his horse, not but what he's welcome to all he can howd an' more till it, for aw couldn't think more on 'im nor do more for 'im, if he wer' my own lad, which aw sometimes awmost think he is, an' yar Ben that set up wi' 'im, an' 'im so clivver at his books 'at it's as gooid as a sermon an' better nor some to yer th' father an' 'im a argeyfyin' an' a argeyfyin' till yo'd think they'd nivver ha' done."

"But what about Lucy?"

"Weel, weren't aw tellin' yo'? Weel, at first when he come he wer' a bit shy, like, o' Lucy, an' her o' 'im; bud one day, a Sunday afternooin it wer, an' th' sun shinin', an' th' sky as blue as weshin'-powder, Tom says it wer' a shame o' Lucy to be cooped up i' th' haase an' ne'er taste th' taste o' fresh air; an' he just up wi' her in his arms, same as yo'd lift a babby, an' carried her aat into garden, an' th' hedge wer' all thick wi' May-blossom, both white and red, an' he gate a lot, an' made a posy for her; an' after that it wer' a regular outin' for her as long as th' weather held, an' after he'd come fro' th' mill, fit to drop, so to speik, he wer' nivver too tired to gi' Lucy her outin'. And then it wer' Tom 'at put into yar Ben's yed to ha' a cheer on wheels, an' he poo'd it hissen up an' daan th' loin, though lads and lasses, shameless hussies some on 'em, made nowt bud fun on 'im an' ca'd him dree-nurse. Bud he sooin garr'd th' lasses howd their tongues an' keep aat o' th' loin—trust Tom for that—an' when th' lads went th' lasses followed, trust *them* for that."

"And how did he make them?" asked Dorothy, laughing.

"Oh! weel, he ca's it moral suasion; but it looked uncommon like feightin th' time aw' see'd it. Ben says it wer' effectual callin'."

"H'm, I don't think I shall like this same Master Tom of yours. He's a paragon, and I don't think paragons and I quite hit it."

"Aw dooan't know what yo' meean bi a Paragon, miss, but there's a Paragon what's a public-haase i' Westgate i' Huddersfielt, an' yo' nivver wer' further off yo'r horse, Miss Dorothy, though aw mak' bold to say so. Why, yar Tom nivver touches a drop stronger nor teea, an's awmost

’verted yar Ben, leastwise he tak’s nowt no stronger nor whom-brew’d an’ *aw* see that’ll nooan hurt ’im.”

“Aye, aye, I see, a paragon, a saint. Oh! I can picture him. Tall, you say? Yes, tall and thin and hollow-chested, stooping, pale, with long black hair as straight as a yard of pump-water; and he turns his eyes up and his toes in, and groans dismally, and his clothes don’t fit him, and he wears black cotton gloves on Sundays, an inch too long in the fingers, and he goes to temperance meetings and prayer meetings, and regularly to chapel twice on Sundays, and attends experience meetings and turns his soul inside out for the world—of Aenon Chapel—to gaze at. Oh! I think I see him now, that quite too precious Tom!”

“Weel, so yo’ may, Miss Dorothy,” said Hannah with a quiet smile. “He’s had his bath upstairs—nivver such a one there wer’ sin Adam for weshin’ hissen all ovver once a week whether he wants it or not—an’ nah, aw’ll be bun he’s mankin’ i’ th’ garden.”

And Hannah went into the back kitchen or scullery at the back of the “house” and, still smiling, beckoned to Dorothy. “Aye, he’s theer, sure enough.”

And this is what Dorothy saw: a young Hercules, stripped, save his vest, to the belted waist, his heels together, his toes out-turned, his knees braced, his breast expanded, his chin in air, and in his outstretched brawny arms whirled about his head a mighty pair of clubs—“it’s a windmill,” whispered Dorothy—“Oh! but he’s a proper man.”

“As ever yo’d see in a day’s walk,” chuckled Hannah,—“more o’ a Samson nor a saint, accordin’ to my readin’ o’ th’ Scriptur’s,—but ther’s neer a Dalilah o’ ’em all ’ll ha’ to cut Tom’s hair for ’im, trust owd Hannah for that.”

“H’m, that’s as may be,” said Dorothy in the maturity of wisdom, finished and formed at a select academy, and, turning to take her leave of Lucy.

“I must run away now, dear Lucy; ’t will never do to let your handsome lover catch me in this fright of a gown. I’ll come again some day when you’re likely to be by yourself. And, Lucy, dear, I daresay he isn’t at all a paragon. There, now, and don’t blush any more, or you’ll be struck so.”

Now although from this time forth Dorothy Tinker made more than one occasion to visit her sick friend, popping in at uncertain times of the day, as Mrs. Garside said, “promis’us-like” it was not till nigh up upon Christmas time, that she ever had speech with Tom. And this is how that came to pass. One day, a week or so before Yule-tide, when the snow lay heavy upon all the hills, no other than Workhouse Jack presented himself in Wilberlee mill yard, looking very like a middle-aged, beardless, lean and hungry image of Father Christmas. He was met in the yard by Sam Buckley.

"We don't want no hands: we're puttin' no fresh 'uns on this side Easter, so off yo' pack abaat yo'r business."

"Be yo' Mr. Tinker, sir?" said Jack.

"Nooah," answered Sam, somewhat mollified by the implied compliment; "nooah, what do you want?"

"Isn't this th' spot at Tom Pinder works at?" asked Jack.

"Aye, if yo' ca' it workin'; some folk 'ud ca' it lakin'. What does ta want to kno' for? no good awm sure."

"Well, aw'n getten a letter for him."

"A letter! Who's it fro'?"

"Aw reckon th' letter tell that for itsen."

"Well, hand it here, aw'll see he gets it."

"It's varry partickler, yo' see," demurred Jack. "It's fro' a woman, an' oo' telled me at aw wor to 'liver it to nob'dy but Tom hissen, an' 'oo's a woman 'at generally has her own way i' our parts."

"Well, yo' can oather gi' it to me or wait outside th' gate till he comes aat. Yo'll nooan see Pinder afore th' mills lose."

"Tha'rt a liar; aw see 'im nah. Hey Tom lad, aw want thee!" and Jack adroitly dodged past the protesting slubber and ran up to Tom. Buckley deemed discretion the better part of valour and took himself off.

"Sithee, Tom," almost gasped Jack in his eagerness, and casting a triumphant glance at the discomfited obstructionist, "sithee, there's a letter for thee. It's fro Betty Schofield at th' Wakey, an' tha's to go back wi me. 'Oo'd ha' put that i't' letter, aw wer to tell thee, but 'oo'd no more ink, an' th' pen gate cross-legged."

And Tom read as follows:

"Deer Tom,

This is to let yew 'no at Mr. Black's bin took vary bad, an's frettin' becos yo' dont com' to see 'im. He's i' bed; wi' a stroke i'th reight side, hopin' you're well which it leaves me, so no more at present from

Yours trewly,

BETTY SCHOFIELD."

Tom's heart smote him. He was conscious that latterly he had been remiss in his visits to his friends beyond the hill. His new life was growing on him, and new interests filling his mind.

"Is it serious, do you know, Jack?" he asked.

"Moll 'o Stute's says another do 'll finish him. He's had two doctors till 'im, an' Moll says his constitooshun' whativver 'oo meeans bi that, couldn't ha' stooid one, ne'er name two. But yo'll come, Tom, an' Betty says yo'll do him more gooid nor physic."

It would have been nothing out of the common for a hand to "jack" his work without saying "by your leave," or "with your leave," but that was not Tom's way. He sought Mr. Tinker in the dingy little office, but he was not there,—he might be in the house, someone suggested; and Tom made for the house, a mere stride, not a stone-throw from the mill-gate. Jack trotted by his side like a faithful dog.

"Weel, I declare, if there beeant big Tom Pinder comin' up th' walk, miss," exclaimed Betty, the cook, wiping her hands on her coarse apron, "an' as shallockin' a lookin' felley wi 'im as ivver yo' clapped een on," and a knock at the kitchen door coincided with her wondering "what's to do naah!"

Now Dorothy was in the very thick of that daintiest of all household doings the making of pastry for the Christmas fare. She was garbed in a pretty print dress, and a white bib and apron, spotlessly clean, became her vastly. Her small and shapely hands were cunningly turning the well-greased tins, and shaping the dough within and above a noble array of large and portly tins crammed with the makings of pork-pies and jimping the edges of lesser tins designed for the mince-meat that, not innocent of the flavour of brandy, scented the warm kitchen air. The sleeves of her dress were rolled up and gave play to as white and rounded an arm, with a dainty dimple at the elbow, as ever delighted the eyes of man. Her cheek was flushed either with the heat of the roaring fire or confusion at being so discovered by eyes whose sudden glance, quick withdrawn, betrayed a startled admiration more speakingly than speech.

"I beg your pardon, Miss, but is Mr. Tinker at home? He isn't in the office, nor about the mill," said Tom, whilst Jack alternate gaped and sniffed.

"Can't yo' shut th' door after yo', Tom Pinder," exclaimed Betty, "or do yo' think yo're big enough to do for a door yersen?"

"Uncle's not at home; he's gone to Huddersfield, I think," said Dorothy, hastily unrolling her sleeves, and hiding the glistening ivory of her arms.

"Mrs. Tinker, perhaps?" hazarded Tom.

"And aunt's in bed, as bad as can be with a sick head-ache. A pretty Christmas *we* are likely to have; but is it any message you can leave?" for Tom had turned to go, "you look in trouble."

"Jack here has brought me a message, Miss. It's from an old friend, perhaps from the oldest, and it concerns the best friend I have in the world. My more than guardian Mr. Black, the schoolmaster at Diggle, is sick, it is feared unto death, and Jack here has won over th' top through th' snow to fetch me to him."

"An' dun yo' meean to say, Tom Pinder," broke in Betty, "'at this yer drowned rat of a man 'at stann's theer gaupin' as if he wer mooin-struck an' drippin' all ovver my cleean floor like a leeakin' piggin' 's come all th' way fro' Diggle i' this weather 'at's nooan fit for a dog to be aat in."

"Aye, Betty," said Tom,—he was a prime favourite with Betty of old, and he knew it,—"not so warm as your kitchen, but it was urgent you see, and Jack's an old friend too, aren't you, Jack?"

But Jack's eye and Jack's thoughts were fixed upon something more to a hungry man's purpose than mere matters of friendship—he had caught the whiff from the oven door—it was the scent of pork pie piping hot.

Dorothy caught the glance that waywards.

"Why how thoughtless I am. Now, Jack, I'm sure, as it's Christmas time"—needless qualification—"you can eat some Christmas fare. And they're the very first pies I've ever made, and I *do* hope they'll be nice. Peggy, why don't you set some plates?"

"And mind yo' hot 'em afore th' fire. Its simply beyond all belief how aw've to tell that girl to put hot plates wi' hot meeat, an' cowd wi' cowd, i'steead o' cowd wi' hot an' hot wi' cowd."

"And you Tom,"—and then with a hesitation as though in doubt, "I mean, Mr. Pinder, you will take something before you cross those terrible hills?"

If Dorothy had there and then asked Tom to sit down and make a comforting meal of dynamite washed down with prussic acid it is odds that he would have set to bowl and platter with a cheerful heart; but to put knife and fork into a rich brown crust that crunched beneath the blade and to see the hot jelly gush out over the plate and to catch the fragrance of the red and brown pork with judicious blending of lean and fat cut into squares like dice, and to see all this flanked by a crested jug of foaming beer.—Oh! Don't talk to me of nectar and ambrosia.

"Yo'r health, miss," said Jack, politely and as distinctly as he could with his mouth full, "and yo'rs, too, aw'm sure"—this to Betty, whose ample form he surveyed with lingering approval "and a merry Chersmas when it comes."

But Tom, even as he plied his knife and fork heard ringing in his ears the words that some instinct or some dim apprehension or prompting of native delicacy had compelled from Dorothy's lips.—"Mister Pinder". Tom had never been called Mister Pinder before in all his life "Gentleman Tom" and "Dandy Tom" he heard occasionally from the lasses of the mill, smarting from that worst of feminine ailments—*injuria formal spietal*,—the quiet unconsciousness of or indifference to advances none too coy. But "Mr. Tom"—'t was the baptism into a new life, the stirring of a new manhood, his accolade; it fell on his senses as falls the sovereign's sword on shoulder of kneeling knight. It was a new and nobler Tom that turned his face that afternoon over the hills to Diggle.

"Go to see your sick friend?" Dorothy had cried. "Why, of course you'll go. I'm sure uncle would say so, and anyway if he faults anyone, why he must fault me."

"An' aw hope his first mince-pie may choke him if he does," wished Betty, but kept her wishes to herself.

Tom was shocked at the change a few weeks had made in the old schoolmaster Mr. Black had, truly, been failing ever since the sudden and unexpected death of the shrill Priscilla some twelve months before. His devoted if exacting sister had gone to that land where there is neither dusting nor teaching, and where she must have received a shaking of cherished convictions if she found any schoolboys. Since then her brother had lived alone, cooking and generally doing for himself, save that one of the boys scrubbed the schoolroom floor and scrubbed the desks, in consideration of being put on the school free-list. More and more as the days wore on the schoolmaster had seemed to shrink within himself, and find a placid joy in the not wholly unpleasing melancholy of reflection and regret. Perhaps Priscilla's faithful girding had been to him like a tonic and an irritant, and saved him from a natural tendency to the introspective absorption of a lonely life. Gradually the nightly symposia at the *Hanging Gate* were abandoned, much to the wrath of good Mistress Schofield, who roundly declared that "if th' Schooilmaster had nobbut gone theer o' neets, takin' th' best chair, an' sittin' i'th' warmest corner, just to be out o' reick o' his sister's tongue, she for one fun' his room as gooid as his company." Perhaps one reason for Mr. Black's inconstancy might be found in the fact that so long as Priscilla lived, he knew there was a shield and buckler between him and the engines and weapons of attack the buxom widow knew so well how to employ. Priscilla gone, he felt himself as a city girt round and besieged, but helpless and defenceless, its strong tower razed to the ground. Reason be what it might the angle nook of the sanded kitchen knew him no more and the friendly circle had a very sensible gap. And ere long the news, the all but incredible news, spread through t' village, and up the valley, and about the steep hill-sides, that "owd Black wer' givin' up teeachin', and what to do wi' th' lads and lasses 'at wer' allus under yo'r feet, or up to some mak' o' devilment till they we' owd enough to go to th' mill, 'ud pass a weary woman's wits to tell."

Tom felt as he neared the school a strangely depressing air of solitude and desertion. The playground no more resounded to the eager cries of boys revelling in a brief freedom, nor from the open windows came the murmuring buzz of unwilling voices droning in unison the tables of multiplication. The schoolmaster he found in his little bedroom, not in bed, indeed, but looking far fitter for bed than up. To Tom's surprise, he found Moll o' Stuarts in attendance on the sick man. She had, it transpired, carried the citadel of the sick-room by assault and taken possession with characteristic coolness and determination, and there she had announced her resolve to abide till the schoolmaster should be either better or worse. As for her more legitimate profession she declared:

"They mun get someb'dy else. Onyb'dy wer' gooid enough to bring a fooil into th' world, but it wer' worth while tryin' to keep a wise man in it. Th' best of men's poor feckless things when i'th' best o' health, but if they nobbut cut their little finger, they're as useless as babes unborn, an' it were well there wer somebody to look after him, sin' those 'at had most reight to kept away for weeks at a time, an' ne'er cam' near till they wer' sent for." And with this Parthian shaft, Molly at a sign from the invalid, withdrew, to give Jack, who had stayed below, gazing open-mouthed at the maps and globes, the benefit of her pent storm of wrath.

"I'm glad you've come, Tom. I knew you would, but hesitated to send for you. I know you have little time away from work, and youth companies best with youth when work is laid aside."

"Indeed, Mr. Black, I had no notion you were so ill or nothing could or should have kept me away. I would have come to help and nurse you if I had had to break my indentures and go before the magistrates for it."

"I know it, lad, I know it; and it was pleasant to think there was one not so many miles away who had a warm place in his heart for the old man. You have been to me, Tom, as a son since first I held you in my arms, and I have even thanked God that to my childless life He sent the blessing of one I could cherish and foster as my own."

Tom could find no words. He pressed the thin and shrunken hand that rested, oh! so feebly, on the arm of the pillowed chair.

"And now, lad, that you are here, you must let me say my say, for my strength is waning fast and a voice within tells me my days remain but few. Nay, lad, never greet my course is run, my work is done, and the vespers ring for eventide. I do not dread its shadows, lad, for a hand will hold mine when I tread the unknown way. Take this key, unlock that topmost drawer and bring me the case you will find there."

Tom silently, treading softly did the master's bidding.

Mr. Black raised the lid of the little casket and thence a small bundle of letters, their ink now faded to a pale yellow. They were tied together with a thin blue ribbon. Mr. Black touched them lovingly and sunk into a reverie from which Tom made no stir to rouse him. The vacant eyes of the invalid seemed to be looking through and beyond the stalwart youth or to be intent on the unforgotten scenes of a buried past.

Then with a wan smile and a gentle sigh the faint voice said:

"If I die, Tom, I trust you to place these with me." Then, like a maiden confessing her heart's secret:

"Ah! Tom, even your old dominie was young once—but there was Priscilla, you know."

And what tragedy of a sacrificed life those letters revealed was never betrayed to the eyes of Tom or other man, for unopened and unread they laid upon the faithful, uncomplaining heart that treasured them.

"And, now, Tom, to business. This you see is my will. A man doesn't die any sooner you know for making his will. When I lost Priscilla, a rare woman, Tom, but over tender for this World, a matchless Woman,—I made a new will. I haven't much to leave, but what there is will be yours. I should like you to keep the books—don't part with them. They have been very precious to me. Perhaps some day you will know how precious books can be. I had hoped, fondly hoped, that you would turn to scholarship and take my seat by the old desk—but it wasn't to be, it wasn't to be," and the schoolmaster shook his head sadly.

Again Tom could find no words—what could he say, how could he tell the master that a few hours before the glance of a young maid's eye and the trill of her glad young voice and the touch of her soft white hand had been of more moving eloquence than a guardian's pleading, and that, as he pushed over the hills that day through depth of snow and stress of storm to the sickbed side, revolving many things in his awakened mind, he had made a great resolve and vowed a deep and binding vow.

"There remains but this," continued Mr. Black. "You have seen this locket before. It was your mother's. The time has come when I may place it where it belongs. You know its story. Wear it ever, and may God in His own good time raise the veil and grant light where now is darkness and certainly where all is fruitless conjecture."

Tom took the locket, pressed it to his quivering lips and hid it in his bosom. "Lucy shall twine it about my neck," he said, "and I will wear it ever."

"Send for Moll now. I must lie down. You won't forget Moll, when I am gone. She is a good soul, and has tended me well."

The old man was assisted to his bed, and sank exhausted on the pillow. There was silence in the darkling chamber, save for the heavy breathing of the fast failing man.

"Read me the twenty-first Psalm," he said, presently.

But Tom's voice failed him, and broke as he read:

"'Yea, though I walk through the valley of the shadow of death, I will fear no evil; for Thou art with me, Thy rod and Thy staff they comfort me.'"

And Tom kneeled by the bedside, and hid his face in the coverlet, nor restrained his tears.

And the light trembling hand of him who had so loved him rested on the bowed head, and the feeble voice was raised in prayer and benediction.

And the night fell and the "peace that passeth all understanding" entered therein and there abode.

CHAPTER VIII.

THE legacy left him by Mr. Black amounted to no less than a hundred pounds, which seemed to Tom a vast sum. Mr. Redfearn was sole executor of the will. Tom took possession of the books,—a few choice Latin authors, the Greek Testament, and many educational works. He selected, besides, a few articles of furniture, of which he made a present to Mrs. Garside; he did not forget Moll o' Stuarts. Out of the proceeds of the portion of the furniture which he sold, there was just enough to pay for a mourning suit of good broadcloth for himself, and strangely ill at ease he felt when first he beheld himself arrayed in the glossy doeskin. But after the funeral, he had only to wear it on Sundays, when most people who could manage it by hook or crook contrived to wear decent suits, mainly of black,—black was the general, if not "the only wear." The reason is not far to seek. Among the working-classes the better suit is a very distinct garment from what are called emphatically "wartday clo'es," and is seldom worn except on Sunday, and at funerals.

There remained the hundred pounds, and the question was not easy of answer, what should he do with it? Under the will, Mr. Redfearn had power to apply the money for Tom's advancement in life, even before his majority when it was to pass into his uncontrolled disposition. Tom cudgelled his brain so much and so vainly as to the ultimate application of this immense sum that he came to be thankful he could not, as yet, touch the bulk, or he would have been tempted to throw it into the river. He did not get much help from Mr. Redfearn.

"Yo' see, Tom," said his guardian, "a hundred pounds is a very awk'ard sum o' money. It's summat like a gooise, which is too much o' a meal for one, an' not enuff for two. Nah this legacy o' yo'rs is summat i'th' same fashion. It's too much to go on th' spree wi', an' ha' done wi' it, an' off yo'r mind, so to speeak, and it's too little to set up i' business on yo'r own account,—at leastwise i' ony business 'at's likely to suit thee. Yo' might start i'th' grocery line, to be sure, but I doubt th' little childer 'ud be feart to come into th' shop if they seed six feet of brawn and muscle behind th' counter. Besides they say it tak's a very light hand to weigh grocer's stuff aat to ony profit. I can think o' nowt else. You might go into th' public line on yo'r furtin in a smallish way, an' there's one thing 'at's i' yo'r favour, yo'd nooan want a chuckor aat."

Tom shook his head emphatically: "Nay," he said, "I will never make my living by giving my brother strong drink to his hurt."

Redfearn laughed, "they'll call yo' 'Parson Tom' in a bit, lad. But happen yo'r i'th' reight on it. For one gooid word yo' can find to say for drink yo' can find a hundred to say agen it, an' then start afresh an' tack another hundred to it. Folk will have it, but them as get's th' leeast has th' best share, an' I'll nivver be one to set a young lad i' th' way o' temptation. But has ta thowt o' onything thi sen?"

Tom shook his head. "I've thought till I'm almost stalled of the thought of the money."

"Well, there's no hurry, that's one comfort. Th' brass 'll nooan get less so long as it's ith' bank, that's a sure thing. An' yo're not be out o' your indentures yet. Tak' yo'r time i' makin' up your mind, an' remember 'at it's th' easiest thing i' th' world to put good money into business, but it's quite another thing getting it back after yo'n once let go yo'r how'd."

On one point Tom was quite resolved. So soon as his apprenticeship should be at an end, and sooner if might be, he would be his own master. He would not live and die a weaver, nor yet be content even to live and die a slubber. Other men had conquered Fate and he was resolved that by God's help, he, too could and would. Why, the whole valley in which he did his daily task abounded with men who could tell of early privations, of years of patient unremitting toil, of Spartan endurance, of privations self-imposed and cheerfully borne, and of a notable success crowning and rewarding in middle life, the efforts of their youth and manhood's prime. And Tom felt that he had him the makings of a man and though he had, as yet, unbosomed the inner workings of his soul to man nor woman, being, indeed more given to seek commune with himself rather than another, yet was his mind firmly fixed either to make a spoon or spoil a horn, as the saying goes. But how?

He had said nothing at home, as he now considered Ben Garside's, about his little fortune, and as for the furniture which he had placed in the little cottage, Hannah declared, and meant it, that though it was "gooid on 'im to think o' old fr'en's, an' like 'im, 'oo wer' nooan so greedy as to do owt but store th' thin's for 'im, till such times as he wer' wed, and warst wish 'at 'oo could wish 'im wer' 'at he'd wed a lass 'at 'ud put as gooid a shine on th' owd table, an' cheers, an' th' oak-chest an' linen-press and charney-cupboard as 'oo'd done, but that wer' past prayin' for now-a-days."

There is no question that in this time of electricity and daily papers, news travels faster than in the times of our grandfathers but it travelled fast enough even then. And somehow it began to be whispered about the village that Gentlemen Tom "had come in for a fortin'." with that delicacy of reserve which is nowhere more to be found than among the better end of the working classes, neither Ben, nor Hannah, nor Lucy spoke to him on the matter. It was his concern, and if he choose to have secrets from his best well-wishers they were not going to force his confidence; though it cannot be denied that when neighbours questioned Hannah on the subject, as she stood with her flour-poke and basket waiting her turn at Split's counter of a Saturday afternoon she could give to her sibs no more satisfactory reply, than to tell them "to mell (meddle) o' their own business, an' 'ood try, God helping her, to mell o' hers,"—a reply which was no more satisfactory to herself than to her gossips, for it not only brought a discussion of a highly interesting domestic topic to an untimely end, but it deprived Hannah of that assumption of exclusive intelligence which is as dear to a woman of conversational gifts as to a newspaper editor. But when Tom became aware by many subtle signs that not only had people heard something of his windfall, but that Hannah was piqued by his silence he resolved to take counsel with Ben. Even should he get no better advice than to seek advice.

"Ah, it's a seet o' brass lad, is a hunderd paands, an' a gret responsibility. Aw dunnot think aw ivver seed more nor ten all at onc't, an' that fair med me gip." It was thus Ben delivered himself one Sunday afternoon as he smoked his pipe before the kitchen fire. "Aw knew tha'd do nowt wi'out speikin' to me or yar Hannah abaat th' job, an' we thowt no waur o' thi' for howdin' thi tongue abaat it i'steead o' makkin a spreead abaat it waur nor a peeacock wi' it's tail as some 'ud ha' done. An' as for wearin' th' brass o' drink an' wenchin', as some 'ud ha' done; why it wer better for thi' 'at tha' sud ha' had a millstone then raand thi neck an' bin plumped fair i' th' middle o' th' mill-dam."

"Yes, but Ben, I can discover for myself what I should *not* do with the money; what I want to settle is what I *should* do with it."

"It's safe enew wheer it is, isn't it?" asked Hannah, anxiously.

"Well, it' as safe as the bank, any way," Tom assured her.

Hannah seemed dubious. "Aw dunnot ma' mich accaant o' them banks. Ther' wer' Ingram's, tha'll mind oo', Ben, i' Hundersfild. It went dahn th' slot an' lots o' folk lost ther brass through it. Aw'd just as sooin put my bit i' th' teea-caddy—but we're nivver safe, as th' lad said when he fun' a sov'rin'."

Ben had puffed his pipe in silence, but now waved the long churchwarden to bespeak attention.

"There's yo'r writin's to think on," he said. "Yo' munnot forget as yo'r bun' to Jabez Tinker till y'or twenty-one, an' thof mebbe nob'dy could blame yo' if yo' just went yo'r own gate as if th' writin's weren't ther; still aw misdoubt me th' law 'ud ha' summat to say: an' if yo' once get into th' lawyers' han's aw reely dunnot think yo' need bother yo'rsen abaat what yo' mun do wi' yo'r fortin'."

"But, Ben, whatever comes I mean to do the square thing by Mr. Tinker. I've served him faithfully up to now, and I don't mean to end up by doing otherwise. But don't you think he would release me, if it were fairly put to him, and he received some equivalent."

"He mote," said Ben, "an' then agen he moten't. But ther's no harm i' axin'."

"Aye, that's just like yo' men," said Hannah, "nowt'll do but goin' at a thing like a bull at a red rag. Tom mun step i' to th' caantin'-haase, an' say: 'If yo' please Mr. Tinker, aw'd like yo' to breik mi writin's, aw'n had some brass left me.' Nah, that's nooan my way."

"Well, what is it, Hannah?"

"Sayin's tellin', an' if aw tell'd yo', yo'd be as wise as me. Th' question is, what mun Tom do when he's free?"

"Aye, that's it," said Tom. "Well aw 've my plan, Tom, if th' missus, theer 'll let a man get a word in edgeways. Nah! Hannah, if th'rt fair run daan aw 'll go on." Hannah disdained to make reply.

"Nah! my advice is," said Ben, "just go on, as it were, quiet, for the next few months; but i'stead o' bein' satisfied i' th' mill wi' just doin' what tha'rt set to, keep thi een oppen an' tak' th' cotton wool aat o' yo'r ears, if yo' happen to have ony in, an' larn all ther' is to larn at Tinker's. He 'greed to teeach thee th' trade o' a clothier, an' aw'll be bun' he has'nt swopped ten words wi' yo' sin a 'prentice yo'n bin an' as for that druffen swill-tub, th' slubber, he might teich yo' th' differ atween th' feel o' a strap an' th' feel o' a pickin'-rod abaat yo'r back, an' that's abaat all. But till th' time comes for thee to oppen aat to Tinker, aw'd recommend yo in a quiet way, to larn all tha can. Get to know th' feel an' th' qualities o' wool, an' th' prices, an' th' natur' o'th' dyes an' acids, an' aboon all mak frien's wi' th' tuner, an' larn to gear a machine, an' tune it when it's aat o' gear."

Tom nodded.

"Weel," went on Ben, "as aw'n said. A hunderd paand 's a seet o' brass, an' if yo' know yo'r way abaat yo' can get a set o' machines wi' it—what 'll do for a start ony road i' a sma'ish way, which is th' best rooad an' choose hah! Yo'll ha nooa difficulty i' gettin' room an' power, an' what's more, if yo' winnot think awm sayin' one word for thee an' two for mysen, if yo' like to start i' manifactorin' o' thi own accaant, owd Ben Garsed's mony a yer o' gooid wark in him yet an' he'll be yo'r man, an' that's more nor he'd say for ony other being 'at walks o' two legs atween here an' th' next spot."

Tom's eyes sparkled with a sudden light, and he leaped to his feet to the imminent peril of his head against the rafters.

"The very thing," he cried, "the very, very thing. 'Oh! wise King, oh! prudent King'—stupid that I was never to think of it before, couldn't see wood for trees.—Lucy, you shall be our book-keeper. Let me see—Garside and Pinder, woollen manufacturers Holmfirth. Carried unanimously. Put it. Lucy, put it and hold up both your hands. My word, Ben, but you've a headpiece if you like. We'st nivver mend o' that idea if we talk fro' now till Doomsday. But will th' money run to it?"

"Ben 'll ha' considered that," said Hannah.

"He's a deep un, is Ben, an' if he wadn't talk so much wod mak' heead way yet; but it's 'im for goin' round an' round a thing an' under it an' ovver it afore he's made his mind up. Yo'n awmost to shak' him to get an opinion aat on him sometimes."

"Aw waren't long i' makkin' up mi mind abaat one thing ony road th' time aw clapt mi e'en o' thee, lass," said Ben, with a wink that comprehended both Tom and Lucy.

"Aye, an' aw didn't gi' time to unmak' it, noather," chuckled Hannah, and cast a glance at Ben that made her look thirty years younger and set him thinking of the days when an apparently chance shaft from Hannah's eyes set his heart a pit-a-pat.

"Aye, lad," said Ben, "there's folk started i' this valley wi' less nor a hundred pun', 'at fairly stinks o' brass naah. It's noan th' brass altogether 'at does th' trick; there's more i' knowin' haa to use it, an' more still in knowin' haa to keep what yo' mak' an' turn it ovver an' ovver like a rolling snowball. There's mony a man can mak' brass but it's stickin' to it bothers 'em."

And so it was settled that Tom should bide his time, making haste slowly, as the Roman sage advises, and that, meanwhile, Ben should keep his weather-eye open for room and power.

And Tom was not content with such knowledge as could be acquired in the Mill. Although his hours at the loom were long enough in all conscience, and he certainly led laborious days, he resolved also to shun luxurious nights, if idling through the evenings with a novel of Sir Walter Scott or doing odd jobs about the house for Hannah Garside or, in the summer, strolling about the lanes and over the moors could be said to constitute a luxury. He joined the classes at the Mechanics' Institute and nightly wrestled with the mysteries of Euclid, chevied the elusive *x* through algebraic equations, acquired enough of statics and dynamics to be appalled by the height, depth, and breadth of his own ignorance, and enough of chemistry to bring him to the same conclusion that the highway to ruin would be to trust to his own knowledge of that weird and fascinating science. But if of learning to be likely to be really useful in the career he had marked out for himself, Tom attained to little enough, his mind was all the better for the mental gymnastics his studies compelled. The books he conned demanded close application and sustained thought, and so, had he learned nothing from them at all, were an intellectual discipline that would tell in the battle of life, and rescued him from that flabby habit of mind that comes from desultory and random reading.

It was noticed too, that about this time Tom forsook in some measure his first love, the services of the Established Church, and became a very frequent worshipper at Aenon Chapel. Ben declared that he couldn't make head or tail of this change from country walks turned to profitable account, as Ben conceived, by Ben's discursive utterances *de omnibus rebus et aliis praterca*, but more particularly and recurringly concerning the high metaphysics of Calvinistic theology.

"There's a screw loose, somewhere," he remarked solemnly to Hannah one Sunday afternoon when Tom, after brushing his suit of woe very sedulously and looking more than once in the little cracked glass to see if his tie were rightly bunched and his "toppin" duly "lashed" and parted had sidled rather shamefacedly out of the house with a hymn-book in one hand, whilst with the fore-finger of the other he assured himself that the coin destined for the collection box nestled securely in the corner of his waistcoat pocket. Hannah stayed her rocking and smoothed the sheen of her silken apron, but was mute.

"Aye," continued Ben, "aw cannot tell whativver's come ovver th' lad. Aw say nowt agen his buryin' his nose i' books e'ery neet, an' hardly goin' to bed till aw'm thinkin o' gettin' up. That's improvin' his mind, that is, at least aw hope so—it's only to be hoped he won't addle it i'th process. But this chapel-goin's beyond me. Mind yo', aw nivver said so mich abaat his gooin' to th' church o' a mornin'. He wer' browt up so, and Mr. Black set a deal o' store on it, so it wer' like honourin' yo'r father an yo'r mother, in a fashion o' speikin'. But, dal me, chapel-goin's like turnin' his back on th' church altogether. What does *ta* mak on it, Hannah?"

"Nowt," said Hannah, and Ben knew from experience that the wife of his bosom thought more than she was minded to tell.

"If it hadn't been Tom," continued Ben in a meditative and perhaps something of a tentative strain, "Tom 'at's as steady as a booat-hoss aw sud be enclined to speckilate ther' wer' a wench at th' bottom on it. What do'st think, Lucy, has he said owt to yo' abaat it?"

"No, father. Tom has said nothing but that the new minister at Aenon 's a very good preacher. One o' th' new school, he says."

"Aye, aye, aw'n yerd abaat him. 'A wind-bag,' some o'th owd hands ca' 'im. Bi all aw can mak' aat he's a trimmer 'at sets his sails to catch the wind o' approval fro' th' upper seats o' th' 'orthodox, orthodox Sons o' auld John Knox,' an' the gale o' applause fro' th' young 'uns 'at 'ud like to kick ovver th' traces. He's noather fish, nor flesh, nor fowl, nor gooid red herrin'—so folk sen, an' goes on refinin' an' refinin' and explainin' till Deacon Whiteley says he's refined and explained th' owd Trust Deed away, an' ther's lots o'th owder end dunnot know whether they're stood o' their heads or their heels. An' they dunnot hauf like th' Band o' Hope 'at he's started i' connection wi' th' Sunday Schooil, though aw'll say nowt agen that missen."

"It 'ud be a gooid thing if they'd ha' a Band o' Hope for th' grown-up childer," said Hannah. "I fancy from what Tom said to me t'other neet—I mean night," began Lucy.

"Neet's gooid enew," interrupted her mother in a sharper tone than Lucy often heard. "Though awm awmost forced to be dumb, when yo'r father's got owt to say, awm noather deaf nor blind, thank God; an' aw'n noticed lately 'at Tom's getten into a fine way o' speikin',—Miss Nancyfied aw ca' it,—an' yo'r followin' suit. There'll be no livin' wi' oather on yo' sooin if it goes on."

"Well, what is it yo' wouldn't be capped at?" asked Ben, by way of diversion.

"If Tom joined the Band of Hope," said Lucy quietly, and, one would have judged, sadly.

"Th' lad's clean off," said Ben. "That brass has bin too mich for his yed. Wi' most folk it runs to drink, but aw reckon it depends o' th' constitooshun. But, dal me, if aw dunnot don missen up very next Sunday 'at ever is, an' gooa wi' 'im to th' chapel an' hear for missen; so, dooant forget, Hannah, to ha' me a clean shirt, for aw munnot shame th' lad."

"Aye," assented Hannah, "gooa, bi all meeans, an' if a fooil's advice worth's takkin', please thissen abaat keepin' thi ears on th' pulpit, but keep thi e'en on th' pews." And with this Delphic utterance Mrs. Garside began to lay the little round table for tea, with a clatter that threatened the longevity of the "chaney" cups and saucers that had descended with the Family Bible, and were almost as venerated.

And Lucy looked troubled with that trouble that seeks disguise in constrained cheerfulness.

"It's a woman, then," said Ben to himself. "Who'd ha' thowt it, but whooa i' th' name o' wonder can it be?"

Pursuant to his resolve, Ben, the next Sunday, volunteered to accompany Tom to Chapel, to Tom's undisguised surprise.

"Well, yo' see, lad," explained the Senior, inwardly congratulating himself on the astuteness of his reply, "what's gooid enough for thee 'll daatless be gooid enough for thi partner 'at is to be."

The Rev. David Jones was a man of middle stature, quick and nervous in his movements, and quick and nervous in his delivery. He had all the fire and not a little of the poetic feeling and imagination of his Welsh ancestry. He had the great gift of being able to see and understand the very crux of an abstruse problem and to state it lucidly. Then, when you held your breath for the solution, he would break into a rhapsody, and, in a torrent of words, metaphor piled upon metaphor in dazzling extravagance of phrase, he would scale the gamut of the emotions, and close the exordium as in the wild frenzy of an ancient seer.

"Ther's a gooid deeal o'clout, Tom," whispered Ben, "but aw'n nooan come to th' puddin'." But Ben spoke to ears that heard not. The rhapsodies of the eloquent Gael were thrown away on Tom. His eyes were fixed on the ample pew in which Mr. and Mrs. Tinker sat erect and listening apparently with much attention to the sermon. Mr. Tinker's regard indeed, appeared to be more critical than appreciative.

"Jabez is too owd a bird to be ta'en wi' chaff," thought Ben. "Th' parson's main clever, reight enough, but there's one yonder's gotten his measure, or awm mista'en."

But neither on his employer nor on the severe face of Mrs. Tinker was Tom's wrapt look so intently fixed. By her uncle's side sat Dorothy, looking, said Ben, in his afternoon account to Hannah, "just as if butter wouldn't melt in her maath. She nivver took her e'en fro' off her Bible or her hymn book or th' parson, barrin' once, an' if 'oo didn't look plainly at Tom then 'oo looked at me, that's all aw can say. But it weren't a look straight out o' her e'en, yo' mun understand, nor wi' her eyes starin' out o' her yead, like some wenches 'll look at a young felly; but just a sort o' a squint aat o'th tail o' her e'en, an' then th' lashes fell part way ovver 'em, an' theer 'oo wer' gazin' at th' parson as if 'ood nivver blinked. It's a mercy 'oo didn't look at me th' same way again, or I'd ha' made a fooil o' missen some road or other, an' chance it. An' Tom, why he went as red as a peony, an' his hand trem'led so he dropped a book an' had to scrat it up wi' his feet by reason o'th pew bein' too narrow for him to get his yed dahn to reick it up wi' his hand i' th' ordinary way. Aw poised his shin for 'im under th' seeat to make him mind his manners for when aw *do* go to a chapel aw like to behave some-bit-like, an' after that he listened to th' sarmon as good as gowd."

"And do you remember the text, father?"

"To be sure aw do, trust me for that. Aw gate Tom to nick it with his thumb in his book, an aw wer' settlin' dahn comfortable to th' exposition when aw gate th' full blast o' Miss Dorothy's look, choose 'oo it wer' meant for. It had liked to ha' bowled me ovver, but aw poo'd missen together, an' aw'n getten th' heads o'th discoorse. Reick us th' Bible, missus. It wer' eighth Romans, thirtieth. Read it up, Lucy."

"Moreover whom he did predestinate, them he also called; and whom he called, them he also justified; and whom he justified, them he also glorified."

"Nah! I thowt to missen, we're in for it. Aw liked th' chap's courage. It's holus-bolus, nah, says I, an' th' owder end they looked up at th' parson wi' a grim sort o' look as much as to say, 'Get ovver that if yo' can' an' then they glowered at th' younger end wi' a look 'at said as plain as a pikestaff, 'he's bahn to throw yo' ovver' nah, wi' yo'r new criticism an' yo'r refinin's.'"

"An' did he?" asked Lucy and her mother in a breath.

And it may be just as well to say here and once for all, for the benefit of those who through no fault of their own, to be sure, but to their great loss notwithstanding, have not the privilege of being Yorkshire bred and born, that half-a-century ago theological discussion was, among the mill-hands of the West Riding, as common as ratting or dog-fighting or as disputing over the form of a foot-ball player in these degenerate days. Any fine Sunday of the year, if you walked in the country, you would come across a group of men, gravely excited, discussing with acumen, and all the artillery of text and commentary, original sin, predestination, effectual calling and the inefficiency of works.

"And did he?"

Ben shook his head. "He's a deep 'un is yon'. They ca' folk 'at go to Church o' a mornin' an' chapel i' th' afternooin, devil-dodgers; but yon's waur, he's a deacon-dodger. He knew as weel as he knew his dinner 'd be spoilin' bi hauf-past twelve 'at ther' wer' owd Split an' Tommy Shaw, not to say Jabez Tinker, at's happen more charity, just simply waitin' to lay howd on a word here an' a sentence theer to condemn; but he slipped past 'em a'. It wer' clivver aw'll nooan gainsay, but it wer' nooan honest. Yo've happen no reight to expect brains i' a parson, but th' leeast he can do is to be honest."

"But yo' dunnot tell us ha he han'led th' text," said his wife impatiently.

"Why th' cream on it wer' this: 'at th' Almighty fro' th' beginnin' had foreordained th' law o' righteousness, just th' same as he foreordained th' law o' gravitation an' he elected to salvation them as walked therein, an' them as didn't were rejected. Same as th' law o' combustion," he said, "if yo' put yo'r finger i'th' fire God had pre-arranged 'at yo' sud be burned, an' sarve yo' reight."

"Why that's common sense enough to please you, father, you couldn't find fault with that."

"Aye' that wer' reight enough; but yo' should ha' heeard th' way he wrapped it up an' dressed it i'th catch words o' th' hard-an'-fast Baptists, so as to mak' them o' th' owder end think it wer' all th' owd dish sarved up a bit different. But it wern't; it wer' common sense an' nat'ral religion dressed up to mak' 'em sound like Calvinism. He caught th' deacons sleepin', as he thowt, an' stole their clo'es; but Jabez Tinker saw through him, aw tell yo', an' so did Ben Garsed, if he *is* an' owd foo."

"And what did Tom say to it all?" asked Lucy.

"Tom! Aw've no patience wi' Tom. He walked all th' way whom as if he wer' dreamin', an' all 'at aw could get out on him wer' 'at pale blue went varry well wi some shades o' yoller. He wer' thinkin o' his dyein', yo' see."

"Was he for sure?" asked Mrs. Garside, "which dun yo' think's th' blindest, Lucy, a bat or a mole?"

But Lucy was looking out of the window and answer made none.

CHAPTER IX.

NEHEMIAH WIMPENNY, of Holmfirth, "Gentleman, one of Her Majesty's &c.," in other words a solicitor, was the only legal practitioner in the village or neighbourhood, and though not more than thirty years of age, enjoyed a considerable practice. His father, Ebenezer, had been a successful manufacturer and a zealous Methodist. Presumably he believed that it is easier for a camel to pass through the eye of a needle than for a rich man to enter into the Kingdom of Heaven. Certainly he shared the common belief that lawyers are very scarce in the celestial regions. But these convictions did not deter him from storing up riches in this world, nor from bringing up his son to the legal profession. Perhaps he had confidence in the axiom that exceptions prove the rule.

Nehemiah was well cut-out for a country lawyer: he had the native shrewdness and common sense, and if he did not know much law he found common-sense a very good substitute for it. His local knowledge was like that of a historic character extensive and peculiar, and his father's acquaintances and business connections who, at first from friendship, gave their business to young Nehemiah, had no reason to complain of lack of his attention to their interests or ability to protect them. In person he was of medium height, of sandy hair and pale complexion, with a cold and fishy eye and a cold and clammy hand. He dressed loudly and flashily, but as the extravagance of his raiment was attributed to a twelve months' stay in London in the office of a town agent its fashion or propriety few questioned. He was fond of jewellery, and displayed a good deal of it on his person, and was supposed by envious young manufacturers and merchants to be a"devil among the women,"—a reputation of which he was not a little vain, and which he sustained by the amorous glances and *doubles entendres* of refreshment rooms and bars. He had spent a week in Paris, and hinted that he could an' he would tell a thing or two about the iniquities of the gay city. This did not prevent Nehemiah from attending with laudable regularity at the Methodist Chapel, and anxious mammas with marriageable daughters, secure in the assurance that a reformed rake makes a very passable saint, viewed with complacency the attentions which it pleased this very common-place Lothario to pay to the virgins of their flock and fold; and the pastor of Zion Chapel himself, doubtless reflecting that he was sent to the lost sheep of the house of Israel, and to heal those that were sick and not those that were whole, was very tender indeed to a church-member who gave weekly signs of grace in the form of substantial contributions to the collection box, and whose quarterly pew-rent could always be depended on. It is only fair to Nehemiah to say that he never permitted his dissipations which were possibly much exaggerated, to interfere with business, and that, however deep his potations of the previous night, he was always to be found at his desk with a clear head and a steady hand, a circumstance, of itself, that secured Nehemiah more appreciation in a hard-drinking community, than would have been inspired by an intimate acquaintance with the whole *corpus juris*.

Among his clients Nehemiah numbered Mr. Jabez Tinker, and he was therefore not surprised when the master of Wilberlee presented himself in the small, dingy, stuffy office which Nehemiah found sufficient for his needs. Mr. Tinker, of course, was well aware of the somewhat dubious moral character of the gentleman he had come to consult; but then he did not go to Nehemiah for morals but for professional assistance.

"Well, Mr. Tinker, and how do you find yourself this morning—warm, isn't it."

"Very," said Mr. Tinker—"it's warm, and it's close for the time of the year. But any sort of weather 'll do for your kind of work, I guess, Wimpenny."

"Rather,—the warmer the better—get me used to a sultry climate. It's as well to be prepared for the future, eh?"—Mr. Wimpenny's expansive smile indicated his own appreciation of a very feeble jest; but his client's countenance was not responsive.

"H'm," said Mr. Tinker. "Well, Wimpenny, let's get to business. I want to make my will, and it's no use putting the thing off. I can always alter it?"

"Yes, yes, certainly—as long as a man lives he can alter his will, always supposing he remain *compos mentis*; and we're all human, Mr. Tinker, we're all human."

"It shouldn't be a very complicated affair either," went on Mr. Tinker. "Unfortunately, except the house I live in."

"Snug little hole, but too near the mill," thought his adviser.

"Except that, practically all I have is tied up in my business."

"And a very good business too, Mr. Tinker, by all accounts."

"I've nothing to complain of in that score; but it is unfortunate as things have turned out that I did not arrange differently. You see, I've no son to carry on the concern after my death."

The lawyer nodded assent.

"I must provide for my widow, of course. She must have the house and furniture for her life, and I thought of, say, three hundred a year—not a penny more, she'd only give it to the chapel."

Again the lawyer nodded, making notes, as he listened, on a sheet of foolscap.

"That's plain speaking," went on Mr. Tinker, "but where's the £300 to come from? That's the difficulty. Mills aren't easy to let, and the bigger they are the fewer people want them. I suppose there's nothing for it but the hammer. It's enough to make us Tinkers all turn in our graves. But there it is.—Even if Dick—you won't remember my brother, Richard,—if he'd had a son, it would have been different."

"But we all know he left a very charming daughter," said Wimpenny with a bow and a smirk.

"Dorothy's right enough," said her uncle, curtly. "But you can't turn her into a manufacturer. Though she's a sort of partner all the same. You know her father died suddenly."

Of course Wimpenny knew.

"And her father was part owner of the mill and business. Well, the girl's money is in the business still."

"Phew! that's bad, Mr. Tinker."

"I know it is, and the worst of it, I've kept no separate accounts. I've treated Richard's share just as my own. But my will must put all that right. Subject to my wife's provision Dorothy must have all. There'll be nob'dy else for it."

Wimpenny did not speak for some time. He chewed the end of his quill instead, a way he had when absorbed in thought.

"It's a bad business Mr. Tinker;" he said at length; "it was scarcely like you to confound accounts in that loose fashion and to put trust money into what was practically your own business. People might call it by an ugly name."

Jabez flushed angrily. "What do you mean, sir? I treated my niece as my daughter, brought her up in my house as my own child, and now I propose to leave her my sole heiress. Nothing very ugly about that, I should think."

"Not as things have turned out," was the reply, "but you know as well as I do they *might* have turned out differently, and where would your ward's money have been? However, it's to-day and tomorrow we're concerned with, not yesterday. Has it occurred to you that Miss Dorothy may marry?"

"Of course she may. One doesn't need to pay six-and-eight to learn that."

"Exactly," said the unruffled lawyer. "Now an adopted daughter and an adopted daughter's husband are often quite two different beings, and should Miss Tinker marry it's the husband we should have to reckon with."

"Well, I could pay him out, I suppose?"

"Of course you could—by selling Wilberlee at a sacrifice, a great sacrifice, or by putting a heavy mortgage on the property if it would carry it. We must remember that there are eighteen years of profits to set-off against Miss Dorothy's up-bringing, and the Court of Chancery does not weigh trustees' profits in a hair-balance, I can tell you."

Mr. Tinker rose impatiently. "I didn't come here to have you raise difficulties but to meet them, nor yet to be frightened by bug-bears."

"Now you are unreasonable, Mr. Tinker. I shouldn't be worth my salt if I didn't put the situation plainly before you. You don't go to a doctor for smooth sayings nor yet for sweetmeats instead of pills. No use getting huffed, you know."

But Mr. Tinker was huffed. He was a Tinker and a magistrate, and had been a man of mark these thirty years, and was not pleasant to be told these things by a young lawyer who might have been his son. But he had the good sense to know that what Nehemiah said was truth.

"Ah, well," he said, "I dare say we are meeting trouble half-way. You know what I want doing. I did everything for the best, and I don't know that I care very much what the world says or your infernal Court of Chancery either, if it comes to that. When will you have the will ready, Wimpenny?"

"Let me see. To-day's Monday. Say Thursday of next week. We close for Whitsuntide, you know."

"Very good, so be it. I'll call in on that day. I'll be glad to have the thing off my mind before the holidays. Mrs. Tinker's at Harrogate, and I was thinking of running over for a few days. Till Thursday, then," and Mr. Tinker went his way feeling less comfortable in his mind than he had done for many a long day.

“Confound the fellow,” he said to himself, wiping his brow, “and confound his stuffy little office, too. It’s worse than the sweating-room at the Bank.”

Left to himself Nehemiah Wimpenny sunk into a deep reverie; and, to judge from the faint smile that occasionally played upon his face, a not unpleasing one.

“So Miss Dorothy’s to be old Tinker’s heiress,” thus ran his thoughts, “and that means probably old Eph. Thorpe’s into the bargain. Guess I rather frightened the immaculate Jabez with that hint of a probable Chancery suit. Talk about men starting at their own shadows, as if any possible suitor for the fair Dorothy would dream of muddling away not only her fortune, but her expectations by going to law with a man who could leave him or not leave him thousands of pounds just as the fancy took him. Should have thought Tinker was more level headed. It isn’t the money he’s frightened of, it’s the scandal. These cold, reserved, proud men are always so devilish thin-skinned. Wonder who the happy man ’ll be.—Haven’t heard of anyone nosing around.”

“By Jove! why shouldn’t I cut in myself? She’s a pretty little filly and a high-stepper too. I’ve had my fling, and it’s about time I looked around for Mrs. Nehemiah. Wonder I never meet her out anywhere. Tinker keeps her up pretty close apparently, perhaps she doesn’t care for high-teas, small talk, and cribbage. Shows her sense.”

“Wonder how I can get to know her. No use fishing for an invitation to Tinker’s. Jove! I have it. Didn’t he say he was off to Harrogate to cheer up the old woman. Let’s see, Jabez is an Aenonite. H’m, I must sweeten the Reverend David—well that’s easy enough. Pity I don’t go to Aenon; but that’s soon got over. One chapel’s as good as another to a broad-minded man. All retail the same blooming rot. I mean they all lead to the same place. Different roads to the same city— that’s the phrase.”

“Whitsuntide is it, next week? Shouldn’t mind a run over to Scarborough. Better than sulphur-water at Harrogate, friend Tinker. Why! there’ll be the Sunday School treats, band, flags, processions stale buns and coffee grounds. The sportive Dorothy’s pretty sure to be doing the cheap philanthropic with the kids—and Nehemiah ’ll be there or thereabouts, you bet.”

“But I’ll make sure how Richard left his money. Hearsay’s all very well, but matrimony on hearsay might turn out a sell. I’ll get a copy of his will. But that’ll be all right, I fancy. Gad, it’s dry work thinking. I’ll step across and have a tiddley at the Crown, and I might as well take little

Polly that pair of gloves I promised her. Heigho, I guess I'll have to swear off lovely Pollys, at any rate till the honeymoon 's over."

But before the sagacious Wimpenny abandoned himself to the delights of gin-and-bitters and the lively sallies of the lovely Polly, he dropped a confidential note to his London agent to procure a copy of Richard Tinker's will and such information as the archives of Somerset House could furnish to the interested or the curious as to the Residuary and Legacy accounts filed by the deceased's executor, Mr. Jabez Tinker, to wit.

This missive despatched with his own hand Nehemiah turned his steps towards the Crown, feeling very much at peace with himself and fully entitled to bask in the sunshine of Polly's ready smile. On the way he chanced across the pastor of Aenon Chapel, who was devoting his morning to calling upon sundry of his flock and getting up an appetite for his mid-day dinner.

"Good morning, Mr. Jones the very man I wanted to see. I've a crow to pull with you. Won't there be the usual school treat this Whitsuntide?"

"Certainly, Mr. Wimpenny We'd a special prayer last meeting for a fine day."

"Well, now, I go to Zion. But we Nonconformists are not so narrow as our Church friends, eh? So long as the good work goes on, that's the main thing isn't it?"

"Most assuredly, Mr. Wimpenny, most assuredly. We're only tools in the great Worker's hands."

"Quite so, Mr. Jones, quite so; my sentiments to a T, only better expressed. Now I know these efforts of the Sunday School cost money. I'm not good enough to be a teacher; but you must let me help in my own way. I hoped you would have called, as your predecessor did, and asked for a subscription, then we could have had a comfortable chat," and Nehemiah slipped a sovereign into the parson's palm.

Now Mr. Jones had gone very recently over the list of subscribers to the various efforts and celebrations of Aenon Chapel, and flattered himself that he knew to a nicety the amount for which every inhabitant of Holmfirth "was good;" but he certainly could not remember to have seen Nehemiah Wimpenny's name for so much as a widow's mite. But perhaps the lawyer was one of those worthy men who do good by stealth and blush to find it known. So he had no qualms about pocketing the coin.

“They say open confession ’s good for the soul,” went on Nehemiah. “I was just on my way to have a nip and a snack at the Crown—just a glass of bitter, you know”—Oh! Nehemiah, Nehemiah!—“No use asking you, I know. The old Vicar, now, always had a glass of sherry with me when we met. But they say you are just ruining the trade, with your temperance sermons and your temperance missions. You mustn’t do that Mr. Jones; for if you shut up public-houses *I* might as well shut up shop too. Well, good day, good day.”

Mr. Jones’s face was beaming.

“Do they really say so?” he asked.

“Of course they do, and mean it. There isn’t a publican in the town but would rejoice to have you popped off like an Irish rack-renter. Oh! By the bye, whose field do you have on Monday for your gala? I might manage to have an hour’s romp with your youngsters—any road I could squander a few nuts and have them racing for oranges.”

“Mr. Tinker has kindly let us have the loan of his paddock at the rear of Wilberlee. We’ve had it for years, till the school almost expect it as a right.”

“I see, I see—a prescriptive right. A better sort of prescription than a doctor’s, eh?”

Mr. Jones accorded the tribute of a smile. “You don’t allow your drier studies to dull your sense of humour, I perceive. By the way, the dear children of Zion are joining us this year both in the procession and the after proceedings, so you will not be hampered by any sense of a divided duty. I must not omit to thank you for your generous donation, but I assure you we shall value your presence among us more highly than any gift.”

“Don’t mention it—a bagatelle. Wish it were more. Make it yearly. But now I really must be off or I shall miss my snack.”

“And your glass of—bitter? I think you said,”

“Ah, well, I’ll make it mild to-day. That’s next to teetotal, you know. Again, good day. Hope to have the pleasure of an introduction to Mrs. Jones on Monday.”

“What a very excellent young man,” mused the reverend divine, as he scurried through his calls. “I wish brother Brown of Zion put more fervour into Temperance work.—He might win that young man to the cause”—a conclusion Mr. Jones might have modified had he seen the wink with which the very excellent young man favoured himself as he took the steps of the Crown Hotel and called for his "usual, and a smile with it, please, Polly."

"Miah's in extra spirits this morning. Wonder who's feathers he's been plucking so early," was the mental comment of the slim-waisted damsel as she handed the "usual" with a coquettish air and neatly evaded the proffered salute.

"There's someone coming!" she whispered, as she skipped away.

"There always is, damn 'em," said that very excellent young man.

Whit-Monday in Yorkshire is the saturnalia of the Sunday schools, a festival to which both teachers and taught look forward with delighted anticipation. A committee of the teachers and those members of the congregation who are supposed to be musically gifted, select the hymns to be sung at the services and at the halts of the procession on its route, and the discussion and final settling of the hymn-sheets are not always attended by the harmony appropriate to the occasion. The lives of the organist and the choirmaster are made a burden to them, and before the sheet reaches the printer there is often a coolness between ladies who had vowed eternal friendship. The scholars are very zealously drilled by the choirmaster, the girls singing with zest at the "practices," the boys stimulating their attention by pulling their hair, but lifting up their own voices under protest. The young ladies of the Sunday School wear a subdued modification of their Sunday best at the week-night practices and as they have neither father nor mother to escort them home at the somewhat late hour to which the practices are prolonged, have to make shift with the arm of a blushing and embarrassed teacher from the Boys' School, and, to do them justice, the young ladies cheerfully submit to be thus accompanied. If it should be discovered during the homeward walk of this sober minded Phyllis and Stephen of the mills that their voices go well together, the practising at the school not unfrequently conduces to domestic duets, never, let us hope, to matrimonial discords. An ingenuous bride, not long ago, assured the writer that she simply doted on the Sunday School. When asked for the reason, she naively confessed that it was there she first met her Billy. As this frank young lady has since sent in her resignation as a teacher, it is to be assumed that she now dotes on Billy to the detriment of the Sunday School; but she has not thought it necessary to return the time-piece presented to her by her fellow-teachers on the eve of her wedding-day.

He must be a very callous individual indeed who does not delight in the sight of the scholars as they marshal under the folds of the School flag, blazoned with the name of the chapel and borne in a somewhat staggering fashion by sturdy teachers who find consolation for their tribulations in the honour of being standard-bearers. Even a slattern mother and a drunken father will make a shift at sacrifice to turn the "childer" out decent for the "Whissun treat." It is indeed the time of year when the yearly Sunday suit is chosen. Poverty must indeed have made its home in the house of a Yorkshire mill-hand if a white muslin frock and brilliant sash and a new straw hat with bright ribbons cannot be found for the girls, and a new suit, be the material never so rough, for the lads. It is a feast to the eyes to see the young coquettes—a maid of five is often a promising if not a quite accomplished coquette—arrayed in all their glory, conscious of their charms and severely critical of the gowns of their comrades. There is the exhilaration of the strains of the brass band—which in all probability will be comfortably drunk before the day is out; there is the fluttering of the silken banners in the summer breeze, and, above all, there is the consciousness of being the beheld of all beholders. The boys look either bored or ashamed of themselves and wish they were nearer the buns and nuts, for which they are gloomily conscious they will have to pay by submitting to the humiliating exactions of kiss-in-the-ring. Every door of the village is open as the long procession winds through the narrow streets, and anxious matrons and elder sisters watch for their own to see the sash has retained its bunch and the flounces have not given: also to receive the soothing assurance that Annie or Lizzie is dressed as smart as the best of them. Then there is the singing of a hymn at the minister's house and before the deacons' and—pleasantest feature of all the day's proceedings—the lifting of the sweet young voices under the window of a sick companion who listens from a tear-stained pillow to the air she may never sing again. The distinction almost compensates for pain.

Among those watched the procession was Ben Garside, Hannah, and Lucy. She had been wheeled to the open door. Her father and mother stood on the other side. Tom was in his bedroom, "fettling hissen," as Hannah put it. Ben had put on his better suit, and shaved himself in honour of the holiday,—the last holiday of the year for working-folk till Christmas should come again. There were no Bank Holidays in those days. Hannah had put on her somewhat rusty silk dress, and would have scorned to acknowledge that it pinched round the waist more than it did a year before. As the rear rank of the scholars and the last banner disappeared up the street, Tom's feet were heard descending the stairs.

"Tom 'll be for off, nah," said Hannah, "pity he couldn't ha' his baggin' so's things wouldn't be lyin' abaat all hours."

"Now Ben," said Tom, cheerily, "I'm ready, are you?"

"By Gosh! Aw sud think yo' are ready: stan' ther an' let's ha' a looik at yo'."

Tom laughed, and stood to attention. "Do the creases show very much?" he asked, "I feel like a draper's parcel wrapped in brown paper."

It was a great event. Tom had got a suit of navy blue serge for the summer, and it fitted him like a glove.

"Aw mun gi' yo' a pinch for new," said Hannah, nipping the upper arm.

"An' put a penny in his pocket," added Lucy, "for luck."

"It should be a shilling if it's to match the pinch," laughed Tom, rubbing his arm. "But where's your bonnet, Hannah, and your hat, Lucy?"

"What's ta thinkin' on, Tom?" asked Ben.

"Why that we're all going to the field together. I'm going to wheel Lucy and stand by her, and you and Hannah are to enjoy yourselves with the other young folk."

Ben protested he wouldn't budge an inch. "Not but what he liked to see th' childer enjoy theirsen, but Whissunday wer' a heathenish festival an' a relic o' superstition."

"But you've knocked off work and donned—I mean dressed yourself," remonstrated Tom.

"Aye at nooinin'. Who could wark wi' that blethrin' brass band brayin' up an' down th' street?"

Mrs. Garside looked at Lucy. "It 'ud be a treeat for th' lass," she said.

"I should like it, but I should only be a hindrance. Fancy Tom standing by me for hours at a stretch and all the other young men in the field enjoying themselves. Take mother, father, and I'll stop at home. No one will run away with *me*." she added bravely, but there was a tear in her voice.

"If you stop at home, I stop," said Tom emphatically. "Besides, as for being tied to your side all the time, when you get tired of me, and mother there's tired of mooning about with Ben, we can take turn and turn about. I couldn't enjoy myself a bit if you were stuck here all by yourself, and what's more, I won't try."

"Well, then, that sattles it," said Hannah. "We'll all go, an' th' haase mun tak' care on itsen. Awst put mi silver spooins i' mi pocket, an' there's nowt else 'at means owt. Nah! Ben, stir thee, mon, an' dunnot stan' theer like a stuck sheep."

"*Aw'm* ready," said Ben, "Aw'n nowt to do but don mi cap an' that won't tak me as long as it'll tak' thee to don thi bonnet. Tom an' me could go to the field an' be back afore yo' an' Lucy 'll be ready."

"Aw said stir thee. Put th' kettle on. What's th' use o' goin' to th' field an hour afore there'll be ony theer. Tha doesn't want a whole field to thissen, does ta? We'll ha' us baggin afore we start, an' then we'st ha' th' day i' front on us."

"But aw could put mi finger dahn mi throit an' feel mi dinner yet," demurred Ben. "It's nooan three o'clock bi th' Church."

"That's noah odds. Aw'm nooan baan to ha' thee worritin' me all th' afternooin becos yo'n nooan had thi baggin, an happen sneakin' off into th' village to get a pint becos tha's a sinkin' i' thi' stomach, an' me lookin' for thi all ovver th' field, wanderin' abaat gawpin' as if aw'd just bin let loise aat o'th 'sylum, an' thee stuck at th' *Cropper's Arms* as large as life, makkin' a beeast on thisen becos it's Whissunday. Nooah! if yo' dunnot want yo'r baggin nah, yo' mun ha' it agen yo' do want it."

Hannah's feet and hands had been as busy as her tongue. She had turned up the skirt of her gown and put an apron over all, spread the cloth, fetched up the bread and the butter, cut and spread thick slices for herself and the men, and thin ones for Lucy, washed the lettuce, radishes, and shallots, smoothed the top of the salt-cellar, set Tom to toasting a couple of currant teacakes, produced a jar of raspberry jam and mashed the tea before you could say Jack Robinson.

"Aw've getten a caa-heel for thi supper, an' tha can bring thisen a pint o' Timmy (best ale) for supper as it's holiday time," she conceded to Ben, evidently in great good humour with herself at the prospect of their outing.

And so as the large field near Mr. Tinker's house—there was but a privet hedge separating it from the house garden—began to fill, as the boys and girls gathered from their respective school-rooms, flushed from their hasty tea-drinking, the lads not without a guilty consciousness of a filched bun bulging their trousers pocket, as the brass band played their final tune before withdrawing to the nearest inn to partake of something better than "spotted Dick an' washin'-up watter," as a member irreverently styled the scholars' repast, Ben Garside sauntered into the field trying to look as if Sunday School treats were an every-day occurrence of his life, Hannah sailed behind, whilst Tom with Lucy brought up the rear. There grew a large beech tree on the slope of the ground, and under its full-leaved branches Tom drew the chair in which Lucy sat, her cheeks faintly tinged with a delicate bloom and her eyes sparkling with the unwonted excitement. Her mother raised her to a sitting posture and settled the cushions and wraps as only she could, and "theer yo' are, lass," she concluded, with a fond look at her darling child, "theer yo' are as right as ninepence." But the mother's heart was full as she remembered the day, but as yesterday, when Lucy's little feet would have skimmed the greensward light as a fairy's dance.

But Hannah was not long suffered to indulge in reflections sad or otherwise she was a popular character in the village, and everyone knew that Hannah's bark was worse than her bite. Soon the good wives of the village began to stroll about the field, scanning each others' dresses, and exchanging kindly greetings, whilst their good men sought secluded corners where they might enjoy a furtive pipe, and talk over the topics of the day; the serious minded discussing the last sermon, the pugnacious revelling in the shortcomings of Parliament and the misdeeds of ministers. A small group gathered round Lucy's chair, some of them rosy-cheeked young lasses, who had worked with Lucy in the mill, and who now brought up their young men to be exhibited with all the pride of conquest. And Lucy had a smile and pleasant word for all, and many a strapping swain, as he lounged past the nook where Lucy held her little Court and let his glance dwell upon the delicate face with its refined and chastened beauty, knew rebellious thoughts against the fate that had put the crippled girl beyond the sighs and vows of man; and grey-headed grandsires, bent with age and toil, recalled the former days when they had suffered and striven for the easier lot their children owned.

"Eh! but it's gran' to see yo', Hannah," one would say, "Why aw declare aw hannot seen yo' donned up an' aat sin' we put owd Susan o' 'Lijah's under th' graand. An' yo' do looik weel to be sure, an' aw will say 'at if theer's a woman i' th' village 'at does her clo'es credit it's yo', Hannah. And your Lucy, too, aw declare oo's quite a colour. Yo're lookin' mony a pund better nor th' last time aw seed thi, Lucy, an' tha mun keep thi heart up, lass, theer's no tellin' yet. See yo' Hannah, theer's yar Jud (George) an' yo'r Ben t'other side o'th' field, an' Jud's shakkin' his fist i' Ben's face, an' Ben's dancin' like peeas on a bake-ston'. It's them plaguing politics, but they're enjoyin' theirsen. An' theer's yar 'Tilda yonder i'th' kiss-i'th-ring an Jim Sykes after her. Run, lass, run—eh! he's caught her. Th' clumsy felly, he'll rive all th' clo'es off her back. Gi' 'im one an' get it ovver. Eh! it fair ma'es one young agin to see th' young folk enjoy theirsen."

Lucy had insisted on Tom joining the revels of the field, the gay and innocent sports of the youths and maidens, and her eyes followed him as he joined in the games at "Tirzy," hand ball, and what not. But Tom's thoughts seemed elsewhere, and Lucy knew that his eyes wandered from the laughter-ringing throngs to the rustic gate that led from Wilberlee to the pasture land.

"He's watching for Dorothy," she thought, and there passed, maybe, a shadow over Lucy's gentle face, "and there comes Dorothy herself. Ah! well, I knew it long ago. God send it may not spoil our Tom's young life."

There was a rush of twinkling little feet to meet the young mistress of Wilberlee as she passed slowly through the gateway, and moved into the field, clad in a loose gown of sprayed muslin of palest blue. She swung her hat in one hand that the soft cool air might play about her face, and the rays of the declining sun gleamed upon the auburn tresses, and gave them a golden sheen.

A dozen youngsters danced up to her, shouting their childish welcome, and more than one little toddlekin did Dorothy catch up in her arms and kiss. They danced round her as she walked up the field, or clasped her hand to claim her for some favourite game. And Dorothy smiled down upon the uplifted faces, and made feint to run away from them, but was captured and prisoned in their midst. And so, surrounded by bright and happy faces, Dorothy moved about the field, speaking to many, and giving a pleased recognition to all she knew,—and there was not a man or woman of Aenon chapel she did not know, not a worker at her uncle's mill she could not address by name.

"As free as th' air, Miss Dorothy is," said one, "but she never demeans herself nor forgets she's th' young mistress." And the hands respected her, the more for it. The working people of the mills knew their place, and were not ashamed of it, nor servile to those above them. They did not care that anyone should assume a familiarity they knew must be feigned and which they were bound to suspect.

The Rev. David Jones was in his glory. He had shaken hands with everyone there above the age of thirteen, had inquired about everyone's health as though he loved them, and their pains were his, had narrowly escaped being decoyed into a game at romps, and had looked as though he liked it when a hand-ball knocked off his hat. This did not prevent him confiding to Mrs. Jones, a placid little woman who took life serenely, that he should be glad when it was all over.

As the afternoon wore to evening and the pastor, wearied of parading the field and repeating stale vacuities, he saw, with the pleasure we experience when we realize what we had hoped for rather than expected, that young Wimpenny had not forgotten his half-promise of a day or two ago. Wimpenny was speaking to the minister of his own chapel, a meek, timid man, but hard-working, sincere and self-sacrificing, beloved of little children and their mothers, and for whom even the hard-hearted operatives had a good word. The lawyer was not long in making his way towards Mr. Jones.

"You see I have been able to come, though I'm afraid I'm a late scholar. Won't you introduce me to Mrs. Jones?" and the introduction was duly made. The three paced together through the changing throng, parted occasionally when some eager urchin, in full cry after the flying ball, darted under the parson's arms or a breathless Daphne, with ringlets streaming in the breeze, fled in simulated fright from a pursuing swain.

"Miss Tinker seems to be enjoying herself," said Nehemiah to Mrs. Jones, after he had duly admired her own numerous offspring whom she had indicated in various quarters of the field.

"Is she as nice as she is pretty?"

"Yes, she is very nice, and seems fond of the people. She spoils the children though,—my husband is sometimes a little put out. She does not take life seriously enough, she says, and he is vexed she won't be baptised, though she is quite old enough to become a full church member. I asked her if she had religious scruples that Mr. Jones could assist her to banish; but she only laughed and said the immersion costume of the girls was hideous enough to account for a bushel of scruples without searching further. But then you know she is Mr. Tinker's niece, and I daresay she is indulged too much at home."

Nehemiah did not think this very likely, but, all the same, he replied that it was a great pity.

"Do you now," he said, "I have never had the pleasure of meeting Miss Tinker in society. She doesn't go out much. I fancy. Would you mind——?"

"Certainly, Mr. Wimpenny, if you wish it. See, she is resting now and fanning herself with that outlandish hat of hers. Shall we join her?" And presently the diplomatic Wimpenny was making a somewhat exaggerated bow before the heiress of Wilberlee.

And Tom's eyes followed the graceful girl as she walked by the side of Nehemiah, chatting gaily and seeming well content with his companionship; and Tom plunged his hands deep into his pockets and stalked moodily with clouded brow about the field, deaf to every entreaty from tempting lips to "choose the girl that he loved best," and feeling that for him life had lost its zest. The blue of the sky was dulled, the music of the lark soaring in the azure might have been the cawing of the rooks, and the gentle summer breeze that scarce stirred the leaves an icy blast from eastern shores.

"What a fool I am, crying for the moon. I, Tom Pinder, apprentice to Jabez Tinker, Esquire and Justice of the Peace. Go to yonder rosy faced weaver with sparkling eyes and towzled hair. *She* will lend a ready ear, you can send her home to-night, her heart in a tumult of delight; in her dreams heaven will open to her, and she will wake with your name upon her lips. Or go down yonder to the *Clothiers' Arms*. There are some jolly fellows there, and you will be all the more welcome because you have been set down as a strait-laced, sour-faced curmudgeon with lead in your veins for blood. Go drink with them and join in their drunken chorus; better that than eat your heart out after fruit that is not for you."

And so with head down-bent he makes for where he had left Hannah and Lucy; and in his abstraction nearly walks into Wimpenny and Dorothy. Mrs. Jones had remembered the wise saying that two are company and three are none.

"Mind where you're walking, will you?" exclaimed Wimpenny, cut short in a very flowery compliment which Dorothy was perhaps not sorry to have curtailed.

"I beg your pardon, Miss Tinker, I'm afraid I was very careless. I did not see. I was thinking."

"Now that is not a very gallant speech, Tom—I mean Mr. Pinder. Mr. Wimpenny would have assured me that he never thought at all except of me, and that he would have divined my presence by instinct a mile off."

But Wimpenny was not to be rallied into good humour. He had put on a very tight-fitting pair of patent-leather shoes, and he suffered from the usual infliction of those who wear tight boots,—and Tom had grazed his foot.

"Mr. Pinder! indeed," he thought, "why, damme, it's one of old Tinker's mill hands."

Now Tom, having made his apologies to Dorothy, was for pursuing the tenor of his way, being by no means disposed to offer any to Mr. Wimpenny.

"Oh, you mustn't go, Mr. Pinder, you must take me to Lucy; but first you must help me to gather some flowers. You know Paris so well, Mr. Wimpenny, and must excuse my accent. Shall I say *Au revoir* or *A bientôt*, and without waiting for a reply she turned in the direction of the garden at the house, Leaving Nehemiah dumbfounded.

"Curse the jade," he muttered to himself, "chucked over for a dirty weaver, by Jove. But I'll be even with her yet. It doesn't do to play tricks with Miss Dorothy, and so you'll find some day. But I can bide my time. I'll go and have a drink at the *Crown*, Polly 'll be glad to see me anyhow."

And Tom walked as in a dream. The sky was blue again, and the lark trilled a clearer note, and all the earth was glad in its summer joyousness.

CHAPTER X

IT is one thing for a maiden to invite a young man to a garden, and quite another to know what to do with him when she gets him there. It would have puzzled Dorothy to say exactly why she had asked Tom Pinder to help her cull flowers. The ostensible pretext given had been the gathering of a bouquet for Lucy; but we all know that a woman's ostensible pretexts are—well, ostensible pretexts. For one thing Dorothy had had enough of Nehemiah Wimpenny, and wanted to be decently free of him for the rest of the day. She had wearied of the mild pleasure of poking fun at his French. But in truth Dorothy had acted from impulse and regretted her words all the more when she saw the sudden light of glad surprise that sprung to Tom's dark eyes. But there is safety in numbers, reflected Dorothy. The back door of the house was not locked. Dorothy looked into the kitchen, into the parlour,—neither Betty nor Peggy was there. She called their names at the bottom of the staircase, whilst Tom bided in the garden, but there was no answering cry from Betty or from Peggy, those handmaidens having very properly conceived that Whitsuntide comes alike for bond and free, and betaken themselves, in gay attire, to the delights of the field. Peggy, at this moment, indeed, was flying, with fleet foot, from the outstretched arms of an amorous young butcher, who 'livered the daily joint at Wilberlee, and the staider Betty was listening with all too ready ears to the somewhat halting wooing of the village constable, who, even in plain clothes, was still a proper man and had, perhaps, a prophetic vision of a village-inn with himself as keeper of order and the purse-strings, and Betty as buxom but bustling hostess.

"It is very tiresome," said Dorothy, as she returned to the garden where Tom was pretending to be wrapt in the contemplation of the beauties of a *Gloire de Dijon*, "I did so want a cup of tea, but Betty and Peggy have played me truant. Don't you think, Mr. Pinder, you had better go find them, and say I want one of them, no matter which, very particularly."

But Tom had taken possession of the handbasket and the scissors, and was oblivious to hints.

"Some of these blooms want cutting very badly," was his only answer, "they will fall in another day." Then there was silence save for the clicking of the scissors, the humming of the bees, the good-night song of the birds, and the laughter and cries from the field. Unconsciously, as the basket filled, the steps of Dorothy had turned the gable of the house. The merry crowd was hid from view. The garden here sloped to the river side, and by its brim was a rustic seat. Dorothy sank upon it wearedly.

"I confess I'm tired," she exclaimed "I seem to have been on my feet for a week," and she put out the tiniest point of a shoe-toe and contemplated it ruefully. "Now, what do you mean, Mr. Pinder, standing there swinging that basket like one of those boats in a fair that make you dizzy to look at them? Can't you find a seat somewhere?"

Tom looked all around. He might have found a seat by climbing on the branch of an adjacent tree. Some such thought may have crossed his mind, for by that magic of association that passes the wit of man came to him the couplet that he had read long ago:

"Fain would I climb, but that I fear to fall,"

with its answering

"If thy heart fail thee, do not climb at all."

Tom did not climb. He sat instead on the edge of the garden seat, as far from Dorothy as space permitted.

"I wish you wouldn't call me 'Mr. Pinder'," he said. "I never feel quite sure you are not making mock of me."

Dorothy had taken a rose from the basket and was looking for leaves to bind it with.

"Well you see, you are getting rather too big for me to call you Tom. And besides, you are a man now, and besides, oh!—lots of things."

This did not seem very lucid. Tom went on:

"I was never called 'Mr. Pinder' in my life till you called me so. Then I was very glad and very proud. It put new thoughts into my mind. It was like a 'new birth,' as the chapel-folk might say. But it has done its work now, and I should like once more to be plain 'Tom' to you."

"Well, plain Tom then be it, if that will please you; but we really must be going, or we shall miss Lucy. Hark! many of the people must have left the ground already. I can hear them talking as they go past the mill. Bring along the basket, Tom, and don't spill more than you can help."

"I don't think I should take the flowers to Lucy in the field. People would say you favoured Lucy more than other folk's children."

"And what do I care what people say; I do like Lucy more than any other girl in the village."

"I was not exactly thinking of what you might care about miss. I was thinking more of what Lucy would feel."

"Oh! Of course," said Dorothy, not without a suspicion of pettishness in her tone. Really, this young man was too frank. To say exactly what one thinks is no doubt commendable in the abstract. But then we should be careful to think only what will fall pleasingly on the ear, if we wish to please. "Oh! of course," said Dorothy.

Tom felt he had blundered. "The air comes very sweet and fresh from the hills" he said, to change the subject. "How clear the stream looks to-night and how softly it warbles over the stones."

"Yes," assented Dorothy, "I love the river when its waters are crystal as now; but you know it is so seldom we see it so bright and sparkling. The dye-water from the mill makes it all the colours of the rainbow, but you take care the colours are dirty enough."

"There's something I wanted to tell you, Miss Dorothy," said Tom, after a lull in the conversation which both felt to be embarrassing.

"Well?"

"You see, Miss Dorothy, I shall be of age soon."

"Really! Well that seems to me a thing you need not look so solemn about. It happens to everyone, more or less, if they live long enough. I shall be of age myself someday, I dare say, but I will try to bear it submissively, if not cheerfully. You'll get over it, Tom. You may even in time get used to it."

"Yes, but it will make a great difference to me. For one thing my apprenticeship to your uncle will be at an end."

"Oh!" said Dorothy, "Well, I should think you'll be glad of that. Uncle is sure to want you to stop on at the mill—I know he thinks well of you."

"It is very good of him" said Tom and smiled as he thought of the day when his master had lifted his riding whip in quick, passionate anger. But that was long gone bye. "But I don't think I shall stop on, in fact I'm sure I shan't."

"You won't leave Holmfirth, will you, Tom?" and she was surprised at the interest with which she awaited his reply.

"You see," said Tom, slowly, and colouring as if he were confessing to a crime "I've had a bit of money left and Ben and me, that is Ben and I."

"Oh! bother the grammar" cried Dorothy.

"Ben and me's going into partnership, and there's a little mill at Hinchliffe Mill where we can get room and power. Higher up the river, you know. We will try not to send you more dye-water down stream than we can help. I shall always think when I draw the plugs that the water will pass your window, Miss Dorothy." Tom was distinctly improving.

"It's a great venture," said Dorothy gravely. "A very great venture. I don't mean so much for you, you have all life before you, but for Ben, and what hurts Ben will hurt Lucy. You see other people besides you can think of Lucy." Now there was a piece of malice here, but Dorothy thought she could now cry quits.

"Yes, it's a venture, Miss Dorothy, a great venture. It is one that perhaps would never have been made if you had never called me 'Mr. Pinder,' so don't throw cold water on our scheme. But it isn't just that I wanted to talk about. There's something more."

"'Pon my word, Tom, you're worse than the brook. The teachers have come and the teachers have gone, but you go on for ever. But in for a penny, in for a pound. What more is there?"

"Well, Ben and I have talked it over and over. Don't think me a Pharisee, Miss Dorothy, but we're going to try to run the mill on new lines."

"H'm; that sounds like adding venture to venture, doesn't it?"

"Perhaps: you see, Ben and I both belong to the working class."

Dorothy bent her head in a somewhat hesitating assent. "I suppose so," she said.

"And we know something of what working folk have to put up with, how hard they have to work, and how little they often get in return."

"Come to that," said Dorothy, "I dare say a masters' lot isn't quite a bed of roses. You'll find that out soon enough for yourselves I'm afraid."

"Granted," said Tom, "but fat sorrow's better than lean; but I don't mean to be a master."

Dorothy rose. "It is later than I thought. Betty must have come in by this, or Peggy. And the field's well-nigh deserted. Whit-Monday's come and gone, Tom, and I must e'en go too. You must take the flowers home to Lucy, and give her my love. Say I will call for the basket some fine day."

But Tom ventured to touch her arm as she made as though to go. "Nay, Miss Dorothy, I would I might say my say—but, perhaps, you don't care to know our plans?"—this wistfully.

"Oh! but indeed I do. Just five minutes then. And indeed it is vastly pleasanter here than indoors. No more romping for me this day," and Dorothy sat down again.

"I said just now I did not mean to be a master, Ben and I are indeed going to add venture to venture. You know something about co-operation?"

"Why, what a question! Of course I do. Doesn't Mr. Thorpe tell us every time he comes to see my aunt that the Co-op's ruining him—and serve him right, Betty says. Aunt says that things at the Co-op are nasty without being cheap, for what they give you in 'divvy'—isn't that the word?—they take out in quality. I hope you're not going to start a Co-op, Tom. I really cannot fancy you in a white apron, simpering over a counter and asking me 'what's the next article, miss?'"

"Then you would give us your custom?" he asked with a smile.

"Oh! Perhaps I might sneak in occasionally for a trifle—for Lucy's sake, you know."

"But you forget, I told you we had taken part of a mill at Hinchliffe Mill. It's there we're going to have *our* Co-op."

"Isn't it rather out of the way? Fancy, having to send all that way for a pound of candles. Oh! I beg Ben's pardon; there'll be no need of candles with such a luminary as he in the shops. You'll be selling philosophy by the yard and theology by the stone. But seriously, Tom, I don't see what a Co-op has to do with a mill."

"And that's just what I want to speak to you about. You see Ben's a Socialist, and all his life he has been crying out against capitalists and capital. Now he declares I want to turn him into a capitalist for we are to be partners in this venture upon a venture."

Dorothy shook her head. "I'm just as much in the fog now as ever," she said, "I see if I want to know anything about this wonderful new departure I must ask Lucy. Do get on; you and your Co-op that isn't a Co-op after all. But you will not be a very bloated capitalist, will you, Tom?" she concluded mischievously.

"We aren't going to be capitalists at all. I'm just going to start the concern with my bit of a fortune—it doesn't look so much of a fortune as it did, now I know what a little way it will go. But any way Ben and I are going to work in it, side by side with the hands. We are all going to be hands together. Of course, in a sense, there'll be a master; but he will be a master in a different sense from what we're all used to. Every one of us that can do a full man's work is to have an equal share in the profit, always provided he does the work he is capable of. There will be shorter hours and less work for the youngsters. But the share of all will depend on the profits we make, and no one is to have a greater share than another."

"But that seems ridiculous, Tom. If you are to turn manufacturer like my uncle, why, you must be a manufacturer. You will have to go to market as he does, and meet and bargain with your customers, to dress like them, to mix with them as an equal. How can you do that on the lines you are laying down? I am only a silly girl, may be, and certainly I don't know much about business, but go on,—this grows interesting."

"I know the difficulties, Miss Dorothy, but the difficulty will not be in Ben, and I hope not in me. The difficulty will be in getting a sufficient number of men, capable, reliable, sober, industrious men who can be brought to see that in our scheme there will not only be an escape from the thraldom of the capital they denounce so hotly, but a realization of that equality and fraternity for which men and women have gone to their graves like bed. The difficulty will be to persuade men not merely that they will be better off themselves, but that they must be content to take part of their wage in seeing a worse workman than themselves better off too. Labour is just as selfish as capital. But in our mill no matter what a man's allotted task, so long as he does his work faithfully, he shall share and share alike."

"But that seems just a little absurd, don't you think?" asked Dorothy, now genuinely interested. "You must make all this clear to me. You don't mean to say that if you, say, are the designer or the traveller, you are to draw no more profit out of the concern than a teamer?"

"That's it, exactly—not a stiver. We're all to be partners together. We'll know neither master nor man at our mill. We're going to try an experiment in grim earnest, and oh! Miss Dorothy, for heaven's sake, don't shake your head and look so glum about it. I feel sure we can succeed. We *will* succeed. I am young and there is no hardship, no sacrifice, no work for which I am not prepared. Perhaps I might get a situation under another; perhaps in time I might start on the usual lines and perhaps in time I might make a fortune for myself. But will it not be a grander thing and in itself a better, a more heart-satisfying future should we be able to gather round ourselves a band of workers, all knit together not merely by the selfish bonds of personal interest, but each rejoicing that he is advancing, too, his brother's welfare, and that in his well-being and in his well-doing each and everyone of us is concerned."

Tom had risen in the earnestness of his soul's unburthening, and now paced the narrow strip of gravelled garden path which skirted the river-bank. His eyes were lit with unwonted fire, a flush was on his cheek, his voice gained strength and cadence as the long-pondered thoughts forced themselves to utterance, and the natural unstudied motions of his hands kept harmony with the spoken word.

"Oh! Miss Dorothy, it may all be a dream, but if a dream it be, surely it is such a one as was dreamed by the Lake of Galilee or the slopes of Olive's Mount. Is it not meet that old men in the time to come should dream dreams, and the young men see visions. Had Ben Garside, good, staunch, true man that I know him to be, had not he dreamed dreams and seen visions could he have had it in his heart to strive and suffer as I know he did, not for himself but for the oppressed ones of his class. And shall not we of a newer time have *our* visions, and mine is of a glad day when the band of man shall be against his neighbour, when this unresting, cruel strife of brother seeking to outvie his brother, building ever the fabric of his success upon the undoing of another shall cease from the land, and the Kingdom of which seers have dreamed and prophets foretold shall be indeed at hand."

Dorothy gazed in wrapt regard at the young enthusiast. She drank in the music of his words with greedy ears, and they sank into her soul. Never had man so spoken to her before. Words like these, if spoken at all, were not, in her experience, words for every day life. They should be reserved to be voiced on Sunday from the pulpit and devoutly ignored and disregarded on the Monday. But as the unpent stream of cherished conviction flowed its impetuous course Dorothy felt that she too was being swept with it, and forgot that she was the daughter of a proud and exclusive race, and he who paced before her with rapid, agitated stride, the humblest of her guardian's henchmen.

But withal Dorothy was a practical common-sense young woman, and as little likely as any of her very practical sex to forget the stern necessities of work-a-day life, in a momentary abandon to the transcendental schemes of an enthusiast.

"Don't you think we had better know more about your Co-op?" she said. "These grand ideas may be all very well as abstract theories. I want to know how you propose to put them into practice and live. I seem to remember that St. John not only permits dreams and visions to you men; he also allows us daughters to prophesy."

"Well?"

"Now I venture to prophesy that if you and Ben set about your new venture in the manner you seem to have contemplated, it is not only good-bye to your small fortune, which, perhaps wouldn't matter very much—but it would be to handicap you at the very threshold of your life with the deadening sense of failure, and perhaps fill your whole future with the bitterness of blighted hopes and unrealized aspirations. Now I think I can suggest to you an attainable Utopia. It would not, perhaps, be such a neck-or-nothing affair as yours, but it should have enough of other-worldliness in it for a sane man."

Tom sat down again by Dorothy's side, but this time he did not take the edge of the seat. His nervous shyness had vanished in the abandonment of his speech.

"Ben says women can neither see nor feel an inch outside their own doorsteps," he said with a smile.

"And a good thing for men, whose wives at all events are centred in their homes and families. But I am not Ben's wife, nor—nor anyone else's," concluded Dorothy lamely, flushing slightly at some unspoken thought.

"And what is your attainable Utopia, Miss Dorothy?" asked Tom, very quietly.

"Well, you must let me think, and, as it were, feel my way to a conclusion; for to tell the truth I have not read or thought much on such difficult problems as the subject seems to bristle with. Tell me, at our village Co-op doesn't a member's dividend depend on the amount of his purchases?"

"I believe so."

"And, roughly speaking, doesn't a man's spending power bear a sort of proportion to his earning power?"

"Practically, no doubt."

"Then you see that practical co-operation benefits a man according to his ability and application."

"Clearly."

"Well, I think that is right. Now if I understand *your* principle of Socialism it makes no distinction between the skilled and incapable.

Granting only equality of industry you reward all alike. Now that is not common justice."

"I think it is," said Tom, stoutly, "a man can but do his best."

"All the same, it isn't. Take the case of a man, a designer, say, in a mill, or a lawyer, or a doctor. He devotes money, time, and the hard sweating of his brains to becoming master of his calling. Whilst he is studying he is earning just nothing at all, in fact less than nothing. When he is qualified for it he rightly expects to be better paid than a man who knows how to handle a spade or pickaxe when his life of toil begins, and knows just as much and no more when his life ends in the workhouse or the grave."

"You say 'rightly expects,' why rightly?" asked Tom.

"Because when the skilled and educated labourer in whatever sphere you like *does* begin to be paid it is common justice that he should be paid, not merely for the present years of harvest, but also for the years of seeding, cultivation, and growth. It is merely the analogy of the farmer. It simply means that the toil of preparation is paid for at a later day. It is payment deferred, but none the less payment of what is justly due. Now your navvy or artisan gets his payment from the first day he touches the mattock or throws a shuttle."

"There seems some justice in what say, Miss Dorothy; but I thought you were going to show me the way to your attainable Utopia."

"So I am. I should imagine that the current rate of wages is very much the measure of a man's comparative worth in this life-absorbing soul-cramping pursuit of wealth you call business. When these are paid and other outlays deducted, there remains, or doesn't remain sometimes, what the capitalist calls his profit?"

Tom nodded.

"And it is against this profit your sensitive soul rebels, your dainty fingers will not touch?"

"If it pleases you to put it so, Miss Dorothy."

"Then quell your soul's rebellion, let not your fingers touch. Distribute your profit among all the workers in the concern, yourself and Ben included, for I suppose your stomach will insist on its elemental right to be filled; but distribute to each a share of the profits proportioned to his wage. For taking it that a man's wage is a rough and ready measure of a man's share in building up the wealth, so, too, would it be a rough and ready method of determine your share in the profits. And now most potent, grave, and reverend seigneur, thy hand-maiden hath spoken, and lud-ha'-mercy, 'tis sick to death I am of long faces and your miserable economics. Did ever before a young man lure a maiden to flowery bower and discourse to her sweet—political economy! I warrant you have smoother sayings for Lucy's ear. And, now, good-night. I heard Betty shouting for me down the paddock this quarter gone. Don't forget my love to Lucy."

And Dorothy tripped away, and Tom made homewards, carrying the basket very tenderly; but the rose that Dorothy had toyed with and cast aside he picked up, pressed to his lips and hid in his pocket-book. Someone found its yellow leaves years afterwards, and made-believe to be jealous because of them.

"Law! Betty," said Dorothy that night, as she uncoiled the tresses of her gleaming locks. "I declare your Tom Pinder is as mad as a hatter; and faith, I think it's catching."

"Smittling, yo' meean, miss. Well, some ailments be if yo' bide *very* near them as has 'em."

And Ben and Tom sat long that night talking over their plans for the near future. Ben conceded there was something in what Miss Dorothy had said.

"By gow, who'd ha' thowt yon' wench had it in her, to pounce reet daan on th' weak spot, what yo' may ca' th' flaw o'th system, all in a jeffy like. But she's a head piece in a hundred. It'll be her uncle 'oo favvers, for her father had more heart nor yead."

"An' what for should'nt Dorothy see what yo' two men blinked yo'r een at?" asked Hannah indignantly, "Haven't aw towd yo' scores o' times 'at a woman 'll lawp ovver a wall whilst a man's gooin' raand gropin' for th' gate. Aw'm fain someb'dy can ding sense into oather on yo'—it doesn't matter which, for what one on yo' says t'other 'll swear to. If 'oo's persuaded Tom theer 'at ther's sich a thing as lookin' after other folks consarns till yo'r own's gone to rack an' ruin, it's more nor e'er aw could do bi thee, Ben. Happen aw'd ha' had more chance if aw'd tried afore we were wed i'stead o' after, but ther's no tellin'. Some folk are born so; an' ther ne'er wer' a fooil brought into th' world but there wer' a bigger born to match him. But aw see hah it is, we'st burn more can'les talkin' abaat th' new venture, as yo ca' it, nor th' takkin's 'll run to i' a gooid season. Get thee to bed, Tom, an' dunnot yo' forget yo're Jabez Tinker's 'prentice lad yet, whativver yo' may be some day when me an' Ben's both under th' sod."

The end of Tom's apprenticeship drew near. Stories of his project had already been whispered about the village, and some of the quidnuncs of the barber's shop, which was the central Exchange of local news tapped their foreheads significantly. "Talk abaat a slate off," the slubber at Wilberlee had been heard to say, "yon' Ben Garside's got a whole roof off, and that d—d young bastard fro' Saddleworth's worse nor Ben." But in time the real nature of the new enterprise was bruited abroad and was much discussed. The novel theme was felt to be a perfect godsend in a community which, like others of its size, becomes more agitated over a runaway horse in its main street than over a European convulsion. The landlord of the Croppers' Arms began to feel quite a glow of gratitude towards the sober, drink-shunning Pinder, so many pints of ale did his nightly customers feel necessary for the ample criticism of Tom's scheme.

"Aw know for certain room an' power's ta'en at Hinchliff Mill," said Jim Thewlis, the landlord. "Th' agent for lettin' Denham's mill, as was, called in on his way fro' Huddersfilt' other day. We wer' speerin' abaat this young Pinder. Weel, aw wanted to do fair like so aw said at th' country talk wor' he'd had a fortin' left; th' worst there wer' agen him, so far as ivver aw'd heer'd, wer' 'at he wer' a teetotaller. Aw thowt that wer' enuff, but th' agent seemed no ways taken a-back. Said it were common as measles nah a days," concluded Jim, heaving a sigh over the degeneracy of the times.

"But what's all this talk abaat a newfangled road o' payin' th' hands?" asked the village bellman, whose pimply face and swollen nose seemed to indicate that "Oyez! Oyez!" were thirsty words.

"They're all to have a 'divvy,' same as they han at th' Co-op," explained one.

"There'll be a new job for thi, Bellman," said another.

"Tha'll ha to go round th' village cryin' th' divvy at Co-op Mill"

"Aye, aye," said another, "Oh! yes, Oh! yes, lost, lost and can't be found, a han'some divvy thowt safe an' sound.'" Thus Josh o' Jonah's, the village wit and poet.

But the light esteem in which their design was held by the topers of the Croppers' Arms did not disturb the equanimity of either Ben or Tom. "Th' more th' job's talked abaat, th' better for it," was Ben's expressed opinion. "An' if it's nobbut fooil's talk, talk's talk, an' that's why we want to start a Co-op. When folk get to know th' lines we're bahn to work on, there'll be plenty ready to throw in wi' us, *yo'* see if ther' isna, Tom lad. We'll ha' th' pick o'th mill hands i' this village if th' consarn goes—an' it *mun* go, Tom; it mun go. Aw'st break mi heart if it doesn't. We'll mak it gee if we'n to sell ivvery stick we'n got to buy coil to fire up wi'. But we'st nooan need to do that. Aw've nooan bin idle, an' what does ta think aw've getten to tell thee?"

Ben had not indeed been idle. It has been said that he was a popular character in the district. Men knew him for a shrewd, hard-working man, "wi' his yead screwed on th' reight road, if he *is* a bit loose i' th' tongue." Of more moment still their wives knew him for a sober man, and the daughters of a good many of them evinced a very sympathetic interest in the scheme in which Tom's name was so prominently associated. Moreover, Co-ops were appreciated by the housewives. Co-operative distribution they understood; Co-operative production they had not before heard of but were quite prepared to take it on trust, as a sort of twin-brother of the system of trading they were already familiar with.

"Aw know one thing," many a good dame declared, "it wer' a gooid thing for yar haase 'at aw put into th' Co-op. Aw allus know th' rent 'll be theer at th' quarter end, an' there'll be summat to buy cloes wi' at Whissunday, an' a bit o' summat extra at Kersmas, an' it's all mi eye an' Peggy Martin abaat th' stuff bein' dear an' nasty. That's Eph. Thorpe's tale, that is. Ther's nob'dy nah'll go to Eph's bud them as cannot pay ready brass for their stuff."

More than one good workman, old friends and cronies of Ben's, had already had long talks with him about the matter. They were men who had a bit laid by and were ready to join the enterprise.

"We will have no one with us," said Tom emphatically, "but those who work in the mill. We will have no one's money unless he gives his labour too. Every worker on the job must have his flesh and blood in it as well as his money. If we take money at all it must be as a loan at low interest. The thing is to have every hand a co-operator in production and a sharer in the profits."

"Tak' as few in as possible till yo' see how th' job frames," was Hannah's prudent counsel. "If it goes all reet yo'll ha' plenty o' backers, an' plenty as'll want to ha' a finger i' th' paw (pie). Aw nobbut hope it winnot be like the gradely 'Holmfirth paw.'"

"What's that?" asked Tom.

"Brokken eggs," said Hannah, shortly, "cow-pie,—custard, for fine."

Of course Jabez Tinker heard of the thing. A few days before the expiration of Tom's apprenticeship he sent for him into the office. The indenture was spread on the desk before him.

"Sit down, Tom," his master said in a not unkindly voice. "So I suppose you are going to shake the dust of Wilberlee Mill off your feet."

"Something like it, sir, I suppose, if you've no objections."

"Nay, it's with my leave or without my leave now. Well, I've had no fault to find with you. Are your plans settled once for all?"

"I've put my hand to the plough, sir."

"Well, of course it's no concern of mine. But don't you think you might have consulted me?"

"I should have been glad of your advice, sir," said Tom. Then added firmly, "but you have never given me any reason to suppose you would have been willing to give it me."

Mr. Tinker glanced sharply at the youth. He saw nothing of impertinent suggestion in Tom's face. Tom had spoken, simply and plain, what was to him a plain and simple matter of fact.

"What do you mean, Pinder? Have you any complaint to make. Haven't I always done my duty by you?"

"I don't know, sir. If your duty was to let me severely alone, you have done your duty. You know better than I whether that is a master's duty to an apprentice. I'm no lawyer. But Mr. Black always told me I was to be taught your trade."

"Well, it seems you fancy you know enough about it to start for yourself."

"Little thanks to you," thought Tom, but what use to say?

"But I didn't send for you to-day, Pinder, to discuss my duty or yours. I think you're foolish to begin on your own account. I have had it in my mind for some time back to put you forward in the mill. I'm weary of Sam Buckley and his drunken ways. He gets beyond bearing. I had thought of putting you in his place—at a lower wage, of course. 'Twould have been a big lift for you, but I've had my eye on you, and I think you'd have done."

Tom's feelings at these unexpected words were of mingled pride, gratitude, and self-reproach. He had never suspected that his conduct in the mill was observed by the reserved, self-contained master. He had done his duty as he conceived it, simply because it was his duty.

He knew, of course, that many of the apprentices shirked their work and gave as much trouble as possible. In acting otherwise Tom had neither sought nor expected notice and approbation. He was conscious-stricken both in that he had attributed Mr. Tinker's reserve to callous indifference, and in that the first use he contemplated making of his freedom was to start in what might seem to be a competition with one whom he knew now to have had his advancement in view.

"I am getting older," continued Mr. Tinker, "As you know I have no son. I must look for a younger man to take some of the work from my shoulders. Of late I have felt the constant strain more than I used to. But, there, it's no use talking, I suppose. I think you're a young idiot all the same to start as they say you're going to. Take an old man's word for it, Tom Pinder, business and philanthropy don't mix. Make your money in trade and give what you don't want yourself in charity, if you like; but business must be run on business lines. It's some of Ben Garside's hatching, I expect; but then Ben was always crackbrained."

"I am sure I don' know how to thank you, sir," began Tom.

"Oh! I don't want your thanks. I was looking out for myself as much as you. Nothing for nothing—that's business you'll find. The question is, are you content to stop on at Wilberlee or 'gang your ain gate,' as the Scotch say. Yea or nay, or would you like to think it over?"

Now Tom knew if he consulted Ben, just the advice that Ben would give—stop on at Wilberlee. He knew also that though Ben would say this promptly, and to all seeming cheerfully, it would be the shattering of the brightest dream his friend had ever dreamed. Besides, to fill Sam Buckley's place would bring him very little nearer—he knew what. No! he could wait and work, and Tom believed in the future foretold for him who knows *how* to wait.

Mr. Tinker took up the indenture, and seemed to read it.

"H'm," he said, more to himself than Tom, "I've signed so many of these things that I forget what they bind a man to. But it's a mere form."

"I'll burn this now, anyway," he said aloud. "Put it into the stove, Pinder."

Tom did as he was bid, and as the stiff paper caught the flames, and the smell from the wax seals invaded the stuffy office he felt as though chains fell from his limbs and incense burned on the altar of freedom.

"Well?" said Mr. Tinker at length.

"I think I must go, sir. But I go thanking you from my heart," was Tom's reply.

"So be it," said Mr. Tinker, curtly. "When you're done up dish and spoon don't come here for work, that's all."

"I won't," said Tom, and went.

And as he walked slowly homewards he resolved to keep his own counsel and say nothing to Ben or Hannah about the offer that had been made to him. It would disquiet Ben and lead to no good. Best say nothing about the matter; let it lie between him and Mr. Tinker. Besides if it got talked of in the village those who believed his statement would call him a fool, those who didn't a liar.

It was all the easier to dismiss the subject from his mind when he found the following letter awaiting him:

"Dear Tom,

Seein it will be your berthday nex Sunday, an you will be twenty-one, me an Mister Redfearn have fixed it up to have a bit of a do here seein as it wer here you was borne. An Fairbanks has sent a goos an a turkey, an Moll has maid a puddin an you are to bring Mester an Missus Garsed wi my respecks to em an welcome, likewise their dowter too. Also to say as Fairbanks will send his trap bi Workus Jack for Missus an dowter an yo an Ben mun cum o Shanks mare. Dinner at nooin an no waitin. So no more at present hopeing this finds yo well as it leaves me.

Yure affeckshinit,

Betty Schofield"

Go! Of course they would go; all of them. Where else could the auspicious day be better spent than in the very house he first saw the light, and among the friends of his infancy. Go! yes though the snow lay three feet deep on moor and fell, and the wintry wind howled round Pots and Pans and whirled the stinging atoms in a very blast hurricane and tornado of blinding blizzard.

"Goa!" exclaimed Hannah, "aw'st goa if aw've to crawl o' mi han's an' knees. Yo' mun write a letter back, Tom, an' say we'st be theer at eleven i' th' forenooin if it's convenient to Mrs. Schofield, an' aw'll gi' a hand wi' th' bastin' an' sarvin' up, so's 'oo can cooil dahn afore 'oo sits dahn to th' table. Aw reckon aw'st want no cooilin' dahn long afore we're ovver th' top."

And then Hannah and Lucy fell to at such a preparation, adjusting, re-adjusting, snipping, snipeing, cutting, hemming, tuckering of shawls and dresses, to such a trimming of hat and bonnet, and such a littering of the house with female finery, that if a wedding or a coronation had been afoot, matters could not have been worse.

"Aw'st nivver howd aat till Sunday, Tom," Ben confided to him. "Aw haven't set tooith into a turkey sin' aw can't remember when an' ivvry time aw think on it mi maath watters soa aw can hardly speik. Do'st think there'll be sossidge wi' it? Tha mieet ha' just nudged her abaat th' sossidge when yo' wrote if yo'd gi'en it a thowt, but aw'm feart it's too lat' nah. An' gooise an' apple sauce, an stuffin', an' plum puddin' wi' brandy sauce—eh, lad, it's a pity tha cannot come o' age onst a week. But aw munnot show greedy. Aw onst knew a felly at a club supper 'at e't a whull leg o' mutton to his own cheek, wi' capers and onion sauce an' breead, an' supped two gallon o' ale. They'd to gie him kester oil for aboon a week at after afore he fair gate shut on it. Nah! aw ca' that a fair abuse o'th' kindly fruits o'th' earth. Nah! tha'll ha' studied ettiket nah tha's ta'en to talkin' townified. How mony helpin's dun yo reely think aw mieet ha' wi' out bein thowt greedy? Aw'm nooan a glutton, like that chap at Gowcar 'at went to a club dinner—Bill o' Natt's, aw think they ca'ed him—an' when he gate whom he rolled o'th' floor, an' all he could say wer' 'Howd, belly, howd, for if tha brusts awm done.' And Ben looked anxiously at Tom for a reply. But Tom only smiled, for he knew that Ben was merely talking to let off steam. So the excited little man went on:

"Tha'll nooan be teetotal that day, Tom. It 'ud be a sort o' slur o' Missus Schofield. Aw tak' it at goin' to a feeast at a public wi' a publican an' ca'in' for cowd watter 'ud be just as bad manners as feedin' wi' a teetotaller an' axin for a pint o' drink. Nah! doesn't it strike yo' i' that leet, Tom?"

But Tom explained that he had had that point over with his good friend Betty many a time before and that he wasn't going to begin his manhood by breaking the pledge he had taken with himself. "You'll have to drink my share too, Ben."

"An' Lucy's, for 'oo's tarred wi' th' same brush as thee, Tom. Aw do believe 'at if yo' took to runnin' abaat th' village wi' a caa's tail atween yo'r teeth like them niggers yo'n read on o'th' banks o'th river Ganges, yar Lucy 'ud do th' same as well as her legs 'ud let her. An' thank God!—an' yo', Tom, 'oo can walk wi'out sticks nah." And Ben pressed Tom's arm as caressingly as ever maiden conveyed message to favoured swain.

"You'll have to be careful, Ben, if you're going to drink for three."

"Aye, aye, if all's weel aw'st be poorly th' day after, sha'not aw? But wi' one thing an' another aw just feel as if aw cud turn cart wheels slap daan th' sides o' Pots an' Pans till aw poo'd up at th' *Hanging Gate*. It is na th' eitin', lad, nor th' drinkin', though them's nooan things to be sneezed at, let me tell yo'. It's thowts at' mi Tom's so well thowt on bi all at's knowd him sin' he wer' a suckin' babe. Aw tell thee, lad, mi heart's so full aw could blubber like a cawf, if aw didn't howd missen in." And then Tom knew it was time for him to look intently in any direction but that of honest Ben's face.

Sunday came, and with Sunday came Workh'us Jack, such a beaming radiant Jack as never village saw before: Jack, with a great white rosette on his breast and a white ribbon on the end of the whip with which he flicked the mare with many a soothing "so-ho, so-ho," and hortatory "come up;" an older Jack by many a biting Winter's lapse since first we met him; a stouter, plumper, rosier Jack, but with the same smiling face and unfailing cheerfulness.

How, with infinite tenderness, Lucy was lifted into the trap, how Tom smothered her with wraps and shawls, how Hannah declared she would rather walk through the village because everybody was, she knew, stopping from chapel on purpose to gaup at her, and how she was hoisted bodily in under protest; how, as a matter of fact the neighbours and the neighbour's children turned out into the street braving the whipping of the gusty snow or peered from chamber window; how it was all over Holmfirth in no time that Gentleman Tom and Lucy Garside were "off over th' Isle of Skye to be wed at St. Chad's," how every gossip in the village insisted that she had expected nothing else these months back, and called upon her neighbour to testify that she had often been heard to say so; how the demure young maidens declared that Lucy for all her quiet ways was a deep one and a sly one, and that it was a shame a fine strapping young fellow should be trapped into wedding a pale faced useless thing, little better than a cripple; how Ben and Tom walked far ahead of the trap all the way up the ascent of road to the Isle of Skye, but were overtaken just as they reached the inn there: how Ben insisted on Jack taking "summat short" to keep the cold out, and Tom would have Hannah drink some hot port-wine negus to keep Jack company, and how Jack had another drink for the good of the house; how the exhilarating influence of the liquor passed by some mysterious process from the driver to the driven so that the old mare rattled down from Bill's o' Jack's to Greenfield, and from Greenfield to the *Church Inn*, at Saddleworth; how it stopped there of its own accord and positively refused to budge till Jack descended from his seat and had another drink; how Hannah made sure that Ben and Tom would be foolish enough to try a short cut over the moors and untimely perish like Tom's mother before them; and how finally the chaise drew up in fine style before the *Hanging Gate*, and Lucy almost fell into Betty Schofield's welcoming arms—all this the reader must imagine.

And there, sure enough in the big room upstairs, with its mysterious cupboard labelled R.A.O.B., the sacred room in which the Royal Antedeluvian Order of Buffaloes declared every lodge night that they would "hunt the buff, would hunt the buff, would hunt the buffalo," though where to find it thereabouts would have puzzled them to tell. In this great room a glorious fire roared and cast its welcome warmth and the walls were hung with the Christmas decorations of the lodge, and the Christmas holly and mistletoe looked yet fresh and green, and the long narrow table down the centre was white with Betty's best napery, and Moll, feigning mighty indignation because Tom had caught her round the waist and kissed her smackingly under the mistletoe, busied about making a great clattering of plates and spoons and knives and forks, whilst a distracting odour of roast goose came up the narrow staircase. Mr. Redfearn was there betimes, and Aleck, all in his Sunday best. Then came the down-sitting, Mr. Redfearn at the table-head, Tom at the foot. Aleck facing Ben, and Hannah, and Lucy supporting the chair and vice-chair. Moll o' Stute's and Jack had their dinner later on. How many helps of turkey *with* sausage and of goose *with* stuffing and apple sauce, and of plum-pudding *with* brandy-sauce Ben had I entirely refuse to tell, but only say with all his talk he came in a very lame second to Aleck.

"It only wanted Mr. Black to make it just perfect," said Mr. Redfearn, "but we'll drink in silence to the memory of as good a man as ever walked i' shoe-leather."

I refuse to tell, too, in what glowing terms Mr. Redfearn proposed the health of Tom Pinder, and many a happy return of the day, and of how Tom completely broke down in acknowledging the toast, and of how Ben proposed Mr. Redfearn's health, and Mr. Redfearn Ben's, and Tom the ladies, and then how they drank Mrs. Schofield's and the ladies with a three times three and God bless 'em, and then started the toast list all over again, till Lucy was more than glad when Moll brought in the tea-pot and cups, and they all drew round the fire, and the men lighted their pipes and sobered down to rational talk.

Be sure Tom had to tell of what he was going to do now he was his own master, and of how Ben had "weighed in" to help him, and he had to explain till he was nearly hoarse before Betty could understand what a co-op mill was to be like. And then nothing would satisfy Betty but she must offer to put £50 "into th' consarn, sink or swim, it were all one to her if it 'ud do 'em any good;" and then Tom had to begin all over again and make it clear that only the actual workers were to have any interest in the mill.

"An' wheer are yo' buyin' yo'r wool?" asked Tom o' Fairbanks.

And Tom and Ben looked grave, for they would have precious little left for wool-buying when the machinery was bought and set up.

"At Hirst's, the wool stapler, in Huddersfield, I suppose," said Tom.

"Now I don't take it friendly of you, or either of you," commented Mr. Redfearn. "I've bales and bales left over from th' last shearing, haven't we, Aleck?"

And Aleck said "To be sure we have, an' fair gettin' maggoty for want o' usin'."

"You must take it off my hands, Tom and Co.," said Redfearn. "I'll let you have it cheap, and you can pay me for it when you've had time to turn yourselves round."

It is very sad that such things should be in a Christian land; but it is none the less true that the wool which later on Aleck carted to Co-op Mill had never coated the back of any sheep that grazed on Fairbank's field or moors, and why, about the same time, Farmer Redfearn should be buying wool in Huddersfield, Charles Hirst, the Huddersfield wool stapler, spent many an hour in vain attempt to divine.

It was a glorious feast and a happy gathering, and happy folk those whose faces shone in the dancing rays of the glowing fire; but happiest of all the happy there was Workh'us Jack when Ben and Tom offered him the post of teamer and handy man at Co-op Mill, for Co-op Mill, the low grey mill at Hinchliffe Mill, had been christened without informal ceremony.

"Aw'd ha' come mysen an' helped i'th mill," confided Aleck to Tom, as he walked a part of the homeward way with him and Ben. "But yo' see aw'm th' only one 'at stan's atween th' mester an' ower mich liquor. It's his only failin'. Nivver thee tak' to sperrits Tom. Be teetotal off *them.* Stick to ale an' nivver sup more nor five quarts at a sittin'. Tha'll nooan get fur wrang on that if th' ale's saand. Gooid neet, lad."

CHAPTER XI

THAT was a grand moment for Ben and Tom when the shuttle of the goit at Co-op Mill was drawn, and the water from the dam began to stream into the wheel-race and catch the buckets of the great wheel, transmitting its revolutions to the main shafting and machines. Little enough stock of wool and dye wares had they, and few indeed the engines for transforming by multiple processes the greasy, clotted fleeces into warp and weft and good broad pieces. But both knew every branch of the manufacturer's art, and each was more than willing to take his part, and more than his part, at scouring, dyeing, scribbling, or weaving. They employed very few hands, and each of these thoroughly understood that he was to be paid not only a fair day's wage for a fair day's work, but also a share of the profits; and it did not take long for Yorkshire shrewdness to discover that the better, the more thoroughly, each one worked, the better for one and all. There was no scamping the work, no idling. And there was no breaking time for sprees, no "laiking" because a chap felt Mondayish, and wanted an off-day or two to get over the effects of Saturday's and Sunday's debauch. Every hand at Co-op Mill began in a very brief time to shake off the enervating consciousness of the subservience of a hired labourer. He would not only not idle himself, he would tolerate no idling in a fellow labourer. There are tricks in every trade, or every trade is solely maligned. There are ways of shirking work, of making time pass in merely *seeming* labour that one would think one as irksome in the long run to the operative as they are undoubtedly unjust to the employer. There was none of that at Co-op Mill. Set a thief to catch a thief, and a man who shirks and dawdles at his work steals the time that is indeed money. But let the man who works by your side be personally interested in the work you do, and the way you do it; there is no room there for shirking and dawdling. The lever of labour is, after all, self-interest, and so ingrained is self-interest that the only thing that can be asked of average human nature is that self-interest should not impinge on the self-interests of another.

Now matters were so arranged at Co-op Mill that self interest was necessarily and unavoidably altruistic, and when this great truth was once fairly grasped and assimilated by the hands a spirit prevailed from scouring house to pressing-room that secured ready, willing abundant and thorough work, and the quality and the quantity of the work soon made themselves manifest in the final output. The finished pieces were a delight to the eye and to the touch. There was no occasion to employ a traveller to push their goods. The goods sold themselves. It had been resolved that suit-lengths might be bought at the mill at a little below ordinary retail prices. This was to contravene the commercial code; but Tom did not see why a man should be compelled to go to a tailor and the tailor to a merchant and pay the profits to two middlemen because of a commercial code that chiefly benefited the middlemen and never the consumer. No, the difficulty did not consist in finding purchasers; the difficulty was in putting out goods enough to supply the demand. But as Ben had predicted, so soon as the system began to be understood, and especially after the first "divvy" had been declared and actually taken home by the men and handed to their wives, there was no lack of proffers of service from men who were able, ready, and willing to put their "bit" into Co-op Mill. At present there was some demur to terms—bare interest on invested capital, no participation in profits over that limit. On this point Ben and Tom were inexorable, adamantine. "It shall *not* be a capitalists' concern, it *shall* be a workers'."

And it was wonderful too, and heartening to note the harmony, the goodwill, the general sense of brotherhood that prevailed from counting-house downwards. There was no cringing, no toadying, no tale-hearing. There was the very presence, spirit, and revelation of a moral resolution. Nothing so ennobles a man as to feel that, so far as man can ever be in this network of human organism in which no thread is self-sufficient and self-dependent, he is his own man, with need to go cap in hand to no other. It is a feeling that, in Yorkshire is perhaps apt to run to truculence and the very savagery of self-assertion; but even so it is better than the cringing, fawning self-abasement of the rural districts of the midland villages where squire and priest are gods of earth and heaven.

A man who threw in at the Co-op was a marked and envied man. The pick of the operatives were willing to take the looms as fast as they could be put up. It was Lucy who suggested that the new concern should go into the making of shawls. Everyone who knows the manufacturing districts of Yorkshire and Lancashire knows the shawl of the mill girl. It is to her what the cloak is to the Irish butter-woman, the plaid to the Scotch shepherd, or the mantilla to the Spanish donna. It was Dorothy who designed the pattern for the first shawl and, as time went on, the warm, bright-coloured covering might be seen over the head and shoulders of the women and girls in every mill in the Valley of the Holme. There was no need to be concerned about the texture or the fastness of the colours. It was a Co-op shawl. That was guarantee enough.

Tom and Ben worked early and late. Tom indeed had had a bed fixed up in a small room of the lower story of the mill. Many a night, indeed often for weeks together every night except Saturday and Sunday, he slept in the mill. He was the one to open the mill-gate in the morning and greet the hands as they streamed into the yard and hand them their time checks. His was the hand that, when the long day, yet all too short for his endless round of duties, lagged to its weary close, fastened the gate upon the last of the toilers; and oft and oft, far into the silent hours, he would bend over stock-book and ledger or, when the moon shone high above the mill, would walk round the mill dam and up the rugged hank of the babbling stream that fed it. His constant companion was Jack, no longer Workh'us Jack, but Jack, plain Jack, or Jack o' th' Co-op, or Tom Pinder's Jack, anything but Workh'us Jack; a new, transformed Jack, wearing his corduroys and smock as proudly as if they had been a Field Marshal's uniform. Sometimes a wag, further learned than others, would dub him "Man Friday;" but it was all one to Jack. He was Tom's body servant, his dog, if need be, to fetch and carry. And who so popular all through that beautiful valley and who so welcome at the hill-side farms and cottages as cheery, smiling, cherry-faced Jack with his kindly jest and merry quip and crank? Why, he was worth a dozen commercial travellers rolled into one. When he led the cart from the mill to the coal-shoots and back, or went his round with the great red-coloured barrel on wheels in quest of the ammonia laden refuse of the house-hold it was a sorry day for Jack when he did not bring back two or three orders for the pretty, taking shawls, and what insight into the delightful vanities of lovely maiden Jack did not acquire on his rounds was really not worth noticing.

But it was on a shawl for Lucy that Jack spent his first week's earnings at Co-op Mill, a dainty, modest shawl of softest fleece, a shawl, Jack declared, you could draw through a finger ring, and perhaps one might if the finger were one of Jack's. The rosy-cheeked, brown-eyed lasses of the little farms and homesteads, and the more forward wenches of the valley mills wasted their becks and nods and wreathed smiles on Jack. He took them all as a matter of course; but a look from Lucy's soft warm eyes, from which the pathetic wistfulness of long suffering had not yet worn away, would set Jack "all of a dither." It was for Lucy, when the season came, that he ransacked the hill sides for the peeping snowdrop, and the hedge-bottoms for the shy primrose; for Lucy that he bore home the nodding blue-bells and the blushing fox-glove, or the rare wild rose; for Lucy that he searched the brambles for the luscious blackberry, and bent his back o'er the purple heather for the nestling bilberry; for Lucy that he brought the thrilling thrush; for Lucy that he nearly broke his neck down the steps of the church belfry the day he secured the wild young jackdaw; and for Lucy that he weaned the perverse bird of its natural addition to choleric speech and general bad language. In Jack's eyes Lucy was fair and beautiful as any angel—and indeed her pale face was very sweet to look upon—and for him Lucy's lightest word—nay, such is the divination of affection—Lucy's unspoken thought was as law. And who so surely as Jack could rouse Lucy from the sad reveries into which her thoughts would sometimes stray, and bring back to her lips the pleasant smile and the gentle repartee that had neither sting nor lash? Who was it but Jack that nearly killed the barman at the *Rose and Crown* because he soiled his lips with an unseemly jest involving both Tom and Lucy; who but Jack that, however urgent his business errands might be, never passed Ben's cottage without solicitous enquiry as to Lucy's health, and what sort of a night she had had, and how she had felt that day; and for whom but Lucy did Jack forswear cakes and ale?

But now the last wild rose of the summer has blushed in the hedgerows, and the bracken of the moors is greying to sickly death; the brooks and rivulets fall from the heights in fuller stream and muttering a gloomier song and the long nights are at hand when men-folk of a social mind seek the creature comforts and the good-fellowship of taproom and bar. And this was the season which Ben and Tom deemed fitting for the launching of still another experiment. They had resolved of a Saturday night— that most dangerous of nights, when the wages in the breeches' pockets seem as if they would stand any inroad for the quenching pint throughout the winter months to have night classes at the mills for their own hands, and for as many of their friends as liked to come. There were to be first of all lessons in English History, and with history was to be taught in the only way it can be effectively taught, the geography of the wide, wide world. And the lessons in history were to be enlivened and made the more seductive by the reading of books of fiction and romance, of fable and poem dealing with the period under study, so that by the light of such heroes as *Hereward the Wake*, and *The Last of the Saxon Kings*, and *The Last of the Barons*, by the deathless pages of Avon's Swan, by the muse of Chaucer, of Spenser, and of Milton, the ages of the past lived before the eyes of these eager sons of toil, and they dwelt in the stately company of kings and warriors, cloistered saints and beautiful sinners, and saw, as in a waking dream, the stately drama of their country's making.

There were lessons, too, in chemistry: and in the explosions of gases, the evolving of composite stenches and the pyrotechnics of phosphorescent combustion the younger hands found a joy that knew no satiety or abatement. But Tom confined his teaching to the veriest elements of inorganic chemistry, those whose interest in the subject clamoured for more must seek their further advancement in the fascinating subject elsewhere. It was to teach, to drive home, the great truth of fixed, unchanging, ruthless law that had been, from the first, the dominating idea. And when his pupils had once grasped thoroughly the idea of the all-pervading law in the material world, what was easier than to lead them, without their realising his drift and purpose, to the conception of the fixed, the immutable in the moral law, and what more easy to expel from minds so prepared the baneful influence of the extra-natural creeds that led so many to repose their confidence in the adventitious, the possible interposition of a *Deus ex machinâ* to rescue them from the disasters they had courted for themselves. That twice two make four, neither more nor less, is a great fact; that H and Cl make hydrochloric acid and not Devonshire cream is also a fact; that happiness ensues upon well-doing and suffering upon sin, this also is a fact; but one the churches attenuate to men's minds by insisting upon a rote punishment that may be averted by timely repentance. Tom taught that punishment, mediate or immediate, direct or indirect, is here, and in this present time.

Now Tom was not such a fool as to dub his discourses Lectures on Religion. He knew well enough that to do so would be to talk to empty benches. The orthodox are suspicious of religious instruction unless they receive it wearing a Sunday dress, and a Sunday face, and in a conventional conventicle established by the State, or by that force which is more powerful than the State, the approval of Madam Grundy. The unorthodox, for quite different reasons, would have shunned his class-room, though it was the weaving shed at Co-op Mill they would have suspected a snare to trap them into saintliness. So the astute Tom called his theses "Lectures on the Science of Living," and succeeded insidiously in making his hearers perceive that the Science of Living and Religion are one and the same thing; by Religion, of course, not being understood that *olla podrida*, or hotch-potch of legend, fable, history, surmise poetry, rhapsody, and morals which so many confound with religion. The expositions of this quite unheard of Science of Living were delivered on the Sunday afternoons and in the weaving shed at the mill. Another novelty was that there was no collection. And the lectures began to be talked about and be popular.

"What are ta' fidgettin' abaat, Luke?" a constant caller at the *Croppers' Arms* would ask as the minute-hand of the clock plodded towards the third hour of the Sunday afternoon.

"A'm nooan fidgettin'; but aw mun be stirring."

"Sit thee still, mon. There's time enough afore turnin'-aat time. Th' churchwardens wi'not be raand afore three an' after. Sup up an' let's fly for another quart. It'll be a long while till th' oppenin' time to-neet."

"Nay aw'll ha' no more. I'm thinkin' aw'll just ha' a bit o' a stretch to sattle mi dinner."

"Aye, weel, aw dunnot mind if aw've a bit o' a walk missen to stretch mi legs. Which way did ta think o' takkin'?"

"Weel there's a nice stretch o' country up by Hinchliffe Mill way, an' we'st get a mouthfu' o' fresh air."

"Tha's no bahn to th' Co-op Gospel-shop, are ta?"

"Weel, aw winnot say but what aw meet look in, just to wind missen. Its' a bit o' a poo' fro' here to th' Top. An' there's no wheer aw can ca' to-day, worse luck."

"Tha'll get nowt at th' Co-op, chuse ha. It's nobbut dry drinkin' they han on tap theer, folk say. But aw dunnot set thi on th' road a bit, an' if tha can stand Tom Pinder's preichin' aw reckon aw can. It's nooan like a regular chapel tha sees."

And thus the lecture room filled.

Now there were two men of all others who received the doings at Co-op Mill with disfavour. One was the Rev. David Jones. That very energetic preacher did not like to hear anyone's praises sung but his own. His Welsh fluency, his striking, daring flights of rhetoric, his excursions into tempting but dangerous speculations on the fundamental truths of the creed embodied, consecrated, and enshrined in the Trust Deed of Aenon Chapel, had secured for him the admiring following of considerable numbers of men who, whilst still clinging as for dear life to the shattered remnants of the old dogmas, turned longing eyes to the rationalism of a new criticism and a faith grounded upon human experience. They were like the frail ones of the softer sex, who concede all favours but the last, their heart or their passions consenting, their timidity restraining. Aenon Chapel was now packed with a new set of worshippers whose presence was not too welcome to the "old end," as the Conservative adherents of Calvinistic theology and tradition were styled. "Owd fire an' brimstone" the irreverent styled their leader and spokesman. But the objections of those chiefly responsible for the maintenance and carrying on of the chapel and school, whose father's money had built and furnished the edifice in which Mr. Jones declaimed his mild heresies, were stripped of their accustomed force by one all-persuasive consideration—the collection box. Never before in all the history of Aenon Chapel had the anniversaries of church and schools yielded so profitable a harvest to the anxious treasurer. The debt, without which it is commonly supposed no religious work can prosper, was reduced. Mr. Jones's stipend was increased. The deacons of former days were consumed with envy, and dolefully acknowledging that Mr. Jones had gone up like a rocket, expressed their hope that he might not come down like a stick, but expressed it in a tone that indicated their hope and expectation were not as one. But the new officers of the chapel exulted in their swelling money-bags, in the well-filled pews, and idolized the preacher of the new inspiration.

And not only in his own chapel, but far and near spread the fame of the Rev. David Jones, and to chapel openings and consecrations, to missions and special efforts, invitations came in showers. He became the rage, and though he protested at any term that savoured of Episcopacy and the Scarlet Woman, he, in his heart of hearts, acknowledged the discernment of an ardent admirer who had publicly referred to him as the Bishop of the Holme Valley. At nights he dreamed of the Presidency of the Union.

And now, when all things seemed to go well, people began to talk of the Sunday meetings at Co-op mill, and of Tom Pinder, who, folk said, spoke out what Jones only hinted at.

"Aw'll tell yo' what it is," said one shrewd level-headed critic, "Aw've heard that pea-i'-a-bladder preich at Aenon Chapel, and aw've heard Co-op Tom fro' th' same text, but Pinder doesn't ca' it preichin', he ca's it explainin'."

"An' what wer' text?"

"Why t' eleventh commandment, and mi own opinion is 'at Pinder sees as far as th' purson, an' spits it aat like a man, upright and dahnwright, and a babby could tell what he meeans: but th' other chap, he goes as far as Pinder, but he beats abaat th' bush, an' he 'perhaps this' and 'may it not be that?' an' he watches th' deacons an' th' chief pew-howders to see ha' it gooas dahn, an' he lets hissen aat an' he poo's hissen in like th' cap'n of a sailin' booat wi' one eye on the clouds an' t'other on th' shoals an' reefers."

"Nah, Pinder just says what's in him, an' if yo' dunnot like it yo can lump it. An' what's more, at th' end o' ivvery lectur', yo' can get up an' just ha' a few minnit's enjoyment o' yo'r own accaant an' pitch into th' discourse like owd Billy, an' th' harder yo' hit th' more Pinder seems to like it."

"An' why canno' Jones speik it aat plain same as Pinder?"

"Well, there's some folk so constitooted, yo' see, 'at they like to swim wi' th' tide an' 'll tak' uncommon gooid care nevver to waste their puff swimmin' up-stream. An' then yo' see, Jones has a large fam'ly, an' my misses says 'at Mrs. Jones wi' her rings an' mantles, an' feathers, an' faldelals can do wi' all 'at Jones can addle an' more at th' top on it."

Now, of course talk of this kind in a village like Holmfirth not only circulates, it percolates and in time the gist and substance of it reached Mr. Jones. He had had hopes of Tom at one time. He had observed with satisfaction that this very intelligent-looking, well-behaved, well-spoken, neatly dressed young man had been an attentive listener and frequent worshipper at his own chapel, and that, on occasions, he had brought with him that quite-past-praying-for Ben Garside, a notorious mocker and a scoffer. Mr. Jones had accepted their presence as one of many just tributes to his zeal and eloquence. One had been rescued from the tepid waters of the Church, the other was a brand plucked from the burning depths of infidelity, and Mr. Jones had duly rejoiced.

And lo! now the neophytes had backslided and people "of a Sunday" would pass the inviting doors of Aenon Chapel and walk some two miles of a sultry or wintry afternoon to listen to one who was not only not one of the Covenant, but who was ordained neither by Bishop, Presbytery, nor Congress. He resolved to speak seriously to this erring sheep; and chancing to meet Tom one day descending the hill from Hinchliffe Mill to the village, stopped him, smiling affably and holding out a condescending hand:

"Good morning, Pinder, I'm glad to see you. How are we this morning?"

"Very well, thank you, Jones. How are you?"

"Ahem! Mr. Jones, if *you* please."

"Certainly; Mr. Pinder, if you please."

"Oh! certainly; you see in my position—"

"Exactly—and in mine."

Now this was not a very promising beginning.

"Well?" said Tom.

"I'll turn with you, *Mr.* Pinder. You are doubtless more pressed for time than I. Parson's Monday, you know, is Parson's Sunday."

"Parsons seem to have a fair share of Sundays to the week," said Tom, but without any malice in the remark. "I remember good old Mr. Whitelock of St. Chad's couldn't bear to see a visitor on Saturday—preparing for Sunday, I suppose. Then of course there was Sunday itself, and on Monday every parson I've ever met declares that he feels like a wet rag or a squeezed orange."

"Well it takes it out of a man to have to preach two sermons a day. But you should know something about it. I understand you have a sort of service at your mill on Sunday afternoons?"

"You can scarcely call our meetings services," Tom replied. "We have no hymns, no sermon, and no collection. We have no preacher and no deacons."

"But I thought you were the preacher."

"Then you have been misinformed. It is true that I select some reading, generally not always, from the Scriptures. Then I try to make its meaning, or the meaning of some particular verse or verses, clear as I understand them. That's all; it's really more of a chat than a set discourse."

"I see."

"Then again the discoursing or preaching or chatting is not all done by one man. My experience is that the combined experience and wisdom of an audience are greater than those of any ordinary individual. We are so fashioned that most of what we read in the Bible is read by the light of the reader's own experience of life, his observations and his reflection."

"Well?"

"And so when I get around me twenty or thirty men of divers habits of thought and each with his own views of life, I have the chance of getting at twenty or thirty different commentaries on a text. That is a gain: another is that no single one of *my* commentators is concerned to square his construction of a passage with a hide-bound creed or with the convictions of any one of his hearers. The only thing we are concerned about is to get at the truth."

"And cannot you get at it in the recognised places of worship. Doesn't it savour of conceit to set yourselves apart as people better and wiser than their neighbours?"

"Oh! Well, come to that, Mr. Jones, you are a Dissenter yourself, you know. You dissented from established orthodoxy. We aren't afraid of dissenting from orthodox dissent."

"But there must be limits, young man; there must be limits."

"Yes," assented Tom. "There must be limits. There are the limitations of the human mind. We don't seek to go beyond them."

Mr. Jones was now thoroughly roused. He was a man of no mean intelligence and of a wide range of reading. If also he was a man of insatiable vanity and inordinate ambition, perhaps the atmosphere of adulation in which he lived, the incense of incompetent judges, were the chief causes. He felt now that he was talking to a man of sense and fearlessness. Now it is a treat to talk with a man who has the sense and the patience and the disposition to think for himself, and the courage to speak his thoughts. Mr. Jones walked in silence for a time, Tom moderating his longer stride to keep time with the cleric's shorter pace.

"I hope," said Mr. Jones, at length, "I hope your teaching is based on the cardinal principles of Christianity?"

"And those?"

"The Immaculate Conception and the Resurrection of our Lord."

"Those are not principles Mr. Jones. They are either facts or inventions."

"And you declare them as facts?"

"I don't myself touch on them at all. I confine myself to the cardinal principles about which you have enquired."

"And those?" enquired Mr. Jones, in his turn.

"The fatherhood of God, the majesty, the wisdom, the sanctity of His laws, and—the brotherhood of man."

Mr. Jones shook his hand sadly. "That is merely Natural Religion," he commented. "Men will find it but a broken reed in the hour of temptation and the time of sorrow."

"It suffices," said Tom "for some of the wisest, the best-living, the most benevolent of men."

"Aye?" questioned Mr. Jones.

"The Jews," said Tom quietly. "Contrast the life of the average Jew with that of the average Christian. Will you find the difference always in favour of the Christian?"

"Surely, yes," said Mr. Jones. "An unbeliever can never have the impregnable assurance that we find in the crucified Christ."

"Not in the loving-kindness of the Father," said Tom. "You exalt the Son at the expense of the Father?"

"Dear me, dear me," said Mr. Jones. "This is worse than I thought. I am afraid you are all astray, my young friend. I beseech you consider your ways, reflect on the danger you are in, the perils that compass you round about. Above all pray without ceasing, pray for light and guidance."

"I do pray, Mr. Jones. I pray every day; I pray at my bed-side, I pray at my work, in my daily walks."

"Ah! But prayer without faith is but a beating of the air. You must have an intercessor with your offended God, a sacrifice for His outraged laws."

"Mr. Jones, I respect your zeal and think you mean well. I do sacrifice. I offer myself as a living sacrifice. It is all I have to offer. When the great account is made up my life must plead for me. If that will not avail, I have little confidence in any other plea. But I did not seek this interview, Mr. Jones nor choose this topic, or is this, main street of Holmfirth, the best place for such discussion as we have drafted into. My main business to-day is to determine how much a bale I can afford to give for the best Spanish wool that is the part of my Master's business that I am intent on just now. If I remember that it *is* my Master's business, I shan't be so far wrong, shall I? And I'm going to try to make a bargain with a Jew wool-stapler, and I'm no more afraid of being overreached than if he were a Christian. But come up to Co-op Mill, and have a fling at my class you'll be made heartily welcome. Fix your own time, but come."

"God forbid," said Mr. Jones, as Tom darted into the railway station, just in time to catch the Huddersfield train.

Jabez Tinker was as little pleased as his spiritual guide with the rumours to which he could not well be deaf, concerning the success of the novel enterprise of his former apprentice. From the first he had predicted disaster for the venture. It was the crack-brained scheme of an addle-pated enthusiast and a misguided, self-opinionated youth. That was his opinion, and he did not keep his opinion to himself. But as time went on and the bankruptcy he had foretold did not overwhelm the Co-op Mill; as old and tried hands who had been with him for years, one after the other, left Wilberlee for the small concern higher up the stream, Jabez began to feel the irritation of the prophet whose vaticinations have come to nought. It would not be fair to say that Jabez begrudged Tom and Ben their success. That success could scarcely be considered to have injured him in his business. The operations, the rise or fall of Co-op Mill, were in his eyes beneath anything but contemptuous notice. But he could not conceal from himself that he would have better pleased to have seen Tom coming to him, cap in hand, to sue for reinstatement at Wilberlee. He had a sort of rankling resentment against Tom for refusing his own proffer of protection and advancement. When he had made that offer he had plumbed himself on his magnanimity—and, indeed, it was a generous offer. Jabez Tinker's pride was wounded, and Jabez Tinker was a proud man.

One day he chanced to meet Nehemiah Wimpenny, the lawyer. It was near the time for the elections to the Local Board, of which Mr. Tinker had been so long the chairman and autocrat that the other members of the Board might just as well have stopped at home as attended the monthly meetings. Wimpenny was the clerk.

"Well, we shall soon have the elections upon us, Mr. Tinker, and I suppose you have heard the news. Rum start, isn't it? What next, I wonder."

"I've heard no particular news that I'm aware of, Wimpenny. I'm no gad-about, as you know."

"Ah, well! It's an old saying that we've to go from home to hear news, especially if it happens to concern ourselves. Not that this is likely to give you much uneasiness."

"Well what is it?" asked Tinker, uneasily.

"Oh! It's hardly worth retailing. Sorry I mentioned it; but they are saying in the village you are to be opposed at the next election."

"Me! Opposed! Well, I'm ready, and pray, who is to be my 'honourable opponent,'—that's the expression, isn't it? 'Pon my word, I'll relish a good stand-up fight. I've been returned unopposed so often that a good, vigorous opposition will do me good."

"Well," said Wimpenny slowly, "I'm not sure you'll think your honourable opponent a foeman worthy of your steel. You'll never guess who they're talking about."

Mr. Tinker rapidly reviewed, mentally, all men of the neighbourhood likely to enter the lists against him.

"I'm a bad hand at conundrums," he said, "I give it up."

"What would you say to that insolent young upstart at Co-op Mill?"

"What! Tom Pinder! confound the puppy. Why, there'd be little honour in defeating him. D——n his impudence. But you're joking, Wimpenny, and I tell you I like joking as little as conundrums. But there,—the fellow isn't worth a thought. A nameless workhouse bastard oppose me! Well, you've had your joke, Wimpenny; next time we meet try and think of a better one." And Tinker strode angrily away, without much ceremony.

As a matter of fact there had been talk of nominating Tom for a seat on the Board, and the matter had been even broached to Tom himself. But Tom had from the first scouted the idea. He had enough on his hands looking after his own concerns, and he had sense enough to know that if a man won't stick to his business his business won't long stick to him. But when it transpired that, had he consented, he would have had to fight his old master, Tom was indignant. What did people take him for, he wondered. He felt that for him to pit himself against Mr. Tinker would have been a gratuitous insult to the man who had been his master for so many years. He knew that it would be to wound that master in his most sensitive spot, and he had a respect for family pride all the greater, perhaps, because he himself had no family ties or traditions to be proud of. And he shuddered to think what Dorothy might say to his presumption and ingratitude should the mere suggestion of his possible candidature reach her ears.

But of Tom's way of meeting the proposal Mr. Tinker was, of course, as yet, quite unaware. He had taken it for granted that Wimpenny was well informed, that he would not have repeated to him a vulgar *canard.*

And Mr. Tinker was therefore in high dudgeon when he spoke to Dorothy on the subject.

"Does that Tom Pinder live at Garside's yet?" he asked.

Dorothy opened her eyes in wonderment. It was the first time she remembered her uncle to have so much as mentioned Tom's name to her.

"I believe so, off and on. But I think Lucy Garside, Ben's daughter, told me they see very little of him except on Sunday night. He seems to spend both day and night at his mill. Lucy says he does the work of three men."

"You seem to be very intimate with these Garsides. 'Lucy' comes very pat to your lips. Do you see much of them? Do you ever meet this Pinder there?"

"Oh, yes, sometimes."

"I think you might remember you are my niece. Such people as we are not fit associates for the Garsides; still less for their lodger."

"Law! uncle, what have they done now? I've known Lucy ever since I could toddle almost."

"That may be. It's your aunt's fault, I suppose. I can't attend to everything. And now your aunt's illness keeps her at Harrogate you do pretty much as you like, I suppose."

"When the cat's away the mice will play," thought Dorothy; but only thought it.

"Well," continued Jabez, "you mustn't visit the house any more. I won't have it. If you don't respect yourself, you must respect me. You must drop these Garsides and Pinder too. By the bye, come to think of it, Wimpenny told me something about you seeming to be very familiar with Pinder at the Whitsuntide gathering. I didn't take much notice of it at the time. But be good enough to ignore him next time you chance to meet him."

"I'm sure I'm much obliged to Mr. Wimpenny for his interest in my movements," said Dorothy. "Are you acting on his advice, uncle? Did he charge you 'six—an'-eight' for it? He must be very smart, for I'm sure it isn't worth half the money."

"This is no laughing matter miss, I'd have you know, I tell you, you must drop these Garsides, and that young puppy too."

"Who? Mr. Wimpenny?"

"D——n Mr. Wimpenny," roared Jabez. "You know my meaning very well. See to it that you heed it. People will be saying next that you are running after the jackanapes."

Dorothy blushed scarlet. There was an angry gleam in her eye. She drew herself up proudly.

"I am a Tinker, sir, no less than you. I was left to choose my friends when I was young and needed, perhaps, a guide. I call Lucy Garside my friend, and so long as Lucy Garside deems me hers, be sure I shall not do as you command. As for Mr. Pinder——"

"Your precious Pinder," snarled Jabez.

"You had better go to him and learn from him how your brother's daughter and your niece should be addressed." Dorothy swept out of the room.

Oh! Jabez! Jabez! How little you know the heart of woman. It is safe to say that from that hour Dorothy never thought of the unconscious Tom without resentment against her uncle, and a feeling that certainly was not resentment for Tom.

Mr. Tinker felt in anything but a Christian spirit when his niece so defiantly left the room, and he knit his brow in angry meditation.

"Am I never to be done with that Tom Pinder?" ran his thoughts. "I pick him up out of the workhouse; he knocks my overseer head over heels; he refuses the handsomest offer I ever made to anyone in my life; starts in business on his own account, and now, forsooth, has the audacity to try conclusions with me at the polling-booth. I've a good mind to let him have a walk-over. There'll be no credit in beating him—that I'm sure to do but if by any chance he should head the poll—but that's not to be thought of. I'll give the cub something else to think of besides canvassing, or my name's not Jabez Tinker. If a man will play at bowls he must expect rubbers."

And as a result of his deliberations the manufacturer once more found himself in the office of Mr. Nehemiah Wimpenny.

"Come to sign your will, Mr. Tinker? It's been ready for you this—I don't know how long. I thought you'd forgotten all about it, and yet you seemed in a precious hurry about it when you gave me the instructions."

"No, it's not about my will I've come. That can wait, I think. In fact I may have to vary my instructions. I'm not quite satisfied with my niece's conduct lately. But we won't go into that at present. It's another, a more important one."

Nehemiah settled himself in his chair and gave all his mind to his client; but Jabez seemed for the nonce to have lost his usual promptitude and decision. He had to pick his words.

"It's a question of water-right," he said at last.

"H'm, ticklish things, very," said Nehemiah. "Nothing more so."

"So I've always understood," said Jabez—"and costly."

"Yes, costly. You might almost pave Holmfirth with the gold that's been spent on law over disputes about water. But let me have the facts. Perhaps it may not be a complicated case at all."

But his client seemed in no hurry to state the facts. He seemed to be more interested in the question of cost.

"Suppose I have a complaint to make against a firm higher up the stream, what are the proceedings to be taken?"

"What do you complain about, fouling or improperly tapping your supply?"

Mr. Tinker took time to reply. "I don't quite follow you," he said.

"Why," said Nehemiah, "water-right cases are usually complaints that a man has fouled the stream with dye-water or chemicals or by diverting ochre-water from above his own head-goit so that it may enter the river below his own mill but above his neighbour's. That's one class of case, and a comparatively easy one. The other is when a mill-owner fancies that the water that has passed over his neighbour's water-wheel is not returned to the stream for his own use lower down the stream. Now that's always a very delicate question, and one for experts. And it's well known that for one surveyor you get to swear on your side, another can be got to swear on the other. They're as bad as vets, in a horse-warranty case. Now which class of infringement do you complain of?"

Again Mr. Tinker had to pause for a reply. "O both," he said. "Yes, certainly, both."

"Why," exclaimed Wimpenny, "whose mill is it?"

"The Co-op Mill," said his client, somewhat shamefacedly, as the lawyer thought.

"What! That fellow, Pinder! By Jove, I'm glad of this. Gad! I'm as pleased as if you'd told me I was own brother to the Prince of Wales. But"—and his face fell.

"But what?" asked Jabez, sharply.

"It'll be lean picking, even if we win. I don't suppose the whole concern's worth powder and shot."

"And why are you anxious powder and shot should be spent on Pinder?" asked Tinker, suspiciously.

"Oh, well I don't mind telling you, Mr. Tinker. The fact is, I was rather hard hit by your beautiful niece, if you'll excuse my saying so."

"Well?" said Mr. Tinker, stiffly.

"But she seemed to prefer that low fellow Pinder's company to mine, and if she's no better taste than that, well, I'm not the one to enter the running against a screw."

Mr. Tinker winced. "You seem to lose heart very easily, Mr. Wimpenny. Young men weren't so easily discouraged in my young days."

"Much you know about it," thought the lawyer. "A spirited young woman like Dorothy Tinker's rather a different sort of an undertaking from old Split's scarecrow of a daughter."

By mutual consent to the men reverted the less embarrassing question of water rights.

"Just explain to me, Wimpenny, what must be done to vindicate my rights."

"Well, you must file a Bill in the Court of Chancery, and you must file affidavits by the oldest inhabitants as to the customary service of the water, and by analysts as to pollution, and you must go for damages, and you'll have to get other manufacturers to assess the damages, and, oh!—yes, you might try for an *interim* injunction."

"And Pinder'll have to set another lawyer on?"

"Of course he will."

"And that'll cost *him* money, win or lose?"

"Rather."

"Then go at him hammer and tongs, and the sooner you begin and the hotter you go at him, the better you'll please me."

"But the evidence?"

"You must find the evidence, sir. I don't care whether I win or lose. But Co-op Mill must stop. For want of water if we win: for want of funds if we lose."

"Do you understand me?"

"You bet I do, and I'll tell you this, I never went into a case with better heart. You may rest easy, Mr. Tinker. Co-op Mill's as good as broke."

It was but a week or so after this interview that Workhouse Jack, loitering about the mill yard, espied a seedy looking fellow peering in at the mill-gates. It was a Saturday afternoon. The engine was stopped, the hands had trooped home, Tom and Ben had gone for a walk, and Jack was in sole charge. He was dressed in his Sunday best, and meditating a visit to the village, and, of course, Lucy. He knew the visitor at once for Wimpenny's process server. The process server did not know Jack.

"Can I see Mr. Pinder?" the man asked.

"Aye, if yo're none blind," answered Jack. "What's your will?"

"Oh, beg your pardon, sir. Didn't know it was you. This is for you, sir, and he slipped a paper into Jacks hand."

"It's a petition in Chancery filed by our client, Mr. Jabez Tinker, against you, sir."

"A 'tition, is it," said Jack "an' what mun aw do wi' it nah aw've getten it?"

"Better see your lawyer about it."

"Oh! an' what 'ud ha' happened, now, just for argyment's sake, if yo'd dropped this ere precious dockyment i'stead o' 'liverin' it to me?"

The clerk was not prepared to say. "I don't know indeed. Perhaps the action couldn't go on."

"Oh! It couldn't, eh?"

"I'm not sure. But any way, I *have* served it: so it's no use going into that."

"Aye, yo'n sarved it," assented Jack. "Just step this way, will yo', while aw run mi e'en ovver it," and so saying, Jack led the way into the boiler-house.

Then Jack deliberately locked the door.

"What does this mean?" asked the clerk.

"It just meeans this. Yo' look as if a square meeal 'ud do yo' all th' gooid i'th' warld, an' aw reckon yo've got to eit this bit o' papper afore yo' cum aat."

Jack flung it at him and sat quietly down.

"Yo' may ta' yo'r time, aw'm no ways pressed mi sen. If yo' feel it a bit dry aw'll find yo' a can o' watter to wesh it dahn wi'; but eit it yo' do afore yo' see dayleet agen."

"But, Mr. Pinder!"

"Mr. Pinder, indeed yo' gorm fooil. A'm nooan Mr. Pinder. Mr. Pinder's a gentleman. Aw'm nobbut his man. Nah, ger agate: Sooiner yo'r' at it, an' sooiner yo'll ha' done."

And in the boiler-house Tom found the custodian of Co-op Mill and his prisoner. To Jack's indignation Tom quietly pocketed the petition and released the clerk with an apology and a solatium.

CHAPTER XII

TO say that the service of the bill in Chancery on Tom was like a bolt from the blue would be but feebly to describe the consternation with which he perused the portentous document, and in time realized its meaning and effect. Tom was absolutely unconscious that either in thought, word, or deed he had wronged any of his neighbours below stream. He had not, to his knowledge, turned more dye-water into the river, or taken more pure water from it than the reasonable working of his mill demanded, and had been afore-time accustomed by his predecessor. He had received no complaint from Mr. Tinker, no request for abatement of any nuisance he might unwittingly have committed, or infringement he might innocently have caused, Nehemiah Wimpenny in his zeal to do his client's behests, and in the animus he himself cherished against Tom, had even pretermitted the usual letter of courtesy preceding the firing of the first shot, the letter which in litigation is like the pourparlers of ambassadors preparatory to the formal declaration of war—an omission by the way, which Nehemiah had subsequent occasion to repent in sack-cloth and ashes. But for the present Nehemiah was jubilant and elate. Affidavits simply rained upon Tom. Photographers and surveyors swarmed about the banks of the Holme above and below Co-op Mill, and its waters were analysed and tested qualitatively and quantitatively as though the fate of empires depended on the issue. It was plain that Wimpenny meant to press the motion for an interim injunction, the effect of which would be to stop, if but temporarily, the work at Co-op Mill, and would of itself be as disastrous to its tenant as a final decree after full trial.

Tom and Ben discussed the situation in all its bearings.

"Aw'll tell yo' what it is," said Ben, "it's nowt but spite. Aw've known this stream, man and boy, for ovver fifty year, an' th' Co-op Mill as mony. An' a hangel fro' heaven couldn't mak' me believe as we'n done owt 'at Jabez Tinker's a reight to complain on. It's nowt but spite, Tom, it's th' owd tale ovver agen o' th' wolf an' th' lamb. He meeans to eit us up flesh an' bone, that's th' long an' th' short on it. An' what for? That lays ovver me entirely. Tha's nivver crossed him i' owt, has ta, Tom?"

And then, for the first time Tom told his friend of the offer Tinker had made to him at the close of his apprenticeship.

"An' what didn't ta tak' th' shop for, Tom? It 'ud ha' been a seet easier for thee nor startin' at th' Co-op?"

"Well, you see Ben, we'd made all our arrangements and—"

"Aye, aye, aw see, lad, tha wer' feeart aw sud think tha'd thrown me ovver. Eh, lad, me and yar Hannah an' Lucy too, for that matter, 'ud ha' gone to th' big house afore yo' sud ha' gone agen yo'r best interests for us."

"Oh, nonsense, Ben. I preferred the Co-op scheme. I never enjoyed my life so much as I have done since we went into it, and I shall never cast a regretful thought over either the labour or the wee bit money it has cost me. What worries me, Ben, so I can't sleep o'nights, is the thought of the men who have joined us and put their life-savings into the concern. I shall never hold up my head again if they are to lose their money through their confidence in me."

"And i' me, Tom, i' me, too. Yo' see, lad, yo' wer' i' a manner o' speikin' a stranger; but they'd known me all my life. But aw'm nooan feeart they'll blame oather on us, after th' first shock's ovver. But if they dunnot ma' Jabez Tinker sweeat for this job, they're nooan th' lad's aw tak' 'em for. If yo' know onybody 'at's interested i' insurance companies just yo' tell 'em to fight shy o' Wilberlee Mill," answered Ben savagely.

"That's nonsense, Ben, and yo know it. Now what's to be done?"

"Let's go see Mister Re'fearn," suggested Ben.

"I'm afraid he may think we want to ask him to help us out. We must take no money, Ben, from anybody. We'll keep our good names if we lose every stick we have."

"Oh! tha needn't be so tetchy, Tom, Redfearn's nooan fooil enough to lend us money to throw away. But yo' know he's had more deealin's wi' th' law nor us, an' though it gooas agen th' grain, aw expec' we'st ha' to put a lawyer on to this job. We mun set a thief to catch a thief, aw ma' no daat."

So Tom and Ben set off for Fairbank's and were fortunate enough to find Mr. Redfearn at home. He would hear no talk of business till all had sat down to a good dinner in his own well-furnished sitting room. "Folk always look on th' gloomy side of things when their belly's empty," he observed, "an' taking too doleful a way o' lookin' at things is just as foolish as takin' too cheerful a one," from which profound truism it will be seen that the farmer had learned something in the school of life that is not taught in academies or college. He listened at first to the story that Tom unfolded with the utmost attention and gravity. He even insisted on Tom reading to him the Chancery Bill and the pile of affidavits, but the prolixity and tautology of the legal phrasing soothed him like a soporific.

"It's like bein' i' Church," he muttered drowsily; and presently to complete the analogy, fell into a slumber from which he was only aroused by the entrance of Mrs. Redfearn with decanters, lemon, sugar and hot water, and a bottle of home-made rhubarb wine for the special cheer of Tom, whose habits she knew.

"Yo' munnot think aw've been asleep" said Fairbanks. "Aw wer' thinkin', an' aw can allus think best wi' mi e'en shut. Th' missus theer 'll tell yo' aw speik th' truth, for 'oo often thinks awm asleep when 'oo's givin' me a leckter upstairs; but aw know ivvery word oo's said th' next mornin' better than 'oo does hersen."

"An' much good my talkin' does you, and much notice you take of it," said Mrs. Redfearn, "but if yo' *have* been thinkin' let's hear what you've thowt on."

"Tell Aleck to put Bob i' th' shafts. We'r' bahn to Huddersfilt. This is a lawyer's job, Tom, an' aw think aw know th' varry man for yo'. Yo' know Sykes 0' Wrigley Mill. He's a lad i' Huddersfilt 'at used to be a sort o' teacher wi' Mr. Black, an' then wer' 'prenticed to a 'torney in th' taan. He's started for hissen now. He's as full o' law as an egg's full o' meit, so folk sayn. But he'll neer ma' much aat awm feeart, for when he gets on his hind legs to speik, d— me if he can say boh! to a gooise. His wits all go a wool gatherin' but he knows th' law, none better, aw'm towd. An' believe me or believe me not aw do think he's honest so that wi' his narvousness an' his honesty, he'll not mak' much aat as a 'torney. Aw'm feart oather on 'em's a drawback i' his job; but *both* together's enough to sink a clivverer man nor Edwin Sykes 'll ever be."

It cannot be said that the anxious trio got much comfort from Mr. Sykes. He told them frankly that at the very best the litigation must be costly and prolonged, and that in the long run the Court would probably be guided by the weight and authority of the expert evidence.

"Now that means purse against purse. And I'm afraid, Mr. Pinder, that our guns are neither so many nor so heavy as our opponent's. And Wimpenny won't give us much rest."

One grain of consolation they did bear away with them, however. Mr. Sykes was able to assure them that there was small likelihood of the Court granting an *interim* injunction.

"The Judge will know that to stop the work at the mill, even temporarily, would mean a probably irreparable loss. He won't prejudge the case on an interlocutary proceeding. That will give you time to turn yourself round, Mr. Pinder, and I should say your best plan would be to look out for a mill lower down the stream, *below* Mr. Tinker's. Then perhaps you can have a fling at him some fine day."

"Eh! he's a deep 'un is Ned for all his quiet ways. Talks like a judge doesn't he? What's that word— inter summat?"

"Interlocutory," said Tom.

"An' just think 'at aw've cuffed that lad mony a time when aw've found him moonin abaat Fairbanks wi' a book i' his hand. It's just wonderful what education 'll do."

It did not remain a secret in Holmfirth that the new Co-op was in Chancery—name of dread import. *Omne ignotum pro magnifico.* The utmost that even the fairly well-informed could tell about Chancery was that it was a bottomless pit from which there was no escape, or a kind of legal den where the lawyers fed on the oysters called estates, flinging out the shells for the suitors to quarrel or get reconciled over. That was the utmost; but it was enough. Tom called a private meeting of all the hands and told them the facts. Their first feeling was one of blank dismay, their next and abiding feeling one of dogged resistance.

"It's the devil's plot, and hatched in hell," said the spokesman of the men who had money in the concern. "But we'll fight to the finish, an' bi what we'n heard abaat this here Chancery, th' finish 'll be abaat th' same time as th' Day o' Judgment."

The news reached Dorothy through the faithful Betty.

"Well, the law can't hurt Mr. Pinder if he's done nothing wrong," said her young mistress "The law is for evil-doers, and I suppose Mr. Pinder is not an evil-doer. He's a very innocent looking one if he is."

"Ah! it's little yo' know about th' law, or me oather, come to that. But aw keep mi ears oppen an' they *do* say,—"

"Which, being interpreted, means 'Serjeant Ramsden of the County Constabulary,'" interrupted Dorothy, with an arch smile. "Well, what do they, *alias* Serjeant Ramsden, say."

"Why," answered Betty in no wise abashed. "He, aw meean they, say 'at it doesn't matter a brass farden i' Chancery whether a man's i' th' reight or th' wrang. It's th' longest purse at wins i' th' long run. Th' Serjeant says, miss, 'at if Tom wins i' one court yo'r uncle can peeal to a higher court, an' on an' on till it reaches th' Lord Hissen."

"The Lords, you mean, perhaps, Betty."

"Weil, it's all as one, for ought aw can see. It's naked we come into th' world, and naked we go aat on it, an aw reckon Tom 'll be stripped pretty stark afore th' case gets up to th' Lords."

"But what's it all about, Betty? Dear me, if being in love makes a woman so tiresome as you are, I hope such a calamity will never befall me. What *has* Mr. Pinder done?"

"Oh!" said Betty, "there's no hope o' yo'r escapin' it unless so be as yo'r minded to play a very one-sided game. But if yo' ax me what th' law stir's abaat, as far as aw can mak' aat th' *mester* says it's abaat th' watter-reets to th' mill, but *folk* sen it's nowt but spite, so nah yo' han it plump an' fair."

"Meaning that my uncle has gone to law with his former apprentice from some petty feeling of jealousy, or just to cripple him or even ruin him?"

"That's th' talk o'th village, choose ha."

"Well, I don't believe it, Betty. My uncle is incapable of such conduct. But I'll soon find out for myself. Get me my hat and cape this moment. I'm going out." And Dorothy walked with quick, resolute steps to Ben Garside's house. She was fortunate enough to find Lucy alone, and of this she was glad, for she was in no humour to enjoy Hannah's garrulous speech.

"What's this I hear, Lucy, about my uncle going to law with Mr. Pinder. I can make neither head nor tail of Betty at home, so I've come to you. It seems to me there's something about law that forbids people to be intelligible when they're talking of it?"

"Your uncle," said Lucy very gravely, "has served a Bill in Chancery, I think they call it, on Tom."

"What in the name of common sense is a Bill in Chancery? I know what a dressmaker's bill is, but the other variety is beyond me."

"I don't quite know all the ins and outs of it," replied Lucy, still very seriously. "But so far as I can make out your uncle complains that Tom fouls the stream and takes more water out than he's any right to, and of course as Wilberlee is lower down the stream it must injure your uncle if it's true."

"And is it true?" asked Dorothy.

"Both Tom and father say there isn't a word of truth in it."

"And you believe them?"

"Of course I do," said Lucy simply.

"Then what is there to look so gloomy about? 'Pon my word, Lucy, if you go on in the dumps like that I'll shake you. I only wish somebody would bring a false charge against me. There's nothing I should enjoy more than making them prove their words at no end of trouble and expense, and then laughing at the faces they'd pull when they failed to do it. If that's Chancery I call Chancery a very good joke."

"Aye, but Tom says it will take all they have in the world to prove that they're in the right, and that month after month, for goodness knows how long, the money that should go for wages and in carrying on the mill must go to their lawyer. So it means ruin, win or lose."

"And that's what they call law, is it?" exclaimed Dorothy. "Anybody could see a set of men noodles made it. But what are they going to do?"

"Just carry on as long as they can, and then I don't know what. It doesn't matter so much for father. He can take to his hand-loom again, and now I'm so much stronger I hope to be a help to him. I can spin wonderful. But it will be a sad blow for Tom. His whole heart and soul were in the mill. Not for the money. I never knew anyone care less for money than Tom. But the hands were so contented and father says it was to prove a social and economic revolution, whatever that may mean."

"It means apparently," said Dorothy "ruining yourself for the general good. Does Tom,—Mr. Pinder, take it much to heart?"

"He pretends not to, always tries to put a cheerful face on when he talks to mother. But I know it's just crushing the youth out of him. But it's because those that went in with him may have to lose their money. And father says there'll be no room for Tom in these parts if th' Co-op's stopped. The other manufacturers are sure to side with your uncle, and they'll none of them give Tom a job if he asked for it."

"Oh! they wouldn't, eh?" Then suddenly. "Is Tom *very* dear to you, Lucy?"

Lucy flushed, and her eyes fell before Dorothy's questioning look. But her voice, though low, was very steady as she spoke.

"I love him very much, Dorothy. Next to the love I have for mother and father there is no one in the world to me like Tom. He is my big brother, you know," she added, with a faint smile.

"Oh! Those big brothers have a way of turning into big lovers," said Dorothy. "That's just their artful way. They get a poor innocent confiding girl to feel like a sister, and then when she begins to feel she cannot very well do without him, nothing will do but a ring and a parson. I know them," said Dorothy viciously.

"Tom will never be *my* lover, Dorothy," said Lucy, quietly.

"And why pray, Miss Pale-face?"

"Because he loves someone else. He has loved her for years."

"What Parson Tom engaged! Tragedy upon tragedy. There are two blighted beings then; the course of their true love, ruffled by this dreadful Chancery. And who's the luckless she? This is a world of surprises. Tom was not such a bat as to look outside this house for a prettier face and a sweeter heart than he'll find inside it."

"I didn't say Tom was engaged," said Lucy.

"I know you didn't. Well, if it isn't I'll not venture another guess. Still, I'm a daughter of Eve after all, and I confess I hope Mr. Pinder is not going to throw himself away on some good-looking empty-head of a girl—a calf-love. You said it was a malady of standing, contracted young, if I remember."

"Yes, she's good-looking," said Lucy.

"*And* empty-headed?"

"You wouldn't like me to say so."

"I! What have my likes to do with it? It's no concern of mine. Really, you stimulate my curiosity. Is it anyone I know? Does she go to our chapel?"

"Yes, she goes to Aenon," said Lucy. "But there, I'll tell you no more."

"Oh! I can guess, and thank you for nothing. It's that apprentice of Miss Baxter's, the milliner. Now don't deny it. I saw Mr. Pinder looking at her very much the last Sunday he honoured Aenon. The girl with the green gloves. The taste of some men—in dress I mean."

"Have it your own way," said Lucy, "you'll find out someday, perhaps."

"Oh! Bother Tom Pinder and his lady-loves green gloves as well. However did we get talking of such a trifle! Now, seriously, Lucy, do your father and the other want to fight this case, and can they win if they can fight."

"They say so. But what's the use of talking. If ifs and buts were apples and ducks!"

"And who knows but they are," said Dorothy, springing to her feet. She kissed Lucy with a bright face. "Don't lose heart, little pale-face. They aren't beaten yet. Tell them not to give in. I say so. Now, good-bye,—you're sure it's green gloves?"

"You know I never said so. But good-bye."

It is never safe to be certain about anything connected with the law; but the opinion may be hazarded that never in the long years of his tenancy did the office of Mr. Edwin Sykes receive a fairer client than the young lady who was closeted with that sedate professor of the gloomy science not long after the interview just recorded. The young lady did not seem in the least impressed by the sombre volumes of statutes and reports that lined the walls of the room, nor yet by the tape-bound bundles of foolscap, draft, and brief, neatly docketed, that were spread on a table by the lawyer's side, so many pot-eggs, the ribald alleged, to tempt the unwary to lay.

Dorothy had accepted the chair Mr. Sykes had handed her, but flicked its horse-hair cushion with a delicate cambric handkerchief before complying with his invitation to be seated.

"How very musty everything is," she remarked in explanation. "If I'd walked the length of New Street after sitting on your chair without first dusting it, everyone would have said either that I'd been knocked down by a tramp and robbed on my way from Holmfirth, or been to visit an attorney. There mayn't be much difference in the consequences," she added reflectively, "but I don't want all the world to know my business. You can keep a secret, I suppose, Mr. Sykes?"

"It is part of my business," the lawyer answered.

"Even from Mrs. Sykes—there is a Mrs. Sykes, I suppose."

"Well, yes, as you are good enough to ask, there *is* a Mrs. Sykes,—and till to-day I thought her the most daring of her sex" he would have liked to add.

"Ah! That's a comfort. Now I can tell you everything. You wouldn't think now I'm in great trouble, and I want you to help me out of it, and not a living soul but you must know about it." As Dorothy looked radiantly happy as she made this doleful plaint it may be assumed that Mr. Sykes argued her case was not so desperate as her words.

"If you will tell me, Miss Tinker, the nature of your trouble I may be able to prescribe for you. We poor lawyers are not so clever as the doctors. We can't diagnose by the looks, or, I confess, I should not advise you to abandon hope."

"And this is the lawyer Ben said couldn't say Boh! to a goose," thought Dorothy.

"Now, how shall I begin?" she said.

"Suppose you try the beginning," he suggested.

"You know Mr. Pinder, of Holmfirth?" asked Dorothy, glancing at a formidable pile of papers on the desk labelled "Pinder at the suit of Tinker."

"If you mean Mr. Tom Pinder, of Co-op Mill, Hinchliff Mill, I think I may go so far as to say I do."

"Come, that's something," said Dorothy. "You are so very cautious you might have added 'without prejudice.' Now is it a very bad case?" she concluded.

"Really! Miss Tinker."

"Now I don't want any humming and ha-ing, you know, Mr. Sykes. I take a very great interest in Mr. Pinder—well, not in him you know. That's ridiculous: but in Lucy, you know" and Dorothy nodded with great significance, whilst the lawyer felt that he was getting deeper and deeper into a bog.

"I confess I don't know," he said, "and I must ask you to be a little more explicit."

"Well,—dear me! How tiresome you are—it's about this quarrel between uncle Jabez and Mr. Pinder."

"Are you Mr. Tinker's niece? Then really, Miss Tinker, I think if your uncle wants to open up any negotiations towards a settlement he'd better send his lawyer."

"What! Nehemiah Wimpenny! How could he? Didn't I tell you no one was to know anything of my visit but you and me, and Mr. Wimpenny's the very last man in the world I'd chose for any errand of mine."

"But in what can I help you, Miss Tinker? You will understand, of course, that I cannot discuss my client's affairs with anyone without his knowledge and privilege,—no, not though an angel drop from the clouds."

"I suppose that's a *rechauffé* from one of your pretty sayings to Lizzie Hudson. Oh! Yes! I know all about it Mr. Sykes. Lizzie and I were at school together, and I thought it just odious of her not to ask me to her wedding."

"And only a minute ago she asked me if there were a Mrs. Sykes," reflected the harassed young man. "Will she ever get to her story?"

"And that's what gave me confidence to come to you, Mr. Sykes. Not the not being asked to the wedding, but because you were Lizzie's husband, and I did think of calling on her and bringing her with me, but she'd have guessed,"—and here Dorothy stopped abruptly.

"Yes, she'd have guessed?" said Mr. Sykes, encouragingly.

"Never you mind what Lizzie would have guessed. It's about this lawsuit I've come. I suppose I'd better come to the point."

"Wish to heaven you would," thought the lawyer.

"Now which do you think will win, uncle or Mr. Pinder?"

"If law and justice were one, Miss Tinker, there could only be one answer—Mr. Pinder."

"But they aren't,—so that means Tom, that's Mr. Pinder, will lose."

"You really must excuse me, Miss Tinker, I've said, even now, more than I'd any right to say."

"But don't you see, I want to help Mr. Pinder to win. That's what I came for. Didn't I tell you? Dear me, I wish I'd gone to Lizzie first. *She* isn't slow, at any rate."

Mr. Sykes smiled. "No, my wife is not slow-witted, and I'm afraid I am. Perhaps that's why she took pity on me."

"Shouldn't wonder. Now the question is, how can we help Mr. Pinder, I mean Lucy, of course."

Mr. Sykes felt his brain beginning to give way in the vain striving after his visitor's drift. "Lucy," he murmured hopelessly.

"Yes, Lucy. She's my dearest friend. And she's to marry Tom,—Mr. Pinder I mean. That is to say she would if he would; but she says he wont, and perhaps she's right. Anyway, she wanted him to win this case, and I want him to win this case, and what's more, I mean him to win this case,—for Lucy's sake, of course, because she says it's all spite, and neither law nor justice, and you say so too, don't you?"

"Yes, I do."

"Now Lucy says it's all a matter o' money, I don't mean matrimony; for goodness sake *don't* repeat that stupid jest. But I've had a long talk with Lucy, and she says it will cost Tom and Ben, that's Lucy's father, you know, heaps and heaps of money to fight the case to the end, and that's just what they haven't got. You're the blood-sucker, I suppose?"

"Yes, Miss Tinker, I'm afraid I'm one of them—for Lizzie's sake, of course."

Dorothy looked sharply at Mr. Sykes, and there was a slight flush of colour on her cheek as she repeated "Oh, yes, for Lizzie's sake, of course." Was it possible that this very sedate young man could guess beyond his brief?

"Now *I've* got some money; at least I suppose so; though I've never seen it. But I've always understood my poor father that I don't remember, made a will, and I was the only child. Now you must get to know all about that, and Mr. Pinder and Ben are not to go to the wall for want of money. Do you understand that?"

"But am I really to understand, Miss Tinker, that you propose to spend your money in helping my clients in fighting your own uncle?"

"I don't care if he's twenty times my uncle, though once time once is enough, thank you. But if he's mean enough to try to ruin Ben Garside—"

"And Mr. Pinder?" put in the lawyer, quite casually.

"And I thought this lawyer stupid," thought Dorothy, but ignored the interruption.

"Then I'm mean enough to fight him with his own weapons, uncle or no uncle."

"It sounds parlously like champerty and maintenance," said Mr. Sykes, more to himself than to Dorothy.

"There's no sham about it, sir. I mean every word of it. I'll let my uncle see he can't treat me as he does poor aunt, like dirt under his feet."

"God grant I'm spared the aunt," groaned Edwin Sykes inwardly "what with her Lucy and her own quite bewildering self there are quite women enough in the case, without introducing an aunt."

"If I follow you, Miss Tinker, you are desirous, for your friend Lucy's sake, to help my client with money to carry on this unfortunate litigation. Have you any idea what the costs may amount to?"

"Not the slightest. But that doesn't matter. The money shall be found."

"I've another question to ask, Miss Tinker, and a very delicate one. May I ask how old you are?"

"And this is the man that can't say Boh! to a goose," again thought Dorothy.

"I suppose if I'd assurance enough for a lawyer I should tell you I'm as old as my tongue and a little older than my teeth," replied Dorothy merrily.

"That's exactly what I'm driving at," was the reply very seriously uttered. "I'm not at all sure that I should be justified in taking your money without my client's knowledge and consent even if you were of full age, but from a minor!"

"Pshaw, I sha'n't be a minor all my life. I shall be twenty one next birthday, and that's on May 21st."

"There's many things may happen between now and your birthday."

"Exactly, your client may be ruined and Lucy may be broken-hearted, and all because of a silly punctilio."

"Have you a copy of your father's will."

"Ah! Now you're talking. I haven't; but I suppose one can be procured. I should like to see one any way, for even a woman may be allowed a little curiosity as to her own fortune. After all, I may be as poor as a church mouse. But you can find out that for me and have no qualms, I hope."

"Oh, yes, I shall be pleased to get you a copy of the will. I apprehend that you come to your inheritance in the general way."

"And that is?"

"If and when you attain the age of twenty-one years, or marry under that age. By the way, that suggests one simple solution of the difficulty, you might marry."

"Oh! That's out of the question."

"Not for, ahem!"—the young lawyer raised his long white hand to his mouth and coughed very slightly "not for Lucy's sake?"

Dorothy rose with some dignity to close the interview. "Let me know please when have got the copy of the will. Meanwhile, I suppose I can rely on your discretion," and Dorothy made to go.

"Nay, Miss Tinker, you have not permitted me to say my say. I am well aware that Mr. Pinder is a poor man. I am also a poor man. I had not intended to trouble my client in the event of defeat for more than the actual costs out of pocket. Those I couldn't afford to advance. If you give me your simple word that these shall be paid sooner or later by someone, no matter who," and here there was the barest suspicion of a twinkle in the young man's eyes as he added, "or for whose sake, rest assured I shall not allow Mr. Pinder's cause to fail for want of professional assistance. More I cannot promise."

Dorothy extended her hand. "And you have my word that if I live you shall not suffer. I do so want Tom, I mean Mr. Pinder, to win if he's in the right. I'll do almost anything rather than he should be borne down simply by his poverty. I say *almost* anything. I draw the line at marrying, you know; besides," and a look of sudden remembrance sprung to Dorothy's eyes.

"Yes, besides?"

"Oh, it's something you wouldn't understand, about a horrid girl with green gloves," and Dorothy tripped away with a smile and a nod.

"This case fairly bristles with women," mused Edwin Sykes. Quintilian was right: *Nulla causa sine femina.*

And the months went by and the trial of the great cause of "Pinder at the suit of Tinker" seemed as far off as ever. First blood had been drawn by the defendant: the motion for an *interim* injunction and an account of profits had been refused by the Court, and the judge had made certain observation as to the precipitancy with which the action had been commenced that made that respectable practitioner, Mr. Nehemiah Wimpenny, who was present at the hearing of the motion, long that the floor of the Court would gape and swallow him to the bowels of the earth,—anywhere out of hearing of that calm, gentle voice dropping vitriol in honeyed accents. In proportion as Tom and Ben and the friends of Co-op Mill rejoiced, so did Mr. Tinker rage and storm. From the very filing of the Bill he had regretted that in his anger he had instituted proceedings that none knew better than himself were purely vexatious and vindictive. The monitor of the night watches had left him little peace. In vain he had tried to silence the still small voice by arguing to himself that to stop Co-op Mill would be to stop the irreligious services which more and more abundantly attracted men from the orthodox ministrations of Mr. Jones and the other chapels of the district. Mr. Tinker was no Jesuit. Again and again he more than half-resolved to bid Mr. Wimpenny stay his hand he would have been glad to be quit of the lawsuit, even if he had to pay the defendant's costs as well as his own. But now that he was smarting under a rebuff, and his enemy was exulting in a momentary triumph,—give way now! No! That was not the stuff Jabez Tinker was made of. To be bested by a boy, a nobody that owed all he was and all he had to him, a serpent whom he had warmed in his breast,—it could not, it should not be.

And Nehemiah Wimpenny artfully fanned the flames of Mr. Tinker's wrath. He pooh-poohed the temporary check.

"It wasn't an engagement, my dear sir; an interlocutory motion is a mere skirmish, a sort of reconnoitering expedition, a simple device to draw the enemy's fire. Now we know where they are. They have had to show their hand, sir. We know where their weak spots are."

"That's all very fine," grumbled Tinker, gloomily. "We may have found *their* weak spot; but it seems to me they've found one or two of ours—and one sore one, too, judging by the way you squirmed when my Lord rubbed it into you."

"Oh! That's nothing," laughed Wimpenny. "I took his salt *cum grano*, and I don't doubt you'll attach the same importance to this little *contretemps*. The trial's the thing."

"You must win this case, Wimpenny, if money can win it."

"Money can do anything in this world," said Wimpenny, "at least that's my professional experience."

Mr. Tinker left the lawyer's office in anything but a tranquil frame of mind. He felt like a conspirator in a sordid crime. The very paltriness of the issues and the insignificance of his opponent galled and fretted him. But how retreat now that all the world was saying that Tom Pinder was more than a match for Jabez Tinker?

CHAPTER XIII.

FROM this time onward for some months there is little to record. The parties to the great law suit awaited with what patience they might the final trial of the all-important issue. The failure of the attempt to stay the work at Co-op Mill pending the final decision secured for Tom Pinder and his colleagues a welcome breathing space. If it were possible all hands bent themselves to their respective tasks with increased energy. The check to the plaintiff gave them heart for the present and hope for the future. Every precaution was taken to guard against any fouling or minishing of the stream.

The people of the Holme Valley are even to this day a litigious, disputatious race. They are law-loving in an inverted sense. An average native does not feel that he has lived his life unless he has at least once been prosecutor or plaintiff in a "law do." With the poet he may be supposed to sing—

> "'Tis better to have sued and lost
>
> Than never sued at all."

And the pros and cons of any *cause celebre* are discussed wherever men foregather long before the fierce light of the Courts beat upon the matter. The "company" of the village public constitute themselves into an informal jury. Generally each side has its adherents. The witnesses, or such of them as frequent the houses of entertainment, tell and tell again the story they are to repeat in Court. The strong and the weak points of the evidence are discussed, criticized, cross-examined, as it were, with all the acumen of the native mind, and all the freedom of irresponsibility, and of the license that ignores the trammelling confines of the laws of evidence. The peculiar qualifications of the local lawyers engaged are discussed with a particularity that would very much surprise, and not always gratify the gentlemen whose merits and demerits are so freely appraised. Illustrations drawn from previous forensic contests are liberally drawn upon. There is generally in the company some man who has purchased by bitter experience the right to speak with authority, who airs his knowledge of the intricate mazes of legal proceedings. His conversation bristles with technical terms. He speaks glibly of writs, summonses, subpoenas, judgments, appeals, bills of costs and the taxation thereof. If by good fortune he possesses a copy of an ancient text-book and can produce text and verse in support of his assertions he is an opponent to be admired, but shunned. In public-house controversy the man who is most dogmatic, who can shout loudest and longest is usually adjudged the victor, especially if he is prepared to back his opinion and table the money; but even he must yield to the visible *dicta* of the printed word. By the time the cause is ripe for hearing, bets have been made and taken; the adherents of the adversaries have ranged themselves; there are the village Montagues and Capulets, and the local attorney goes into Court the champion of a score of clients whose very existence he is unaware of.

Now in Holmfirth Jabez Tinker's defeat had been celebrated at the *Cropper's Arms* by a beast-heart supper. The landlord had provided the beast-heart in the due recognition of the policy of throwing a sprat to catch a mackerel. There had been some talk of inviting Edwin Sykes to preside at the supper, but even Holmfirth hardihood has its bounds. Tom Pinder, the landlord had shrewdly surmised, would prove a kill-joy, and as for Ben Garside, though every feeling of his heart said "yes" to the invitation, he was kept away partly by his own sense of propriety, but still more by the emphatic injunctions of his better half.

"Tha'rt nooan bahn to shaat, Ben, afore tha'rt aat o' th' wood, an' when tha does shaat, tha mun do thi shaatin' i' decent company, an' not amang yon' beer-swillin' hogs at th' *Cropper's Arms*. What do they care whether yo' win or looise? There isn't one on 'em but 'ud sell yo' for a quart o' ale. Yo'r nooan bahn to lower yo'rsen bi mixin' amang that lot, it says i'th Book theer 'at i' vain the net is spread i' th' seet o' ony bird; but th' kind o' bird at th' net o' th' *Cropper's* is set for mun be bats darkened wi' brewer's grain, an' that's all t' grain some on 'em feed on."

It did not lessen Jabez Tinker's irritation and general sense of all things being awry that he was in many ways made conscious that the only public opinion that he really cared about—that of his own neighbourhood—was dead against him. Mr. Tinker affected to despise the sentiments of his neighbours, and he certainly could not be accused of stooping to court popularity. But no man is really indifferent to the good or ill-word of his own little world. And Jabez was aware that even his own household was not on his side. To be sure in the rare visits he paid to his ailing wife at Harrogate he was sure of one sympathetic listener as he unfolded in brief, terse sentences the story of his wrongs, in which he had almost persuaded himself to believe, and of the indignities which he concluded must be patent to everyone. But Dorothy he knew to be openly and avowedly in the camp of the enemy, and this was an ever rankling sore. Jabez had declared to himself that his niece was the illest of all birds fouling its own nest. She was a Tinker, his brother's daughter, and it was her bounden duty to take his side and fight his battle whether he were right or wrong. The mere stranger and passer-by, they might scan and scrutinize; but for the girl who slept under his roof and sat at his table to condemn her heart, was the blackest treason and gross ingratitude Jabez had never heard of Walpole's reply to the county member who promised his vote whenever he should think the member in the right. "I want men who'll back me right or wrong: through thick and thin." But Jabez had the same views as to the countenance he was entitled to expect from his niece.

And Dorothy was made to feel that her uncle's feelings were very bitter towards her. The subject of the lawsuit was never referred to, but Jabez, never a demonstrative or genial relative, now became cold, repellent, caustic. If there was a death in the house, Betty declared, it could not be gloomier, and if it wasn't for leaving Miss Dorothy she wouldn't care how soon she changed her name and state.

All this was, one may be sure, not conducive to Dorothy's serenity. She had, too, at times, a sense of treachery to her uncle. Was she justified in secretly aiding and abetting his enemy, even if that enemy were an enemy *malgré lui*? How was she to be certain that what most people said was true, that her uncle was merely persecuting a rival in trade to crush him? Could she, indeed, believe that of that stern, austere man, the pillar of Aenon Chapel, quoted and esteemed throughout the whole Baptist denomination who of all other men, she had thought, however unlovable was at least a just man. These considerations were of themselves sufficient to disquiet a young and sensitive mind. There was another. Was Dorothy honest with herself? It was Dorothy who asked the question. And when man or maid has come to the pass of asking so searching a question it is odds that conscience has a ready "No." Was it *par exemple*, quite the truth, the whole truth, and nothing but the truth, that it was only for her friend's sake, and for the triumph of abstract justice against an unholy conspiracy that Dorothy had so overleaped the bounds of maidenly reserve and perilled her fortune in the quicksands of the law. And when Dorothy, in the still watches of the night, thus put Dorothy's self into the witness box, and her fluttering heart gave its blunt reply, Dorothy was fain to draw the coverlet over a winsome face and hide the crimson blushes e'en from the sightless eyes of night, and toss and turn upon her uneasy couch courting and yet dreading the sleep that brought dreams that should not be for maids uncourted and unwon.

And to nights thus harassed followed days embittered by her uncle's harsh, forbidding aloofness, and, to fill her cup to the brim, by the now unmistakable attentions of Nehemiah Wimpenny. That young ornament of the law had fully satisfied himself that Dorothy was worth the winning. He had even gone so far as to transfer his valued custom from the *Rose and Crown*, and Polly was left lamenting but sustaining her desertion with more philosophy than Ariadne or Dido.

"Good riddance of bad rubbish," was all she said, and forthwith reserved her sweetest smiles and most languishing glances for the village surgeon, who had long sighed in vain, eclipsed by the greater attractions or,—may it be suggested?—by the deeper purse of the village attorney.

Nehemiah was now a constant visitor at Wilberlee, and by Jabez Tinker was always welcomed with a warmth that increased when the manufacturer perceived that the attorney's visits were not purely professional. Jabez saw in his niece's marriage relief from a daily source of irritation. True, the day drew nigh when he must be prepared to produce and vouch his accounts as executor and trustee of his late brother. But Jabez flattered himself that if anyone could be counted on to keep Wilberlee out of Chancery it would be Nehemiah Wimpenny, if Nehemiah Wimpenny were also Dorothy's husband.

"Lawyers are fond of law, but it must be at somebody else's expense," he argued. "Wimpenny won't be such a fool as to share my cake with others, when sooner or later he can have it all himself."

But Nehemiah found the wooing of Dorothy up-hill work. The Holmfirth "Don Juan" was accustomed to the easy conquests of the bar-room and the side-wings of the Huddersfield Theatre. He found it difficult to teach his tongue the language to which it was a stranger, and after a painful hour or so spent in the parlour of Wilberlee in the attempt to interest or amuse the young heiress, his whole being cried out for the unrestrained freedom of Polly's conversation, and for the ready appreciation Polly had always vouchsafed to his jests and innuendos which even Nehemiah knew would ensure his prompt expulsion from Wilberlee, probably at the point of the owner's toe.

But as yet, at all events, he felt himself securely in Mr. Tinker's goodwill. He had even gone so far as to drop a not obscure hint as to the aspirations he cherished in what he was pleased to call his heart.

"Win this accursed law-suit for me," Jabez had said, "and we will talk about matters less important. Meanwhile, you had better make as sure of my niece's consent as you may of mine. Not that Dorothy would stay for that. I wish you joy of her, that's all. Women are kittle-cattle to shoe. I don't think you'll find my niece an exception to her sex."

But Nehemiah, despite the guardian's favour, confessed to himself that if he progressed at all in Dorothy's good graces, his progress was crabwise—backwards. What *could* he talk about? He feigned an interest in the sermons of the Rev. David Jones. But Dorothy yawned at the very mention of the minister's name. Then he affected an interest in her Sunday School class, but Dorothy said Sunday School classes were generally a combination of scholars who didn't want to learn and teachers who didn't know how to teach, and as she felt herself to be one of the latter class, she was determined to give her class up. Then the desperate lover essayed his powers at the retailing of local gossip, telling with unction how young D— was supposed to be casting sheep's eyes at Nancy N—; how the plain daughter of the vicar's warden was shamelessly setting her cap at the new curate, and how the hue of Mrs. J—'s nose-end was erroneously attributed to poverty of blood.

In one topic only could he prevail on Dorothy to take an interest at all, and that was a topic on which Nehemiah was eloquent enough at first, but of which in time he became uncommonly shy,—the vexed question of water rights, with especial reference to the great case of "Pinder at the suit of Tinker."

"So you've lost your application for an *interim* injunction?" Dorothy said demurely one night after tea, when her uncle had hurried off to a deacon's meeting, promising speedy return, and hospitably pressing his guest to stay for the substantial supper of cold meats and pastry with which our hardier fathers braved the terrors of nightmare and dyspepsia.

"Oh, that's nothing, Miss Dorothy," said Nehemiah jauntily, glad of a subject of conversation in which he flattered himself he could shine, "nothing at all, I can assure you."

"Then you expected to lose?"

"Well, not say expect, but fortune of war you know, fortune of war, glorious uncertainty, and all that, don'tcherknow."

"But you are certain to win in the end, or is there a glorious uncertainty about that?"

"Oh! yes, sure to win in the long run. Pinder can't stand the racket. Expected he'd have caved in long since. Can't understand it. Sykes must be risking more than I'd like to. Sticks like a leech at all points."

"There's an old saying, Mr. Wimpenny, that Tear'em's a good dog, but Holdfast's a better. Perhaps Mr. Sykes is one of your Holdfast breed."

"Ah! Ah! very good, indeed, Miss Tinker. Must remember that. But we shall shake him off yet, you bet."

"Thank you, I don't bet."

"Beg pardon, Miss Tinker, only a way of speaking, don'tcherknow. No offence," and Nehemiah told himself that Dorothy was a very difficult girl indeed.

"So you think you'll wear Mr. Pinder out. Do you mean his patience or his means?"

"Oh! patience is cheap enough. I dare say Pinder has plenty of that. It's the poor man's assets, don'tcherknow."

"I'm afraid that's often too true, Mr. Wimpenny."

"Well, I could have sworn it was about all the stock-in-trade Pinder had to break him in. But somebody's finding the money, or else Sykes is a bigger fool than I take him to be."

"Money, money, money, you men seem to talk and think of nothing but money."

"And they say, Miss Tinker, that women have a very pretty notion of spending what the men think and talk about."

"Well, I for one would rather talk of something else. You're sure, now, uncle is going to win this case?"

"Well, of course I *think* so, or I shouldn't have advised the proceedings."

"But I suppose you advised the application for a what-do-you call it injunction. But you failed in that? Now I want you to tell me all about uncle's grievances against Mr. Pinder. It is so delightful to find a lawyer who can make things so beautifully simple to a poor ignoramus of a girl like me. I can see now why you have so many cases in the Courts."

"Oh! Dorothy, Dorothy."

And forthwith the willing victim of woman's guile talked at large of water encroachment, of unlawful ochre-water diverted from its natural course so that it passed by the head-goit of Co-op Mill, and only entered the river as it sped on to Wilberlee, to Mr. Tinker's great damage and detriment. Never was Nehemiah more eloquent, never had he so wrapt and intent a listener.

"She's just the woman for a lawyer's wife," thought Nehemiah, as he talked. "I'll practise my speeches on her."

"But, after all, it's no use wearying you with all these details, Miss Tinker. We shall never reach a final trial. Your uncle isn't the man to take a beating, and if we're trounced in one Court we shall go to another. Pinder can't stand the racket. I call it downright dishonest of him taking the savings of those deluded Co-opers, as they call them, and spending it on Sykes. Of course it's all the better for me. But the whole thing'll fizzle out in the Bankruptcy Court, and I take it there'll be no necessity to wait for the Court of Chancery's decision. Want of shekels will decide the question before we're much older, mark my words."

"How very charming!" quoth Dorothy. "Really, Mr. Wimpenny, I don't know how to thank you for making everything so clear to me. Now these water-foulings by Mr. Pinder, I suppose anyone can see them? You've interested me so much I've a good notion to turn myself into an amateur expert; if that isn't a contradiction in terms."

"Not more anomalous than a woman with sense," reflected Nehemiah. But he said with something of an effort.

"Well, the fact is Miss Tinker, there isn't very much to see. It's the eye of science, don'tcherknow, that we go by in these cases. The eye of science," he repeated, evidently pleased with that phrase.

"Well, anyway, I'll try what the eye of a woman can see some fine day. Perhaps I may find out something that has escaped all you clever men, and then you'll have to take me up to London as a witness, I hope."

It was, perhaps, in pursuance of this quite commendable resolve, that Dorothy one bright, cloudless day in August, clad in a close-fitting costume that permitted the graceful movement of her limbs without concealing the charming lines of her form came suddenly upon Tom Pinder in the neighbourhood of the Isle of Skye. Dorothy, who had, as far as the nature of the ground permitted, followed the course of the stream as it flowed from its source down the valley, was warm and flushed from the toilsome ascent, but the glow of health was on her cheek and its sparkle in her eye. Tom, on the contrary, was pale and careworn. Too sedulous devotion to his necessary work, too little rest of mind and body, but above all the constant anxiety and uncertainty for the future were telling their tale upon his robust, vigorous, elastic frame. But a glad light sprang to his eyes, and a happy smile to his lips as he met Dorothy's outstretched hand.

"You are quite a stranger, Mr. Pinder; it is ages since I caught more than a glimpse of you. Betty is quite fretting that you never go to see her now. Vows she is wearing to skin and bone; but it must be by the eye of faith she attests the process."

"No. I do not often get to Betty's kitchen now," said Tom, with something very like a sigh. "More's the pity; you see, I can't very well go openly, and you wouldn't have me go like a thief in the night."

"No, I would not. It's all this wretched law business, of course. But which way were you going, uphill, or down?"

"Bilberry! Well, there'll be a breeze from the water's face. But I think I ought to be turning homewards."

"May I accompany you, Miss Tinker? You pass near my own mill, you know."

"La! *my* mill! how grand it sounds. I think I should like to say *my* mill, and to feel that the hands were *my* people. 'Tis a relic of feudalism, I suppose."

Tom raised his eyebrows almost imperceptibly. He had not credited Dorothy with much historical knowledge.

"Oh, you needn't look so superior, Mr. Wiseacre. I've read a book or two, though I don't teach classes on Sunday, like a naughty, defiant unbeliever, as some folk are. But there, you shan't accompany me homewards. That will perhaps teach you to veil your superiority."

"I assure you, Miss Tinker," began Tom, but boggled at his disclaimer, for he was a poor liar, and Dorothy had; divined his thoughts shrewdly.

"Instead," said Dorothy, enjoying his confusion, "instead I will go on with you to Bilberry Reservoir: I've as much right to the cool breeze from its surface as you have, and if you've no very great objection, Mr. Pinder, you may give me your arm up the hill."

Tom flushed to the brow and, feeling weak as water, hoped that Dorothy's ears were not as quick, as her eyes, for sure she would have heard the beating of his heart.

"Do you know, Miss Dorothy, I think it's the very first time I've been asked to give a lady my arm."

"Been asked?" said Dorothy, and part withdrew her little hand.

"Or given it, of course. I should never dream of giving it unasked."

"Oh!" said Dorothy, and her hand stole back again. "What, not to Lucy?"

"Oh, well, you know. Well, perhaps Lucy may have taken it sometimes when she felt overdone can't say for sure. One doesn't think of these things."

"Oh! don't they?" queried Dorothy, and her hand again made for retreat.

"Not with Lucy, I mean," added Tom.

"Oh!" and the hand now was restful.

They walked slowly towards the reservoir, leaving the highway, and treading on the soft close-cropped grass that fringed the moor. A grouse, occasionally, whirring low near the heather, cried its alarmed "Go-back, go-back," and the faint sound of the sportsman's gun was borne upon the wind. Silence fell upon the two, a silence that Tom knew not, nor cared to break.

"And what about Miss Baxter's apprentice?" at last spoke Dorothy, very softly.

Tom did not seem to hear. In truth he walked in a blissful trance. The question fell upon his ear, but the words, as words will when the mind is dreaming, tarried ere they reached his senses.

It seemed to Dorothy as if there had been a long gap in their conversation when he spoke.

"I beg your pardon, what did you say, Miss Dorothy?"

"I said, what about Miss Baxter's apprentice?" and there was no mistaking the withdraw of the hand now.

"Miss Baxter's apprentice!" said Tom, blankly. "Miss Baxter, the milliner, you mean."

"Of course I mean her *and* her apprentice."

"Well, what about them?" asked Tom, "and how came we to be talking about them?"

"What's her name? I hope it's a pretty one."

"Why, Miss Baxter, to be sure."

"Stupid! I mean her apprentice. The one that wears green gloves. She's one of the teachers in our Sunday school. Oh! You know very well, sir."

"I suppose you mean Miss Pounder."

"What a horrid name: but what could you expect from a girl that wears green gloves. You really must buy her a pair of another colour. But there's no great change from Pounder to Pinder. That will be one comfort for her. But I meant her Christian name."

"Upon my word," said Tom, "I haven't an idea. It may be Jezebel for aught I know or care."

"But I thought…."

"Yes, you thought?"

"Oh! nothing," said Dorothy, "and here, thank goodness, we're at the reservoir at last. Oh! isn't the view down the valley just lovely?"

"It is," said Tom, but his eyes were on Dorothy's beaming face.

They lingered for some moments on the embankment of the vast sheet of water, each wrapt in thought. It was Dorothy who spoke.

"Wherever does all the water come from and how could they manage to trap it like this?"

"Oh, this reservoir is almost made by Nature. Yonder is Hoobrook Hill and there is Lum Bank. It needed but to throw a bank across the intervening space, and behold, the reservoir was made. The water comes from Holme Moss and the hills running up to Saddleworth. You would scarce think that this huge dam contains nigh a hundred million gallons of water, and that there is a pressure of several hundred thousand ton weight on the bank on which we stand."

"Oh! Tom! if it were to burst!"

Pinder looked very grave. "I have often thought of that. It would be a calamity such as daunts the heart but to think of. I come here often of a moonlight night when I have made up my books for the day. It is sweet to be alone with God, and thoughts that come from God and turn to Him. But there seems some weird fascination that draws my steps hitherwards. Had I ever contemplated suicide…."

Dorothy's hand sought his involuntarily "Never that Tom, never that."

"I should have thought there was an unseen hand beckoning, me hither. This great expanse of water, so still, when the clouds brood over it, so sullen, so seeming peaceful confined, so terrible for infinite woe if it should I o'erleap its barrier, has cast its spell over me."

"How gloomily you talk, Mr. Pinder!"

"It was 'Tom' but a moment gone."

"Well, Tom, then—as we are such old friends."

"Yes, Miss Dorothy, my heart misgives me about this slumbering giant. I doubt the strength of his chains. See here"—and he led toward the centre of the embankment. "Where we stand the surface is nearly a yard lower than the mouth of the culvert."

"What's the culvert for?" asked Dorothy.

"It is the safety valve of the reservoir."

"I'm afraid I'm rather stupid."

"You see, when the reservoir gets over full the excess should go down the culvert. As things are it would begin to overflow just where we stand. Indeed, more than once when the wind has set this way, I've seen the water trickle over here. Let that trickle be but continuous and a rill would become a gap, the gap a yawning aperture and this huge burthen of Nature's most innocent fluid would hurl itself down the valley, and what or who could withstand it!"

"But, Tom, whose duty is it to see to these things?"

"The Commissioners. Your uncle is one of them."

"Oh! I will speak to him, I promise you, and that right urgently. Would you, could you speak instead of me? Uncle is very wroth with me these days, and, oh! Tom, life is so dree at Wilberlee, I could find it in my heart at times to cry my very eyes out. And it's all your fault."

"*My* fault!" he repeated.

"Yes, yours, Tom why couldn't you let uncle alone with your horrid law. You know he will have his own way, and, I think, your having been his apprentice makes it more galling."

"And a workhouse brat at that," said Tom, bitterly.

"Oh! never think of that, Tom. No one does. I don't, and I don't care if I do. It isn't that: but uncle cannot bear to be thwarted. Can't you let it drop?"

"Faith, I'd only be too glad. But it is Mr. Tinker that attacked me, and there is only one way to stop the law that I know of. Your uncle must give the word. But he wont, and I can't."

"Couldn't you just let him have his own way; it will please him, and it won't hurt you, nor your precious Co-op either."

"I don't know what you call hurting me: it will just ruin me, and what's worse it will ruin a dozen others or so, poor Ben Garside among them."

"But couldn't you go lower down the stream? Mr. Sy——, I mean somebody,.... I mean" and here Dorothy lost herself altogether, and stood dumb-founded.

But Tom's mind had seized upon the first suggestion of her words and he was unconscious of her embarrassment.

"Yes, if some good fairy would transport Co-op Mill below Wilberlee, we might manage very well. Say we had that carpet we read of in the *Arabian Nights*. But what's the use of talking? I cannot stop the litigation, and your uncle wont."

"Couldn't you allow him the name of a victory if he promised to let things go on just as they were, and you had nothing to pay those greedy lawyers? I'm sure he is not an unreasonable man, only you've crossed him, somehow, Tom."

"I couldn't send him more water or power if I tried, I know that."

"And do you think he doesn't know it? Will you just go to him and humble yourself to him. I'll engage he shall meet you half-way."

"I'm shot if I do," said Tom stoutly, "he began it and he must end it."

"I thought you preached the gospel, Tom."

"Aye, aye, that's all very well; but there's nothing in the Bible about eating dirt, or letting a man make a door mat of you for him to wipe his feet on. Besides, there's others to think of, Miss Dorothy. There's Ben, for one, and all those whose money is in the concern. They'd never be willing."

"You shan't hide behind Ben, nor yet the others. You know very well they'll say aye to anything you said. I know I should, Tom."

Is there ought so subtle in this world as a woman's cozening tongue.

"Do promise, Tom," and here Dorothy seemed parlously near letting flow the tears she had threatened a while back; "for Ben's sake, for Lucy's sake."

"I cannot, Miss Dorothy, do not ask me. You do not know how hard it is for me to say you nay."

"For *my* sake, Tom; because *I* ask you. Oh! I am so unhappy amid it all. I know not what I say, nor ask."

"For your sake? Miss Dorothy, for your sake!"

"For mine, Tom," whispered Dorothy, with down cast eyes and burning cheek.

How Tom at that moment constrained himself, and withheld the words that leapt to his lips, he could never tell.

"For your sake then, Dorothy," was all he said.

She placed her hand within his arm, and in a silence that neither cared to break, they turned by mutual impulse to descend the hill homewards.

CHAPTER XIV.

Tom Pinder lost no time in waiting upon his solicitor and acquainting him with his desire that the proceedings should be stayed even if to stay them meant an ignominious surrender. Mr. Sykes did not conceal his surprise.

"What about the plaintiff's costs?" he asked. Tom said he had reason to hope these would not be insisted on. "It is yours I'm much concerned about."

"As to them, make your mind easy. I shall make out an account of my actual disbursements, and you must pay me off by such instalments as you find convenient."

"But your labour?" protested Tom, "the days of manna are over long ago, and I suppose that if popular opinion were ought to go by lawyers would be the last body of men in the world for whom a special dispensation from the general rule would be made."

"Ah well! popular opinion is sometimes wrong, let us hope, despite the saying, *Vox populi vox Dei*."

"I thought you were a Radical, Mr. Sykes."

"Yes, yes, but I am not so ardent a lover as to be blind to the faults of my mistress. But about this stay of proceedings. I must sound Wimpenny. I'm afraid he'll be for his pound of flesh and all the other blood he can squeeze out of you. He's very sore about that interim injunction and the judge's remarks at the time would scarcely be as balm of Gilead to him."

"I suppose Mr. Wimpenny will take his orders from his client."

"Oh! of course. Well, we shall see what we shall see. That's oracular, if it doesn't convey much information. What about your scheme of Co-operative production on advanced lines? Is that to die an untimely death? It seemed to me a most promising essay in social economics. So long as you were content to work like a slave and be a poor man, with no prospect of being anything but a poor man, the system seemed flawless."

"Systems for the regulation of human affairs will never be flawless, Mr. Sykes, till the men and women who are the flesh and blood of all systems are also flawless. Now I am far from being that."

"I presume not," said the lawyer, with something like a sigh. "I suppose you've got tired of this sacrificial altar and have secured a lucrative berth, and, like all the others, are going to worship the golden calf. *Sic transit gloria mundi.* I shed a tear to the memory of Co-op Mill and all the high resolves it enshrines. Who shall write its cold '*Hic jacet.*'"

"Nay, Mr. Sykes, I am not a Latin scholar; but if you will change your goose quill for the graver's chisel, you shall inscribe on the corner stone of Co-op Mill a proud, a defiant *Resurgam.*"

"What! You intend to try again?"

"Certainly, I am already looking for premises *below* Mr. Tinker's Mill. Unless the Holme takes to flowing uphill, I shall be safe from my present adversary, at all events."

Mr. Sykes rose and grasped his client's hand warmly. "That is good hearing, Mr. Pinder; you are a man. Ah! I don't wonder at Miss —"; but here the man of law checked himself.

"Confound it. The murther was nearly out," he muttered.

"I'll write to Wimpenny at once," he said, "but I mustn't seem too hot for a settlement or he'll hold out for all he knows. I shall begrudge him every penny that goes from your pocket to his. Well, good day. I wish I were a manufacturer, I'd turn world-mender too."

"Oh! If you shew the world the example of one lawyer who has an idea beyond his bill of costs, you'll have done your share," laughed Tom. "Convert nine others and Huddersfield need not fear the fate of Sodom and Gomorrah."

Pinder had more trouble with Ben Garside and his colleagues than he had encountered from his solicitor. Ben was for a fight to the finish. "Tinker's shewing th' blue feather," he opined. "What's come ovver thee, Tom? Tha'rt nooan bahn to duff when things are lookin' up a bit? Besides, th' best terms we can mak 'll be to pay us own 'torney an' gi' up Co-op Mill. We med as weel be hanged for a sheep as a lamb, and if we're to be ruined we med as well be ruined gradely as hauf ruined. Aw reckon th' bailies 'll be bun to leeave us a bed to lig on, an we'st scrat along some rooad till they put th' coffin lid ovver us. Aw say feight to th' deeath. Talk abaat bowin' th' knee to Baal?"

"Baal!" quoth Hannah curtly. "Baal wer' a respectable sort compared wi Jabez Tinker; an' as for that Wimpenny, oh! If aw wer' a man, wouldn't aw just. That's all."

What "just" the irate dame would have done, words failed her to express, but judging from Hannah's gestures it was something that would not have improved Nehemiah's personal appearance.

But the negotiations with that gentleman which Mr. Sykes opened up did not promise to bear immediate fruit. It is possible that Mr. Wimpenny saw everything to be gained and nothing to be lost—by himself—in the sweetness long drawn out of proceedings in Chancery. The defendant's overtures were not met in a conciliatory spirit, and Sykes advised that nothing further should be attempted in that direction. Tom felt that he could do no more, and when he told Dorothy the steps he had taken to fulfil the promise she had wrung from him, Dorothy expressed herself content.

"You can hold out till May 21st?" She only asked.

"Oh, dear me, yes. From what I can judge when a lawyer in a Chancery suit contemplates a move in the proceedings, he takes a month to think it over, then he takes counsel's opinion, then he takes another month to think over counsel's opinion, then he rests for a month to recuperate his energies after their unwonted strain, then he writes to his London agent indicating the step he wishes to be taken, the agent takes a month to think over his principal's letter, and another month to reply to it, and at the end of all the country solicitor changes his mind, and the process circumbendibus begins *de novo.*"

"You ought to have been a lawyer, Tom," commented Lucy. "You have been thinking over a certain step to my knowledge for more than twelve months, and you haven't taken it yet."

"And what's that, Lucy?" asked Dorothy.

"Oh! you'll know soon enough when he takes it," was the most explicit answer that Dorothy could obtain, and with that she had to be content.

"I wonder why Dorothy mentioned the twenty-first of May next?" asked Tom of Lucy, when they were alone together.

"Why she comes of age then, stupid," said Lucy, as shortly as ever she was known to speak.

But some months must elapse before that eventful day was due in the ordinary progress of the leaden-footed months. The Christmas of 1851 was for all in whose fortunes we are concerned, but a cheerless and anxious season. Work continued fairly good, and on that score there was nothing much to complain of. The winter months were open and depressing. The old adage that a green Yule makes a fat churchyard was amply verified. Low fevers were rife. The strains of the waits on

Christmas Eve failed to arouse the sense of Christmas in the heart. Plum pudding and roast beef failed to stimulate to cheerfulness when all around was a damp, drizzly, clinging blanket of rain-charged atmosphere. For days together a pall of moisture settled over the Valley. The moors were soaked, and oozed like surcharged sponges. Every rill became a rivulet, every rivulet a river. The lower lands contiguous to the Holme were flooded. The dams were charged to the brinks, and in the mill-races the pressing waters strained the stoutest shuttles. From the hillsides the swollen streams brought rocky fragments rolling, tumbling, splashing. It was a man's work to watch the river immediately below the tail-goits of every mill, to prevent the goit being blocked by the flotsam of the stream, and the water-wheel thrown into back-water.

It was an anxious time for Tom and Ben on more than one account. The apprehensions that had long possessed Tom as to the safety of Bilberry reservoir did not leave him. Rather he saw daily reasons for the more concern. The new year of 1852 saw little improvement in the weather, Almost daily Tom made his way to the banks of the great dam, surveying it with anxious eye. When he spoke his fears to old residents, they were pooh-poohed. It was the old cry of "Wolf." The people in most immediate danger had been told so often that something was wrong with Bilberry embankment, and for so long had the gloomy predictions of the local Cassandras come to nought, that Tom spoke to deaf ears. None heeded him. Even Ben accorded him only the attention of politeness. The people lower down the Valley based their indifference to his suggestions of possible peril upon the indifference of those nearer the reservoir. If the people who lived cheek by jowl as it were with the big dam could afford to laugh at Tom's dismal forebodings, why should they put themselves about. They recommended Tom to permit the Commissioners to know something about their business, and more than hinted that he had enough to do to look after his own particular concerns without worrying himself about what was after all a matter for the public authorities. It did not occur to them to reflect that if a man is drowned it does not matter much to him whether he has met his death through public or private defeasance.

On Tuesday, the 4th of February Tom had been as usual to market. He had done his business early in the afternoon, but had been detained in town by the necessity of seeing Mr. Sykes in connection with the eternal lawsuit. Then he had to wait for a train so that it was long past the hour for the evening meal when he reached Ben Garside's house in Holmfirth. The tea-things had long been cleared away, but Hannah was soon bustling about preparing an appetising meal of broiled rashers, poached eggs, and tea and toasted teacake. The meal was grateful after the long wearying day. It had been a depressing day. The market had been slackly attended: the weather had something to do with that. It had rained pitilessly all day, a steady, persistent, dogged downpour, ceasing at times for the fragment of an hour, only to commence again, and so on, as if it never meant to stop. And as it was on the Tuesday, so it had been for three or four days before. At the "ordinary" at the Queen Hotel, kept by Mrs. Beevers, in the Market Street, the manufacturers from the valleys of the Colne and the Holme were full of talk of choked tail-goits water piled back into the wheel-race so that the wheel refused to turn upon its axis. The merchants shook their heads gloomily over the mild, open weather. They declared, as their grandchildren declare to-day, that when they were boys winter was winter; but now there was no depending on the weather, and the almanac was a snare and a delusion.

Tom lingered over his meal, luxuriating in the warmth of the room, and the pleasing rest of mind and body. But about nine o'clock the rain abated. The moon glided high in the heavens, sailing in and out among the masses of the drifting clouds. It looked as if the weather might take up after all. It was time it did. But wet or fine Tom had work to do he had fixed to do that night, work which could only be done at the mill, and which were better done that night. That done, the morrow would be clear for the morrow's work. He would have an hour at his account books, he told Ben, and sleep at the mill, and Jack—you have not, reader, forgotten Work'us Jack—should bear him company. Hannah protested in vain that "Tom was killing himself with overwork. Flesh and blood couldn't stand it, and Tom would never make old banes if he went on at that noit. It was bad enough to kill one's self to keep one's self, but it was ten times worse to kill one's self building a house o' cards, only to be blown down by that Jabez Tinker."

So Tom and Jack turned out into the night and set forth up the valley toward Hinchliffe Mill. Their road lay at times by the winding serpentine course of the river, and when the watery moon glanced downwards with bleared eye from among the clouds they could see the swollen waters. They met scarce a soul. It was late and a'ready the lights in the village and on the hillsides were being extinguished in the "house" or chamber. An occasional cur sadly bayed the moon. The swollen waters of the river rolled in their bed with sullen sob. It was a night of dread through which the growing wind wailed amid its tears. The gloom of the hour and scene fell upon the comrades. Scarce a word passed between them, as with bent heads and cloaks close drawn they made their way through the mire of the high-road and the sloughs of known bye-paths little trod. It was hard on ten of the night when the mill was reached. Jack kindled a fire in the office-grate and sat beside it for a time to dry his shoon. He made a brew of strong coffee for his master to cheer him through his task. Then Jack in stocking-feet sought the wool-hole where he had improvised a bed of unscoured pieces, greasy, but snug and warm, and anon his loud breathing might be heard above the beating of the storm without.

Up to something near the weird midnight hour Tom bent over his invoices and books, fighting against the waywardness of thoughts that seemed intent on anything but accounts. At length he abandoned his task half done. He felt strangely wake and alert. At all times able to do with little sleep,—that is a feature of your mill-worker—to-night he felt that he should woo slumber in vain. Donning his pilot jacket that had been steaming and drying on a chair-back before the fire, and lighting a lanthorn and taking in his hand his stout gnarled shillelagh, bought from an Irish hay-maker last harvest-time, he set forth alone on his usual round of the mill-yard, leaving the outer door of the mill on the latch. His round finished, led by what impulse, moved by that presentment he did not stay to consider, he left the mill-yard and began to climb the hill towards Bilberry reservoir. He walked sharply, for the night air was biting shrewdly, and Tom was a noted walker. His long strides soon covered the distance that lay between the mill and the reservoir bank. Tom hummed an air to keep him company in that vast solitude. The sky was clearer now than an hour or two before, but the night was still dark enough to make the feeble glimmer of the lanthorn grateful. Tom moderated his pace as he neared the embankment. Was it worth while to climb its steep face or should he turn his steps downhill. He could hear the water above his head lapping against the copings of the bank. Still, as he had come so far he might, he thought, as well walk the round of the embankment. He was on the huge abutment that turned its breast towards the valley the long barricade that cooped up the vast pile of water, and slowly, the lanthorn dangling by his side and swaying in the wind, he began to tread the path on the embankment top, slowly for in the uncertain light, a slip might cost him a sousing, and it was no hour for a cold bath. But, as he walked, peering ahead to pierce the gloom, and watching carefully his steps by the lanthorn's pale glimmer, he came, midway in his course, upon a sight that checked him with sudden halt, and made his heart stand still. There, at his very feet the water was trickling over the bank, and down the outside. A thin flow, perhaps, a couple of feet in width, had worn the upper soil, and now a continuous stream, not a quarter of an inch in depth, was gently, silently ebbing over the embankment. Even as Tom gazed spell-bound, he was sensible that the opening widened, the water that overflowed was deeper, and its escape in quicker time. A great fear seized on Tom, a dreadful thought well-nigh crushed his brain. He felt powerless to move. Then, with a cry, he rushed heedless along the embankment to the culvert. Not a drop of water flowed over the culvert's lip. The pent giant had found an outlet for itself, and was making for it. Tom ran back to the gap he had but just left. Even by this faint light he saw the breach was wider, the furrow deeper. Sick at heart, scarce realising what he did, Tom with stick and hand tried to tear up stones, cobbles, or sods that might stem the growing current. He spent his time and in vain. Fast as he made his tiny barrier, the licking wavelets undermined it and washed it gently down the embankment side; and the stream that now, oh! so silently, so grimly wore away the surface layers, bit and gnawed into the vast barrier and the clinging earthwork. But to Tom, with action had come perception. Vivid as lightning's flash the whole sequence of the possible, nay, the seeming inevitable, was borne upon his mind. He sprang to his feet, dashed down the embankment side. Not two hundred yards below the reservoir some houses stood darkling in the night, their inmates locked in sleep. With fist and stick Tom hammered at the door, thrust his stick, his fist through the windows of the bottom room, where oft the turn-up bed was stretched.

"Rouse ye, rouse ye!" he cried. "The reservoir! Flee for your lives!" Down to the Co-op Mill he dashed, racing as sure only as those do speed who know that Death follows hard upon their heels, and ever as he sped and passed some silent, lowly cot he paused a breathing space to rend the midnight silence with wild, yet wilder cry, "The flood! The flood! Haste ye, save yourselves." He reached the gates of his own mill, dashed to the corner where Jack still slept in dreamless sleep. He kicked his prostrate form, he shook him, dragged him to his feet.

"Don yo'r breeches. Here's yo'r' clogs. Haste, man! Bilberry's brust. Damn yo' wakken. Ar't deead?"

In that time of frenzied haste the language of his childhood came back to his lips.

Then as Jack, half awake, bewildered, donned his nether garments with but one idea, that Co-op Mill was on fire, Tom rushed to the stable where their one horse was housed. He threw a halter over its head; there was no time, no need for saddle. Jack had followed, thrusting his arms into his coat sleeves as he came. Tom sprang to the horse's back. The gate still opened wide.

"Clutch mi leg, Jack, an' stick to me an' yell wi' all thi might."

Tom's first thought had not been of Ben or his household; but gratitude, duty alike, made them his first care. He must reach Ben at any cost. The horse, urged by Tom's prodding heels and by the sticks that beat upon its flanks, galloped down the hill. Jack could not keep pace; panting, gasping, clinging, he stumbled and fell.

"Make for Ben Garside's," shouted Tom, and was swallowed up in the night, the horse's hoof beating the rain washed road with dull thuds, its heavy pants audible afar.

It was one o'clock and after when Tom made Ben's cottage He thundered at the door, and in a marvellously short time that seemed eternity to Tom, the upper window was raised, and Ben's capped head thrust forth.

"Th' pub's lower dahn, tha' druffen fooil," said Ben's voice drowsily.

"Open, Ben, open for God's sake. Th' embankment's burst at Bilberry."

But ere Ben had ceased to gape out of the lattice, Hannah, in her petticoat, had run down the slender, narrow stairs, and unbolted the door.

"Quick, quick, where's Lucy? Wakken her! Don yo', Hannah. Ben, Ben, haste thee, man. Oh, here's Jack; that's reight lad, aw feart tha'd be longer."

Lucy, pale, trembling, but calm, had come down, part dressed.

"Ar't sure, Tom?" asked Ben.

"It's giving bi inches, it cannot howd. What shall we do? Oh! What shall we do?"

"Mak' for th' hills, for sure," gasped Jack, as he drew deep draughts of breath.

Then Tom felt a quiet hand upon his own, and Lucy by his side drew him part aloof.

"There's Dorothy lower down," she whispered, "and if flood come, oh! Woe is me for all at Wilberlee. Hark! the alarm is spread. Race to Wilberlee; and Tom! kiss me, it may be good-bye."

Tom kissed the tremulous lips raised to his. "God keep you, Lucy, God keep us all. I cannot leave you."

But Hannah, too, had thought of Wilberlee. "There's Dorothy. Yo' mun give th' alarm at Wilberlee."

"And you?" asked Tom: but even as he asked he had turned to the door where the horse, all untethered, stood.

"Ben an' me 'll manage," said jack. "Up wi' thee, Tom. By gosh! hark to 'em screechin' up the valley."

Aye, aye, the warning cries had been heard and heeded, and as Tom wrung Ben's hand and vaulted to patient Bess's back the wind bore to his ears the startled cry, "The flood! The flood! It's come at last," and as the mare, spinning cobbles and pebbles behind its clattering feet, galloping as though the foul fiend pursued, dashed past farm and mill and house Tom cried loud and ever tender, "Oh, rouse yo', good folk, rouse yo'. Bilberry's on yo'. The bank's brust," and the small-paned windows were raised with quick grasp from within, and startled faces with widening eyes peered forth into the night, and still Tom raised the cry, now hoarse, now shrill, in voice that almost failed. "The flood, the flood!" And loud and louder still behind him grew the cries, deep toned of men, anguished shrill of women, wailing tones of children roused from cradle and from cot. The sleepy valley behind him slept no more. It had roused to panic, to the sudden apprehension of ravage, ruin, death. Whither flee? How save the little hoarded wealth; how bear the infirm mother, who by inglenook declined daily to her grave cheered by the babbling prattle of her daughter's bairns; how save the bairns themselves! And even as Tom rode the cries behind him swelled in volume till they fell upon his ears as a hoarse roar, broken by shrill and piercing shriek, and if his ears betrayed him not, above the din of human voice he heard the growl of gathered waters loosed. No use to look behind, the darkening skies veiled the sight. Thank God! Here is Wilberlee. Well Tom knew the entrance to the yard. Pray God the gate yielded to his thrust! It did. By there, through the yard, was the shortest cut to the house. He swung from the back of the beast, now blown and trembling. The panic had seized upon it. Grasping its mane Tom led it through the yard, round the mill gable. Here the noises from above were broken by the mill's flank and hushed. Not a light shone through the windows of the house. All was silent within, but at the garden foot the river roared, and Tom in the dim light saw that on its foaming breast it bore objects, strange, hideous, torn from the fields, floating stacks of hay, ponderous engines and machines, the dark outline of animals swept quickly by.

"Oh! rouse yo'! rouse yo'!" shrieked Tom. He tore a boulder from a rockery by, and with it crashed at the stout outer door. It shook and groaned but yielded not. Tom remembered that the window of the sitting-room or drawing-room came to within a foot's step from the ground. It was a moment's work to dash the window open with his feet, and Tom amid the falling of the glass and the creaking crash of woodwork was within the dark room, his clothes rent, his face scratched, his hands bleeding. There were sounds above of awakening life. Tom sprung to the foot of the passage stairs, finding the inner door he knew not how. "Wake ye, wake ye," he cried hoarsely.

Then a light glimmered above, on the landing. It was Jabez Tinker in his dressing gown. A candle was in his hand that he shaded from the upward current.

"Thank God, yo're up," shouted Tom, bounding up the steps. "Dress yo', quick. Rouse the house. Bilberry's burst. Oh! hark yo'."

Some building higher up the river had fallen with a groan into the stream and frantic cries rent the leaden skies mingling with the crash of stone and iron and stout timbers torn like mere sprigs.

Suddenly from the well of darkness shone the gleam of a lanthorn. It was impossible to see who held it. Mr. Tinker cried out:

"Who's that?"

"It's me, Sergeant Ramsden," said a calm, stentorian voice. "Glad you're up, sir. Time to flit. Had to wade here. Where's Betty?"

"I'm here, George; but yo' munnot think o' coming up till aw've med mysen some bit like."

But the tramp of the sergeant was on the stairs already. His was a welcome presence. The hurry and agitation of the past hour had told on Tom. He felt sorely the need of help. Mr. Tinker seemed paralysed not so much from fear as the sudden waking from sleep to stand face to face with what perils none could tell. Betty clung to her constable, but he was probably used to being clung to for protection by the weaker sex.

"Where's Peggy?" asked Tom.

"Gone to Harrogate to fetch aunt home."

It was Dorothy who spoke. She had partially dressed, but her long, curling, beautiful glossy hair fell like a veil upon her shoulders to her waist she was pale and anxious, but she retained a great measure of composure. She had drawn to her uncle's side but her eyes were on Tom.

"Are we safe here?" asked Mr. Tinker. "Is there any chance of my being able to get across the yard to the office?"

"Can't be done, sir," said the Sergeant, touching his high hat as well as he could with the hand that held the lanthorn. His other arm supported Betty.

"The garden's three feet deep and more. Same in mill yard, no doubt, and rising every second; had to wade in. Glad to find window broken down."

There was a sudden shriek from Betty. Through the door of the parlour that opened into the passage at the stair feet came a torrent of water nigh as high as the doorway itself. It flooded the passage, and, step by step, quicker than a man could mount them, scaled the staircase to the landing on which they stood. Small articles of furniture and ornaments were borne from the room, tossing and colliding as if in a grotesque dance.

"Make for the attic," said Mr. Tinker, and led the way, followed by the women. Tom was hard upon them. The sergeant followed with an agile departure from his professional staidness, deliberation, and dignity of gait that only stress of circumstances constrained. If a withering glance could have arrested it the rapidly rising, gaining flood would have stayed its inroad.

The attic was a low, barely furnished room, immediately under the roof. It was lighted from above by a thick sky-window. It held two low beds of plain deal—the chaste couches of Betty and Peggy. There were two chests of drawers, one doubtless sacred to each maid. There were two chairs, a washstand, a portrait of the sergeant, staff-in-hand, and the like of a soldier over which Peggy was supposed to weep out her heart in moments of despondency.

"I doubt we're not out of it here," whispered the sergeant to Tom. He cast his light through the doorway. "See, the water mounts quickly. 'Twill be on us, and we mun drown like rats in a hole."

"Can you swim?" asked Tom, under his breath.

The sergeant nodded.

"Doff your boots; keep your cloak and breeches nothing else. Get into that corner. Give me the light. Don't let them see you doff. They're fleyed enough."

There was no time even for suspense. The water was already in the attic. Tom dragged a bed beneath the skylight and with a blow from his stick shivered the thick glass.

"Yo' mun get through th' skylight, Ramsden," he bawled. The turmoil of the waters drowned all lower speech. "I'll pass t'others to you."

Ramsden nodded. The habit of discipline is invaluable in the hour of emergency. Tom had taken the command even in his old master's house, and it seemed natural that he should order and others obey.

With difficulty he twisted the portly constable through the aperture. It was a tight squeeze.

"Tear up some of the slates. Widen th' hole," shouted Tom, as he dragged a trunk to the top of the bed to stand on. "Now Dorothy," he whispered, "you next."

"No, uncle," she said, drawing back. This was no hour for ceremony. Tom almost lifted Mr. Tinker bodily on to the trunk, the sergeant from above seized his wrists, and Tom, with a mighty heave, hoisted him aloft.

"Now you, Betty," said Dorothy.

It was well for Betty the stone slabs had been wrenched with little difficulty from the sounding lines of the aperture. She was stout and heavy as seemeth a cook, and if there had not been strong braced thighs on the stack, and arms like iron beneath her, Betty would have slept that morn her last sleep on earth in the tiny attic she had known so long.

"Now, Dorothy," said Tom. She was already on the chest. He pressed her hand tenderly as she turned her face towards the gap through which the Sergeant had passed. Tom lifted her through almost bodily. "Come you, now," she said as she left his arms.

"Here, sergeant," bawled Tom, "take these blankets and things. It'll be cold up there." And Tom hastily passed blankets, sheets, and counterpanes through the window. Then those above heard him tearing at the bedsteads like one possessed. He rove them asunder by main force and passed the sections to the sergeant. Then springing on to the chest he thrust his arms to either side of the roof, and with a thrust of the feet that sent the box flying, forced and prised himself to the roof.

They could see little even by the light which the constable still retained. They were sure only that Wilberlee House was all but submerged, and that the devouring waters as they swept by them crawled up the sloping roof. From the thick darkness came shouts and wails and cries, and the thundering crash of falling buildings. By the lanthorn's glare and the casual glimpsing of the moon they saw, as they strained their visions to pierce the black encircling pall, what looked like huge pieces of machinery that broke from the tomb of the night before their eyes and then were gone again. More than once, almost level with the house eaves, a face of a man or woman, a white, pallid, drawn face, with eyes distended in speechless horror, would flash above the waters and then be borne away like chaff in a mighty blast, or the long white trailing of a woman's dress would shoot beneath their feet, come and go ere they realised it was come. And ever and anon those awful, thrilling, sickening cries, whose dread import they but too surely guessed. The night was bitter cold. They clung together, crouching low, their absorbing thought—would the house stand the shock of those pounding waters, would the dinning flood go on for ever?

Tom only had been engaged. Getting what hold he could by the low chimney of the house, he fastened together with the cording of the beds the disjointed laths, making a very passable raft. This he lowered to the verge of the roof. It might be needed, who might say? The very house seemed to shake under them as they crouched and waited in agonised suspense. Had it been less stoutly built it must ere this have been swept bodily away as rows upon rows of houses that night of doom were swept away by the devouring torrent—many bearing with them husband, wife and child, scarce roused from sleep ere the flood clasped them in the embrace of death.

And still the surging water rose higher and higher, now creeping slowly up the thatch, now sweeping swiftly upwards and now falling as suddenly for a foot or two, giving a momentary hope the violence of the storm was over—but only to surge nearer and nearer to those who now clung to the ridge of the arched roof. Tom contrived to crawl cautiously to Mr. Tinker's side. With difficulty making the dazed man hear him above the roar of the waters and the dinn that stunned their sense, Tom made him understand that they must now trust to the frail raft he had improvised.

"It's our only chance, sir. The bindings of the roof are giving. And look, look!"

Tom pointed across the mill-yard. The moon was clear of the clouds, and for a few moments the scene of desolation and the waste of waters might be seen by the silver light.

Mr. Tinker's gaze followed the direction of the outstretched arms. Across the yard towered the long mill chimney, and it was rocking and swaying like a drunken man. There was not a moment to be lost. The sergeant and Tom slipped the raft on to the bosom of the racing flood. It was all but torn from their grasp.

"Get you on it with the women," cried Tom. Betty was with difficulty placed upon the frail support. Mr. Tinker followed her. The sergeant, obedient to Tom's gesture, sprang upon it.

"Now, Dorothy, jump for your life"; but even as the words left his lips, the bark was torn from his grasp. There was a shriek of terror from those aboard, and Ramsden cried, "The chimney. Oh! God! It's falling!"

Tom breathed a prayer.

"It's you and me for it, Dorothy. Can you trust me?" He passed his arm around her; she pressed her lips to his, and Tom, with his almost unconscious charge, leaped far out into the centre of the headlong current. And even as he leaped the great chimney-stack, its base destroyed, swayed towards the house, and in one unbroken mass fell upon the roof that had been their refuge, and Tom and Dorothy were lost in the crested billows that leaped with angry roar to meet the very skies.

CHAPTER XV.

SOME ten days or so after the events recorded in the last chapter, a stout woman past the middle age sat by a large four-posted bed in a spacious and well-furnished bedroom. The eider-down coverlet of the bed, its damask hangings, the prie-dieu by its side, the rich covering of the walls, the silken curtaining of the windows, the full pile of the carpets, the costly paintings on the walls indicated the abode of wealth and refinement. The woman by the bedside, on whom fell the genial rays of a bright-burning fire, was plainly but neatly dressed. The anxious glances she cast upon the figure stretched upon the bed seemed to bespeak a greater, a tenderer concern than that of the ordinary professional nurse. There was no sound in the room save the ticking of the massive marble clock upon the mantel, and the regular breathing of the patient. The nurse turned the pages of a ponderous family Bible, but as her attention was confined to the highly coloured illustrations it is probable the printed page was a dead letter to her eyes.

So absorbed was she in the contemplation of the ornate plate depicting the sale of Joseph by his brethren that she almost dropped the heavy book from her knees as a faint voice issued from between the curtain folds.

"Has th' buzzer gone, Hannah?"

"Sakes, alive! If he isn't wakken," the nurse exclaimed, drawing back the curtain. "Eh! Tom, lad, it's fain aw am to yer thi voice. But tha munnot talk nor fash thisen."

"Has th' buzzer gone?" the invalid asked again. Then his eyes wandered slowly and somewhat vacantly about the room.

"Where am I?" he asked.

"Aye, tha may weel ax, lad. Thou'rt at Mester Willie Brooke's at Northgate House i' Honley, an' here tha's been awmost ivver sin they sammed thi up i'th churchyard all swoonded away; an' long it wer' afore they knowed reightly whether tha wer' wick or deead."

"Have I been poorly?" asked Tom. "What am I doing here? Where's Ben? Is he at th' mill? There's those pieces for Skilbeck's want 'livering. Why isn't Lucy here?"

"Poorly! Tha may weel say that, an' off thi yed for days together, an' of all th' stuff 'at ivver a man talked, all abaat 'junctions, an' love, an' ferrets, an' rabbits, an' then tryin' to swim, an' it took two on us to howd thi i' bed. But theer, it's time tha had thi physic, an' then thi mun go to sleep agen, an' th' cook 'll mak thi some arrowroot, an' thou'rt to have a glass o' port wine in it, th' doctor says, teetotal or no teetotal, which aw nivver did howd wi' i' time o' sickness, an' agen th' law o' natur' in a way o' speikin'." But Hannah's views on this grave question were lost upon the invalid. He had again sunk into deep and refreshing sleep, and as Hannah laid her hand gently upon his brow, the slight moisture told that the fever in which he had tossed and raved had succumbed to care and treatment.

When Tom awoke Hannah's place had been taken by a tall, grey-haired man of spare form, broad shoulders and slightly bent, his forehead lined with the tracery of time and care. His eyes had been long fixed upon the features of the sleeping youth and seemed from their expression to seek for some flitting transient likeness they bore a moment but to lose the next. It was Jabez Tinker. From the face so often, so minutely scanned, the eyes of the watcher turned at times to a small gold locket he held in his palm. It bore in pearls the letters.

A.J.

It was the locket taken by Moll o' Stuarts from the slender neck of the way-worn woman the *Hanging Gate* had received more than twenty years before, the locket confided to Tom by Mr. Black, and which, ever since, night and day, sleeping or waking, he had worn beneath his vest. Presently Mr. Tinker became aware by that subtle uneasy sense we all have felt, that Tom's eyes were fixed inquiringly on his face. He rose somewhat stiffly to his feet and bent over the bed. He took the hand that lay upon the coverlet.

"Are you better, Tom?" he asked, very gently. "We have been very anxious about you."

Tom looked upon the features, usually so stern, with puzzled interest. He seemed to be searching for some elusive memory of the past.

"I dreamed you were dead, drowned," he said at length. "But I seem to remember so many strange things for an instant or two. Then it is all blank again. But mostly I seem to be fighting with some awful, pitiless enemy that tosses and whirls and throttles me till I choke. And then again all is dark and vague, and I remember nothing."

"Well, you see, I am not dead yet, Tom, thanks be to God, and under God to you. 'Tis you, Tom, that have been nearer Jordan than I."

"Jordan!" said Tom, musingly. "Jordan! I was right then. I knew there was a flood, somehow, but I thought it was Bilberry burst." Then, as if the very words brought a flash of crowding memory and peopled his mind with vivid visions, he cried aloud:

"Dorothy! Dorothy! Where is Dorothy! Oh God, I've let her slip again," and a look of anguish, of hopeless despair was on his face, and with trembling hands he covered his face, and burying his head in the pillow, sobbed as though his whole being would dissolve in tears.

Mr. Tinker beckoned to one who stood by the door. She had entered the room very quietly, fearing to wake the patient. It was Dorothy, looking frail and fragile, but not unhappy, for Hannah had told her that Tom was coming to his senses, and the long, weary waiting and fearing was at an end. As Dorothy with noiseless step approached the bed Mr. Tinker drew aside. Dorothy touched gently the hand bent upon the pillow, and stooped low, very low, so that her lips were very near, and her breath played upon his cheek.

"No, Tom!" she whispered. "Not lost—won." And as Tom raised his face and gazed upon her as men upon the lineaments that are dearer to them than life, when life is sweetest, her eyes drooped beneath his ardent gaze, and the mantling colour suffused her cheek. She stole her hand into his, and for a while they were still. Jabez came and stood by his niece's side.

"Leave us for a time, Dorothy," he said. It was the voice of Jabez; but not the voice she had so long been used to hear. It was almost caressing in its gentleness. Dorothy smiled her assent.

"I'm to bring your arrowroot up, Tom, and I've made it myself. I know the port wine's nice. I tasted it. Don't let the food be spoiled, uncle, and, remember, Tom's not to be bothered or upset. If he is, won't Hannah give it you, that's all," and she tripped away with a glance at Tom that did him more good belike than arrowroot or wine.

Mr. Tinker waited until the door had closed upon her, then he drew a chair to the bedside.

"I mustn't agitate you, Tom," he spoke. "But, oh! If you could realise what my feelings have been since you have lain between life and death, my dread lest you might pass away and make no sign, the fears, the hopes alternate holding sway, the doubts, the prayers you would forgive much to an old and stricken man." He opened the hand in which he still held the locket. Involuntarily Tom raised his to feel for the trinket he had so long cherished.

"Can you tell me the meaning of this locket? It was found upon your neck, they say, when you were picked up unconscious, scarce breathing, your heart but flickering, in the churchyard yonder, after the Flood had abated. You had saved Dorothy, how, she scarce seems to know. But she lay very near to you, her head upon your breast. They thought you both dead. But Dorothy was soon no worse. But this locket, speak, Tom, what does it mean?"

"It was my mother's," said Tom.

"And she?"

"She died the night I was born."

"But her name? Who was she? For heaven's sake, Tom, tell me all you know. You cannot divine how much hangs on your words. They mean perhaps as much to me as you."

Then Tom told him the tale of the night on which this story opened.

"And Fairbanks, the landlady, the midwife? They can tell me more, they can speak to this. Does this Moll o' Stute's still live?"

"Oh, yes, Moll's safe enough. Did you know my mother, Mr. Tinker?"

"Know her! Oh! my God, know her! But ask me no more now, Tom. Not a moment must be lost. Brook will lend me a horse. Mine went with the Flood. I'll see you to-morrow. Now have your arrowroot and sleep and get strong and well. Whether my hopes are well founded or not, you're my son from this day, Tom, for you saved my life, lad, and you saved Dorothy's. And I'm proud of you, lad, I'm proud of you—Tom Pinder, foundling, and there isn't a man in the valley that wouldn't like to call you son, nor a girl you couldn't win. Hannah and Dorothy'll look after you till tomorrow, then."

It was the afternoon of the next day before Jabez Tinker returned from his quest. In the interval between his departure and return, Hannah had yielded to Tom's importunity, and sent for Ben.

"Eh! Lad," was Ben's greeting, as he wrung the invalid's hand with a grip that made Tom wince, "aw could awmost find it i' mi heart to call it an answer to prayer. Yo' munnot let on to Hannah, but mony a time a day this last ten days an' more, aw've been dahn o' my marrow-bones a prayin' tha med be spared Th' laws o' natur's all vary weel, Tom, for th' intellec' but there's times, lad, when th' heart o' man turns to its Maker like a babby to its mother i' its pain. An' this has been sich a time, aw reckon. Eh! man! its fair heart-breakin' to gooa dahn th' valley. Near on eighty folks drahned, caantin' th' childer in, an' as for th' damage to property, a quarter million pund willn't cover it, folk sayn. Th' Co-op. Mill's gone, choose yah, an' Wilberlee House an' all. Yar bit o' a whomstid's safe, an' that's summat to be thankful for; but, eh, mon, aw dunnot know wheer we'st all ha' to turn for summat to do, there's thaasan's an' thaasan's o' folk aat o' wark, an' no prospec' o' ther getting onny, an' i' thick o' winter, too."

"It's all a dreadful muddle to me, Ben, I can't seem to remember much about it. How did you escape, and how came I here?"

"Well, aw nivver did!" exclaimed Ben. "Didn't yo' com' an' wakken me up, an' didn't Jack an' me awmost carry th' missus an' yar Lucy till we gate 'em on to th' 'ill-side. An' if we couldn't see mich on account o' th' dark we could hear enough. By God! aw thowt th' end o' th' world wer' come. An' th' skrikin'! Eh! lad, it wer' enough to freeze th' blood i' yo'r veins. But that didn't last long. It were short shrift for most on 'em. An' then wonderin' an' wonderin' what had come on yo'. Aw thowt Lucy'd go fair daft abaat yo'. That's a heart for feelin', if yo' like. Then Jack couldn't stand it no longer. He said he could swim down to Wilberlee if he could nobbut be sure of findin' th' road. He said 'at if tha wer' deead he'd as lief be deead, too, an' aat o' th' gate. An', by gosh, he off, an' 'atween runnin' an' wadin' an' swimmin' he gate theer, but theer wer nooa signs o' thee, or onybody else, for that matter, an' nowt but part o' th' mill truck to be seen. Th' chimbley wer' clean gone. But it wer' Jack that fun' thee all th' same up in Honley churchyard liggin' ovver a gravestooan. An' Miss Dorothy. Gow! lad, ha tha mun ha' hugged her. It's a mercy tha didn't squeeze th' life aat on her. Aw've nooan seen 'em missen, 't isn't likely," and, Ben winked; "but yar Hannah says oo's black an blue wheer thi arm held her. But oo'll think none th' worse of thee for that."

"Get on with your story, Ben, and don't be frivolous. Where's Jack?"

"Oh, Jack's all reight, barrin' 'at he says he's supped soa mich watter o' late that nowt but owd ale an' plenty on it 'll tak' th' taste aat of his maath."

"But you mustn't let Jack get into evil courses Ben."

"Oh! Jack 'll be reight enough when he's getten summat to do. But it's the owd tale. 'Satan finds some mischief still for idle hands to do.' Yo' see ther's a seet o' folk come fro' all th' parts o' Yorkshire an' Lancashire to see th' course o' th' flood and th' deborah, as th' newspapper ca'd th' muck an' th' rubbish 'at's left. Holmfirth's more like a fair nor owt else. It's as bad as Honley Feeast time. An' all th' seet-seers 'at can get howd o' Jack mun treeat him. If he does get a bit fuddled afore bed-time it's little wonder. Aw've often noticed 'at folk 'll pay for a pint o' ale for a chap 'at wouldn't gi' him a penny-teea-cake if he wer clammin'. Dun they let yo' smoke i' this fine room, Tom? Aw'm fair dyin' for a reek o' baccy."

But now Dorothy entered with a tray covered with a napkin snowy-white and on it a basin of arrowroot, and Ben slipped his clay and flat tin box into his pocket.

"Aw rekkon aw'll be gooin', Tom, or Hannah 'll be flytin' me. Nivver yo' get wed, Tom, if yo' want to ca' yo'r soul yo'r own. It's just awful' th' way a felly's put on after he's once getten th' noose raand 'is neck. Tak a frien's advice Tom an' be warned i' time."

And with a wink that meant volumes, Ben conveyed himself away, walking on tip-toe, as if afraid of waking a sleeper to whom sleep might mean life or death.

"Now, Tom, you've got to eat this just now," said Dorothy, "wait till I see if it's cool enough," and she touched the lip of the spoon with hers and affected to taste the odorous compound with the air of a connoisseur. "It's just nice, sir, and if that doesn't cure you, nothing will."

"I could drink a bucketful," protested Tom. Couldn't I have a chop or a steak? I'm as hungry as a hunter."

"Chop, indeed! I should think not. Later on you shall have a cup of chicken-broth and the weest slice of toast. You've no idea how ill you are." Dorothy spoke lightly, but suddenly the woman gushed into her eyes, and it was a poor, faltering voice that said, "But you're better now, thank God. Oh! Tom, if you had died!"

"Would you have cared very much, Dorothy?" asked Tom.

"Is that what you call eating arrowroot, sir? Listen, that's uncle. How soon he's back." Dorothy had gone to the window and drawn aside the curtains. "The horse is covered with foam, and uncle looks ten years younger and as glad as a bridegroom."

A quick step was heard on the stairs, and Jabez Tinker stood at the door of the sick-room.

"Is he awake, Dorothy?" whispered Mr. Tinker.

"Awake, yes, and likely to be, as far as I can see, what with one and another. Call this a sick-room. Better call it a show and charge for admission. It takes one maid's time to attend to the door. If Mr. Brooke doesn't send in a bill for a new knocker and fresh paint, he's a saint."

"There, there, chatterbox," exclaimed Jabez, gaily. "Out you go, Dorothy, and don't come up again till I ring. Then you may come, no one else."

Mr. Tinker looked radiant, and, as Dorothy had said, younger by ten good years. In his impatience he almost pushed his niece from the room. Then he strode to the bed and held out both his hands to Tom.

"It's true, Tom, it's true, every word of it. Oh! that ever I should live to see this day. I've dreamed of it, I've prayed for it, and now it has come to me, this my great joy, out of the deep waters. Truly God moves in a mysterious way."

Tom had risen to a sitting posture. Jabez flung a loose shawl—it was Dorothy's—over his shoulders.

"You mustn't risk taking cold," he said, very gently. "Are you quite sure you feel strong enough to hear a rather long story, Tom, or would you rather wait?"

"I would rather hear it now, sir."

"Then hear me to the finish and don't judge me too harshly. God knows I've suffered enough without your condemnation. But it might have been worse, it might have been worse."

Mr. Tinker was silent for a time, as if to arrange his thoughts or choose his words. Then very gravely he spoke:

"My father, Tom, was a very strict, stern man" ("I'm not surprised to hear that," thought his listener) "and with an overweening sense of family pride. He was very proud that he was a Tinker, and, indeed, Tom, we are as old a family as there is in the valley. Never forget that. And we have an unsullied name. My father had another failing, if failing it be called. He was inordinately fond of money. He expected, he took it for granted, that both Dick and myself would marry not for money, of course, but where money was.

"But both his sons disregarded their father's wishes. I, secretly, while he yet lived; Richard, as you know, after his death. It was my fate, at the house of a customer in Liverpool, to meet sweet Annie Lisle, the family governess. She was an orphan, alone and unfriended, in the world. What else she was, how sweet, how winsome, how patient, how true and how trustful I cannot bear to think of, still less speak. I won her love. I dared not speak of my passionate devotion at home. My father with the burden of age had become each year more exacting, less tolerant of opposition to his will. I feared to anger him. It was in his power to disinherit me by his will. I was absolutely dependent on him.

The homestead was his, the mill, the business, were his. I was not man enough to face poverty, expulsion from my home, loss of social status—not even for my loved one's sake. Call me a poltroon, Tom, a coward, a cur, if you like. I have used bitterer words than those to myself. I knew it would be hopeless to ask my father's consent. He would have had one word—'Go!' Then I began, with a satisfaction I strove in vain to banish, to observe, nay, to gauge, the sign of my father's failing health. I persuaded myself he was not long for this world, and in my heart of hearts I was glad. But my passion ill brooked delay. I urged Annie to a secret wedding. Reluctantly she consented. She procured a week's holiday from her employer, and we were married by special license at the parish church of Seaford, on the south coast, a small fishing hamlet little frequented by the tourist or holiday-maker. It was a week of Paradise. Then my wife returned to her employment, I was to find a favourable opportunity of breaking the news to my father. Meantime anything might happen. I conjured my wife to keep our secret. I kept the certificate of our marriage, so afraid was I lest it should fall into another's hand. My wife was not even to write to me lest my father's suspicions should be aroused. I continued to call on my Liverpool customer as usual, and when he asked me as usual to dine or sup at his house, I treated my own wife with the distant courtesy one shows to a governess. One day, early in the winter of 1830, I called at the house of Mr.——, I was determined to take my wife away. My father had softened much during the past few months. He had agreed to pay me a fixed salary, instead of doling out a pound or two for pocket money. I had resolved to place Annie in some small cottage not far from Holmfirth I had thought of Greenfield. I could see her there each week. And there was another reason why another home should be found for her. Judge of my consternation when Mrs.—, in answer to the inquiry which I made with assumed indifference as to the health of the children and their governess, told me that Miss Lisle had been dismissed her service, dismissed ignominiously, without a character. I controlled myself as well as I could. Mrs. —— said enough to convince me that my darling had been dismissed under the darkest suspicion that can rest upon a pure, unsullied woman. But even then I did not disclose the truth. My wife had vanished and left no trace behind her. She had been true to her promise to me, even when a word would have cleared her name and confounded the angry jealous woman who spurned her from her home. Almost penniless she turned into the world. She never wrote to me or sent me word. Judge how I searched in all places likely and unlikely for her. Secretly, with what scant means I could procure. I instituted inquiries on every side; but my wife had disappeared as effectively as though she had never been. She had never worn her wedding ring; she had borne my name only during all that too brief week of wedded bliss at Seaford. Time went by; I knew my wife, if she still lived, must be a mother. I feared, then at last I persuaded myself, that in her shame and grief she had destroyed herself. I called upon my head the curse of the Almighty, but God seemed heedless of my blasphemous ravings. From that time life for me had lost its savour. I lived only for work, for business success. They were my distraction. Then, as you know, I married. But of that I need not speak. My wife bore me no children, and when I took Dorothy as my ward I almost hated the child because I could not love her as my own."

There was a long silence. Tom feared to speak. He guessed the rest too surely.

"One present only had I given to my sweetheart. It was a locket with our initials intertwined, and a love-knot of our hair inside. It was a whim of Annie's. Tom, my boy, my son, you have worn that locket about your neck. Can you forget the wrong I did your mother, and forgive the father who can never forgive himself?"

"Nay, Mr. Tinker, nay, father, if indeed I am your son," faltered Tom.

"I've seen Moll o' Stute's. I've seen Mrs. Schofield. They remembered the features of your mother as though she died but yesterday. Besides—but there can be no question of it."

"Well, father," said Tom, very solemnly, "I thank God that I am indeed your son. It is not for me to judge or to forgive. I will try to be to you all your son should be."

Jabez bent over the bed and kissed Tom's brow, and the tears streamed down the face of the elder man, his pride humbled, his cold reserve broken down, the man of iron melted to a gentleness he had never known before.

"Do you know, Tom," he half laughed, half sobbed, "you're not unlike what I was at your age. You're a Tinker, whether you like it or not."

"And a Lisle," added Tom, and lay back upon his pillow in great comfort. Then he added:

"So Dorothy's my cousin."

Jabez nodded.

"Can I come in?" spoke Dorothy's voice outside. "Open the door, uncle, I've both hands full."

"I'll leave you together, Tom. I know more than you think I know," whispered the old man, and quitted the room.

"Of all the born conspirators commend me to Jabez Tinker, Esq., J.P., of Wilberlee Mill, that was, and to Mr. Tom Pinder, of Co-op. Mill, also that was. Here's your chicken-broth, sir, and you're to drink a glass of champagne—doctor's orders."

"Put it on the table, Dorothy, for a moment. I want to speak to you. Come, stand here, please."

Dorothy pouted, but obliged, "Behold, thine handmaiden," she said, "what wills my lord?"

"Dorothy, be serious for a moment. Your uncle has told me a strange story. I cannot repeat it all. Can you credit it? I am your cousin!"

"Oh! poor fellow, he's raving again. I knew how it would be, all this talking. I'm sorry to hear it, Tom—I do so hate cousins. I've dozens of 'em, and not one nice one in the lot."

"And I'm not Tom Pinder, either."

"And who may you please to be?"

"Only Tom Tinker, son of Jabez Tinker, of Wilberlee Mill that was and is to be."

Dorothy part withdrew from the bedside and looked long and fixedly on Tom.

"And is that all you have to tell me, Mr. Tom Tinker?"

"No, Dorothy, I have another secret to tell you. But you must come closer, closer still. Dorothy, I love you. I have loved you for years. Will you be my wife?"

Dorothy made answer none. But when Tom drew her face to his she suffered him.

"My darling, oh, my darling! I love you more than life," murmured Tom in her ear.

"And is that what you call telling me a secret? You silly boy, I've known it ever so long."

"And you, Dorothy, how long have you loved me?"

"Ah! that's my secret."

The story I set about to tell is told. Another house stands by Wilberlee Mill; another mill stands upon the ruins of Wilberlee, and

Tom Tinker is master of the mill, and nominal master of the house. There is a Young Jabez plays about an old man's knee, and a sweet fair-haired Lucy prattles and babbles on its godmother's knee. Lucy Garside was bridesmaid at Dorothy's wedding, and was sponsor for her daughter at the font. She remained unmarried through her life, and she, too, had a secret; it was one that was never told.

Wilberlee Mill prospered. The hands were paid on the same principles as Tom and Ben had introduced at Co-op. Mill, and prospered with the mill. If Tom was never rich as this world counts riches, he was rich in a wealth above a miser's dream.

"What about the action 'Pinder at the suit of Tinker,'" asked Nehemiah Wimpenny of his client.

"Judgment for the defendant with costs," was the curt reply.

"Happy to draw the marriage settlements," ventured the unabashed attorney.

"Thank you, Edwin Sykes will do that," was the reply.

Wimpenny returned to his siege of the facile heart of the lively Polly, and in time wedded her. But their marriage was not a happy one. Nehemiah's attachment to the bar of the *Rose and Crown* survived Polly's translation to a loftier sphere of life. He became a confirmed tippler, and his clients left him one after the other. He became in time that most pitiable of objects—a pot-house lawyer, and only escaped the last disgrace of a lawyer's life because no one would trust him with their money.

Ben Garside took to Methodism in his old age, and wore glossy black-cloth o' Sundays. But he always averred that he had fallen from his best ideals, and suffered the fear for his own soul to deaden his concern for the souls of others. He and Jack smoked many a pipe together in the calm summer months of peaceful and prosperous years, seated on the crumbling walls of Co-op. Mill, and mourning over a vanished dream.

The last sage dictum of Ben to be recorded in this narrative suggested its title. It was uttered on the eve of his friend's wedding.

"Aw reckon, Tom, as ha' tha'll be goin' to Aenon Chapel after tha'rt wed?"

"Why so?" asked Tom

"Cost tha'rt one o' th' elect."

"I don't take you, Ben."

"Why, mon, doesn't elect mean chossen."

"I suppose so, Ben."

"Why, doesn't ta see, tha'rt Dorothy's choice?"

THE HOLMFIRTH FLOOD.

As many of the readers of "Dorothy's Choice" may not be conversant with the facts upon which that story is based, and as those who are may wish to have in concise form a historical narrative of that great catastrophe the following account, taken from the author's "History of Huddersfield and Its Vicinity," is appended:— "The Bilberry Reservoir is situated at the head of a narrow gorge or glen, leading from the Holme Valley, at Holme Bridge, to a high bluff of land called Good Bent, and was supplied by two streams flowing through the cloughs running to the north-east and south-east of Good Bent, and draining the Moors of Holme Moss on the one side and the hills running up to Saddleworth on the other, including some thousands of acres of moorland. The confluence of the streams takes place between two large hills, called Hoobrook Hill and Lum Bank, and which run parallel to each other for a distance of about one hundred and fifty yards, when they open out and form an extensive oval basin of not less than three hundred yards diameter. The reservoir formed by blocking up the valley below the basin enclosing some twelve acres of surface. It was defective in its original construction, and was for a long time known to be in a most dangerous condition. At the time when the embankment gave way the quantity of water in the reservoir would not be less than eighty-six million two hundred and forty-eight thousand gallons or the enormous and fearful amount of three hundred thousand tons in weight. It burst a little before one o'clock in the morning of February 5th, 1852. The moon shone bright over the varied and romantic landscape; the streamlets swollen by recent heavy rains, filled the river to its banks; the industrious population were recruiting their wasted energies by sleep, when all at once, in a moment, the ponderous embankment was carried away by the force and weight of the pent-up waters, and desolation, ruin, and death overspread the rich and fertile valley for miles around. Trees were torn up by the roots and hurried onwards by the rush of waters, roaring with renewed fury as they swept each successive obstruction. The death-shrieks of scores were hushed as the flood passed forwards to new scenes of destruction and death, leaving in its track ponderous pieces of rock weighing many tons; the dead carcases of horses, cows, goats, and other cattle; here and there broken machinery, bags of wool, carding machines, dye pans, steam engine boilers, timber, spars, looms, furniture, and every variety of wreck. It would seem as if the whole body of accumulated waters had tumbled down the valley together, sweeping all before them, throwing a four-storey mill down like a thing of nought, tossing steam engine boilers about like feathers, and carrying death and destruction in their progress. In consequence of the narrowness between the mountain bluffs on either side, a vast volume of water was kept together, which spent its force upon Holmfirth, where the mass of houses, shops, mills, warehouses, and other buildings was expected to present a formidable barrier to its further progress. The check, however, was but momentary for the flood, with the mass of floating wreck which it carried in its bosom, shot through buildings, gutted some, and tumbled others down, until it found a further outlet and passed on, doing more or less damage lower down the valley at Thongs Bridge, Honley, and Armitage Bridge. After passing the last place mentioned the flood got more into the open country spreading itself out in the fields, and swelling the river down below Huddersfield. Much might be written on the details and incidents connected with the catastrophe. A few of the most striking may be mentioned. A few hundred yards below the reservoir stood a small building two storeys high called Bilberry Mill, the occupation of Joseph Broadhead, and used as a scribbling and dressing mill. The end of the mill was caught by the sudden swell, and about ten feet in length and its gable were washed down the valley. A little further down the valley, and on the same side as Bilberry Mill, stood Digley Upper Mill, lately occupied by Mr. John Furniss, woollen manufacturer. The building was a block of stone work, consisting of a factory, a large house, farm buildings, and outhouses. The end of the mill was washed away, a quantity of machinery, and a large amount of property in the shape of pieces, warps, etc., destroyed, and the gable end of the house, which was comparatively new, and the farm buildings swept away. In the latter were twelve tons of hay, three cows, a horse, and several head of poultry, which were all carried down the stream. A short distance below stood Digley Mill property, which consisted of a large building sixty yards square, four storeys high, built of stone; a weaving shed, containing thirty-four looms and other machinery; two dwelling-houses, seven cottages, farm, and other outbuildings, making altogether a small town. Adjacent to it in the valley and on the hill side were several fields of rich and fertile land; the whole forming a secluded but compact estate, valued at from twelve to fifteen thousand pounds. In one of the houses built on the river side, resided Mrs. Hirst, widow of the late George Hirst; and in the other resided Henry Beardsall, her son-in-law. The cottages were occupied by work people. The buildings formed a mass of solid stone work; but the torrent swept it away like a straw, carrying its ponderous machinery down the valley, and tossing its boilers about with the greatest ease. The engine was carried from its place, and became embedded in the mud lower down in the valley. The house built on the hill-side remained, but the cottages and all the other buildings were carried away, except a tall engine chimney. With the buildings were swept away four cows and a valuable horse. Bank End Mill was the next building in the valley. Its gable end and one window from the top to the bottom of the building were washed away. It was completely gutted in the lower rooms and the machinery in the upper storeys was thrown together in heaps. The dye house and stove, about twenty yards long, were completely cleared away, leaving nothing of them standing above the ground. The property belonged to Joe Roebuck whose loss was estimated at from two to three thousand pounds. The valley here widens until it reaches Holme Bridge, a small village composed of a few hundred inhabitants. The stream here is crossed by a bridge of one arch, about forty yards on one side of which stands Holme Church, in the centre of a graveyard; and about the same distance on the other side stood a toll gate and a number of dwellings. The bridge was swept away to its foundations. The wall surrounding the church was ravished by the speeding torrent, and the few trees planted in the yard were uprooted and carried down the stream. The interior of the church and the graveyard, as seen a day or two after the flood, presented a melancholy spectacle. Inside the church the water had risen about five feet. The floor was torn up—the pews had been floating, and the floor was covered with sand and mud several inches thick. In the centre of the aisle was laid the body of a goat which had been washed from Upper Digley Mill, and within a few feet of it, resting on the seat of one of the pews, lay the coffin and remains of a full grown man. Both these relics, with others not found, had been washed up from their graves by the whirlpools formed by the current, as it passed over the churchyard. The roads and fields from the reservoir downwards to this point were almost covered with huge masses of stone and other loose substances, of which the bank of the reservoir had been formed. Down to this point no human life appears to have been lost; but a little lower down, at the village of Hinchliffe Mill, the loss of life was very great. This village was on the left bank of the river, and consisted principally of cottage houses. The factory, which gave its name to the village, was a large building five storeys high, built on the opposite side of the river, and which remained, though the water had passed its first and second floor, and done great damage to the machinery. The mill was for some time blocked up to the windows in the second storey with huge pieces of timber, broken machinery, and wreck of various descriptions, which the torrent brought down from the mills above. On the village side of the river, six dwellings which formed "Water Street," were swept down and hurled forward with the flood, and thirty-five of the inmates perished. The following is the list of the occupants of the houses that were swept down. The first house was occupied by Miss Marsden and three others; the second by Joseph Todd, his wife and children; the third by J. Crosland and seven others; the fourth by James Metternick, and nine others; the fifth by Joshua Earnshaw, his little girl, and two sons; and the sixth by John Charlesworth, and nine others. The houses in this neighbourhood not washed down, were in some cases flooded into the chambers; and in one of them—the endmost left standing—were sixteen individuals, who saved their lives by getting on an adjoining roof. In the adjoining houses, five persons perished. Of the five persons who were overcome by the waters in the houses above Hinchliffe, three were drowned in one house, viz.—James Booth, his wife, and a lodger. In the same pile of buildings, the wife of Joseph Brook (who was endeavouring to save herself and child) was drowned with her infant in her arms. The country grows wilder below the last-mentioned place; and in the centre of a wide valley stood Bottom's Mill. From the open country here offered to the stream, the factory, which was a very large one, sustained comparatively little damage. After leaving the mill, the torrent assailed the machine shops and works of Messrs. Pogson and Co.; proceeding thence to Harpin's Victoria woollen mill, doing great damage. Machinery was broken, cottages carried away, and much property destroyed. At the time of the calamity twenty persons were in these cottages, and were only rescued by a communication being opened up through the walls with the end house which was rather higher up away from the flood. Here in one chamber, the poor creatures were huddled together expecting momentary death, when at last the water abated sufficiently to allow of their being removed which was scarcely effected before the house fell in. Within a short distance of Victoria Mill stood Dyson's Mill, which was occupied by Mr. Sandford in the yard of which Mr. Sandford resided. His house was swept away, and with it himself, his two children, and servant. The factory sustained very serious damage, both in its walls and machinery. Mr. Sandford was a person of considerable property, and is said to have had three or four thousand pounds in the house at the time. However this may be, it is known that he had just before been in treaty for the purchase of a considerable estate at Penistone, and that he had only that very week given instructions to a share broker at Huddersfield to buy for him a large amount of London and North Western Railway Stock. His life was also insured for a large sum. The bodies of Mr. Sandford's two daughters and his housekeeper were found a few days after the flood; but the body of Mr. Sandford was not found till February 20th. His friends wished to find the body in order to prove his death, without which they would not have been entitled to receive the amount secured by his policy of insurance. A reward of ten pounds was therefore offered in the first instance for the recovery of his body, which sum was increased to one hundred pounds. Procklington or Farrars' Upper Mill stood next, the large dyehouse of which was completely destroyed. The damage was estimated at two, or three thousand pounds; and one of the boilers, weighing six tons, was carried by the water to Berry Brow, a distance of three miles. These were the property of Mr. J. Farrar. The factory known as the Tower Mill, situate a little below, was built across the stream; but the torrent rushed onward and carried the greater portion of the mill along with it, leaving the two ends standing. The mill was filled with valuable machinery and woollen material, and was the property of Mr. Hodson Farrar. In the factory yard two children were drowned, and a little further down a third child was found dead. At the *George* Inn, near this place, nine bodies, principally recovered from the stream, were laid. At Holmfirth, hundreds of dwellings were inundated, some of them were filled to the top storey, compelling the inmates to escape through and get upon the roof for safety; indeed, the houses were thoroughly gutted. Happily no lives were lost; but the most heart-rending scenes occurred to the inhabitants of some of the houses on the opposite side of the street. On the left hand side of what the day previous was a narrow street stood the toll-bar house, kept by S. Greenwood, who, with his wife and child, were swept away. He was seen to come out of the house with a lighted candle in his hand return into the house, close the door after him, and in a moment or two not a vestige of the house was to be seen. Lower down, on the same side of the street, was an extensive warehouse occupied by Messrs. Crawshaw, carriers, which was swept away. To the left were some extensive blue dye works; the destruction of these premises was most complete. A little above the mill and between that building and a stable, stood two small cottages, one occupied by S. Hartley and his family, the other by R. Shackleton and family. All the members save three of these families, were swept away with the cottages. Victoria Bridge was dismantled. On the right hand side, over the bridge, was a new row of shops, built in the modern style, every one of which was flooded. The loss sustained by the various occupants was great. At Smithy Place (a hamlet about two miles north-east of Holmfirth) the water rose to a fearful height, and but for the alarm which had been given, the loss of life must have been great. Whole families had to leave their beds and betake themselves out of the way of the flood with no other covering than what they slept in some quite naked; and the shrieks and cries of children for their parents, and parents for their children, were heartbreaking. The damage done in this place was very great. From Honley to Armitage Bridge the wreck was fearful, the front and back walls of St. Paul's Church, at the latter place, being completely destroyed. Two children were found dead above the "Golden Fleece" Inn, one of them on the water side, the other washed into a tree; they were conveyed to the inn. A young woman, about eighteen years of age, was found dead and naked in a field near Armitage Fold. Beyond this part there was some slight damage done. From a statement published soon after the occurrence, it appears, that so far as could be ascertained, 77 lives had been lost, 38 of them being adults, and 39 children; 26 were married, 12 unmarried, and 12 children were left destitute. The estimated damage and summary of property, in addition to the loss from devastated land under tillage was as follows:—Buildings destroyed: 4 mills, 10 dyehouses, 3 stoves, 27 cottages, 7 tradesmen's houses, 7 shops, 7 bridges, 10 warehouses, 8 barns and stables. Buildings seriously injured: 5 dyehouses, 17 mills, 3 stoves, 129 cottages, 7 tradesmen's houses, 44 large shops, 11 public-houses 5 bridges, 1 county bridge, 4 warehouses, 13 barns, 3 places of worship, and 2 iron foundries. Hands thrown out of work: Adults, 4,896; children, 2,142 total, 7,038. The total loss of property was estimated at £250,000. The coroner's jury, who viewed the bodies of the persons drowned by the flood, in addition to the usual verdict of "Found drowned," made a statement to the effect that the Holme Reservoir Commissioners had been guilty of great and culpable negligence in allowing the reservoir to remain for several years in a dangerous state, with a full knowledge thereof, and that had they been in the position of a private individual or firm they would certainly have subject themselves to a verdict of "Manslaughter." Generous subscriptions were raised for the sufferers in various parts of the country, amounting altogether to £68,000. A large surplus of the fund was left after relieving the sufferers, which was devoted towards the erection of five almshouses, the first stone being laid in 1856. A brass plate bears the following inscription:—

"The foundation stone of the Holmfirth Monumental Alms Houses, erected to commemorate the great flood caused by the bursting of the Bilberry Reservoir, on the 5th of February, 1852 (by which upwards of eighty lives were lost), and also the munificent liberality of the British public, was laid by the Provincial Grand Lodge of Freemasons of West Yorkshire, on Monday, the 24th of April, 1856, 5856."

GLOSSARY

Towzer,

a lock-up or a police-cell.

THE END.

Milton Keynes UK
Ingram Content Group UK Ltd.
UKHW020837200524
442968UK00005B/704

9 789357 956499